Presented to the Library of

CORPUS CHRISTI COLLEGE
CAMBRIDGE

by

the author.

The West Highland Galley

The West Highland Galley

DENIS RIXSON

First published in 1998 by
Birlinn Limited
Canongate Venture
5 New Street
Edinburgh EH8 8BH
Internet www.birlinn.co.uk
info@birlinn.co.uk

British Library Cataloguing-in-Publication Data
A Catalogue record of this book is available from the British Library

ISBN 1 874744 86 6

The publisher acknowledges subsidy from

THE SCOTTISH ARTS COUNCIL

towards the publication of this book

Printed and bound in Finland by WSOY

Contents

Figures

Maps

List of Plates

Introduction

THIS BOOK IS ABOUT West Highland galleys. At first sight this may seem an unrewarding field of study. We have not a single surviving plank from such vessels. Mediaeval boats from the remotest corner of Europe, a subject of neither interest nor importance surely!

My justification is simply that these boats were central to the Hebridean way of life. There are dozens of major islands in the Hebrides, hundreds of smaller ones. The whole fabric of island life is dependent upon the sea. Colonies were established, raids mounted, rents exacted, goods exchanged, cattle ferried, funerals carried – all by sea. First and foremost Highland galleys existed in wood – as commercial or military vehicles, but they also had life in wax or stone – as images of power, and as metaphors in thought and language. The birlinn was not just a material artefact, it became a cultural symbol.

In the course of this book I will argue that for 800 years galleys supported the Hebridean economy. That until 1266 the islanders were at the crossroads of an international trading empire. That their boats were up-to-date and that they were as close to Bergen by sea as they were to Edinburgh by land. That the loss of Norwegian sovereignty in 1266 condemned the Isles to commercial isolation and economic decline. The Hebrideans had nothing with which to oppose the Norse, for whom distance was no object, remoteness no security. To the Scots they became an intractable military problem.

By transporting mercenaries to Ireland, galleys subsidised island life until the Union of Crowns. Despite a perception to the contrary they were not overwhelmed or destroyed by the Scottish state. They were not defeated by the English off Ulster or by the Scots in their own waters. Galleys were fully contemporary until the late thirteenth century. They fell behind as the Norwegian connection was severed. They survived because they were perfectly suited to their environment and to the hit-and-run tactics of a warrior aristocracy. In the end they disappeared for a combination of reasons: the ending of mercenary service in Ireland, the defeat of Clan Donald South by the Campbells and the effects of relative economic disadvantage. They could only survive in a situation of political and military independence. Norse sovereignty largely allowed them this. Between the Treaty of Perth (1266) and the Union of Crowns (1603) these conditions were removed.

Galleys were clinker-built wooden boats that could be rowed or sailed. They had a single mast bearing a square sail. They could carry 40 oars and a crew of up to three men per oar. Both stem and stern were steeply pitched. From the first glance it is apparent that they are direct descendants of Viking ships. The most important single difference is the replacement of the steering-board by a stern rudder. For 800 years the galley was the dominant boat-type in the Hebrides.

One of the hallmarks of West Highland culture during the late Middle Ages was its stone sculpture. We have over 600 surviving grave slabs and some 60 stone crosses from the years 1300–1600. Many are badly worn but enough survive in good or reasonable condition to indicate both the skill of their artists and the cultural vitality of the society that produced them. These monuments were richly decorated with representational and geometric art. Like their ancestors, both Pictish and Irish, the Highland sculptors had a fondness for interlace panels, interwoven foliage and foliated crosses. Whilst the decorative patterns are wonderful in execution, they are not, perhaps, as *interesting* as the representational motifs that appear alongside them.

We have hunting-scenes, armed warriors, churchmen and civilians. We have men and women, monks and nuns. We even have half-sized slabs to children. There are figures at prayer, scenes from the coffin, horses, archers, huntsmen and animals. There are strange magical beasts with human heads, mermaids and unicorns, weapons and trade symbols. We also have galleys – over 80 of them – appearing on roughly one in eight of the surviving stones. In fact galleys are amongst the most important recurrent motifs, sure proof of their contemporary role as well as their aesthetically pleasing quality. Most are badly weathered but a detailed study can reveal a good deal about the boats themselves. (In the text a reference such as 'Lochaline (20)' refers to the list of these slabs in the Appendix. Map 2 indicates their distribution.)

We are not dependent on the stones alone. The sculptural record is supplemented by considerable literary and documentary evidence.

Naval traditions in other countries, boat-building techniques, loan-words, wax seals, manuscript illuminations can all give us clues about mediaeval boat-building in general and Highland practice in particular. Unfortunately no galley has survived but so many once sailed here and so frequent must have been their loss that some relics may lie preserved on the sea-bed.

The history of the Hebrides between *c.* 800 and the last Norse invasion of 1263 is troubled and volatile. It is not all 'dark'. We know quite a lot from Irish Annals, Icelandic sagas and the Chronicles of the various peoples of Britain. It was a long and turbulent period – in many ways a revolutionary one. The Hebrides were on a geographical crossroads; forced into contact with richer cultures in Scandinavia, Britain and Ireland. Despite the violence and social dislocation, this brought a wealth and vitality to the area that contrasts with the slow, isolated decay characteristic of more recent centuries. In that particular crucible was forged a Hebridean culture which attempted independence in the early Middle Ages. It was eventually snuffed out; disjoined from Man and Dublin, isolated from Scandinavia and suppressed by Scotland. It lacked the economic and military resources to sustain itself. But there is evidence of a vibrant, local Gaelic culture. From the early Middle Ages we have a remarkable series of stone castles. From the later mediaeval period we have some equally remarkable grave-sculpture. We have the image of galleys – the vehicles of power and communication. Less attention has been paid to these early achievements than to later dreams.

Through a telescope of sentiment it sometimes seems as if the Hebrides led a charmed and independent life for long periods during the Middle Ages. Until 1266 they were part of the Norse empire – linked politically to Scandinavia, culturally to Ireland, by blood to both. They were briefly at the crossroads of an international maritime culture rather than on the subsidised periphery of Europe. From 1221–1266 they were a centre of conflict as Norway and Scotland fought for dominion. Geography, and Scotland, won. Absence of strong central power in Edinburgh meant that for the next 250 years the Hebrides led a quasi-independent existence both politically and culturally.

The Lordship of the Isles can be seen as a political extension of the previous Kingdom of Man. This continuity was enhanced by the triumph of the Islay Macdonalds over their mainland cousins, the Macdougalls, during the Wars of Independence. It was reinforced by the longevity of John, Lord of the Isles from 1336 to 1387. It climaxed in the extraordinary cultural flowering between 1350 and 1550 whose hallmark is the fine series of grave-slabs and crosses. However the notional charm of this 'Golden Age' was probably lost on the majority of the population for whom life was exaction and toil. The Hebrides have always been a harsh environment, the sea an unforgiving element. Politically the Lordship was a unique institution – forever threatened by Scottish ambition. Over many years the West Highlands and Islands, under the leadership of Clan Donald, fought to maintain a measure of independence. Their final political failure was marked by the forfeiture of the Lordship of the Isles in 1493. By 1506, when it was captured by Huntly, the Scottish kings had made their presence felt even in furthest Stornoway. From then on it is a sad story.

One of the many disservices of the Jacobite myth is that it has conjured us into believing that the issues of Highland autonomy were decided in the eighteenth century. In purely dynastic terms they were. In other respects the Jacobite Risings appear as a disastrous diversion. In the context of political competition between two starkly different cultures the real issues had been decided centuries earlier. The irony is that the Highlanders remained so loyal to a family that had brutally diminished their own independence. Perhaps we can tell something of this Gaelic culture by focusing on its galleys; symbolic then, symbolic now, of the power and reach of that maritime world.

This is not the definitive work on galleys. That will not be written until several wrecks have been found. It is instead an exploration of research to date and an indication of profitable lines of enquiry. There is still an enormous amount that can be done in the context of place and personal names, linguistic analysis, poetry and folklore. Field surveys of nousts, galley-ports, beach-clearances, piers, jetties and yairs are only in their infancy – as are studies of the available manuscript illustrations. Exchequer accounts, customs records and the prices of raw materials can give us data for comparisons over space and time. Research into early Highland castles, churches and trading contacts may open up further avenues. It is then, very much a first attempt at a neglected subject, and I should be delighted to hear of any galley-related material which is omitted through ignorance or oversight.

The book falls structurally into two parts:

Part 1: The History, gives a historical perspective in narrative form. It does not claim to be completely comprehensive since we are dependent on such documentary evidence as chances to survive. Unfortunately the availability of official records and the paucity of other material encourages us to view galleys purely as warships. We know little of any commercial, fishing or ferry activities they may have undertaken.

Two periods give particular insights into the military role played by West Highland galleys. The first is the naval struggle on the west coast during the Wars of Independence. The second concerns Hebridean mercenary activity in Ireland in the latter half of the sixteenth century. In both cases the Highlanders came up against the English and sufficient of their records survive to enable us to make some judgements about the military importance of galleys. I have also given some reasons for their late survival and possible causes for their demise. Further chapters deal with the themes of ship-service, the likely numbers and sizes of boats, and naval warfare.

Part 2: The Evidence, deals with the various types of evidence available to us in the form of carved stones, manuscript illuminations, seals, poetry etc. Here I have culled the sources for specific details to give a picture of what the boats were like. The largest and most unambiguous body of evidence is provided by the mediaeval grave-slabs and crosses. This is followed by the seals and the literature, official or not. Manuscript illuminations, the Bayeux Tapestry and other forms of visual evidence can also give background information which enables us to draw reasonable analogies for the situation in the West Highlands.

Acknowledgements

EVERY HISTORIAN SEES THE PAST from the shoulders of his or her predecessors. Some of what follows is a distillation of the work of the many earlier students of the period. Further sections, such as the surveys of the stones and charter-grants, are wholly original. Otherwise I have tried to credit the principal contributors in the text, bibliography or footnotes.

Studying in a remote location presents considerable logistical difficulties. My thanks are due therefore to Highland Council Library Service for their ready assistance. I am grateful to Mr J Bruce of the Mobile Library, Mr N Newton of Inverness Reference Library and particularly to Mrs M Williams, formerly of the Reference Department, for her unfailing help in tracking down so many obscure references.

I should like to thank: Morag Malcolm, Dalmally Historical Association, for permission to reproduce her excellent drawing of a slab at Inishail, Loch Awe; Lieutenant-Colonel Niall Campbell of Strachur, for information about, and illustrations of, the seals of the Campbells of Strachur; Mr B Thynne of the National Maritime Museum and Dr J Andrews for generous advice about Irish maps; Mrs M Howie and Mrs M MacLellan for information about boats in Moidart; Mr H Cheape of the National Museums of Scotland; Mr A Campbell of Airds; Mr A Ailes of the Public Record Office; Dr N Mills of the Scottish Record Office; Mr I MacDonald of the Gaelic Books Council; Mr S O'Seanoir of Trinity College Library, Dublin and Miss W Thirkettle of Manx National Heritage.

I am also grateful to the following authors and/or publishers for permission to quote from their works or translations:

Dr G Broderick and Manx National Heritage for permission to use extracts from his translation of the *Chronicles of the Kings of Man and the Isles*; Wallace Clark for permission to use extracts from *The Lord of the Isles Voyage*; Professor D Thomson for permission to use translations from *An Introduction to Gaelic Poetry*; The Scottish Gaelic Texts

Society and Scottish Academic Press for permission to use extracts from W J Watson's *Scottish Verse from the Book of the Dean of Lismore* and A M Mackenzie's *Orain Iain Luim*; Scottish Academic Press for permission to use extracts from Alexander Carmichael's *Carmina Gadelica*; The Royal Commission on the Ancient and Historical Monuments of Scotland for permission to use extracts from the RCAHMS inventories; Everyman's Library J M Dent for permission to use extracts from *Egil's Saga*, *The Saga of Grettir the Strong* and *Heimskringla*; Edinburgh University Press for permission to use extracts from G W S Barrow's *Robert Bruce and The Community of The Realm of Scotland*; Faber and Faber for permission to use extracts from *Norse Poems* by W H Auden and P B Taylor; Paul Watkins for permission to reproduce extracts from A O Anderson's *Early Sources of Scottish History* and *Scottish Annals from English Chroniclers*.

Part I
The History

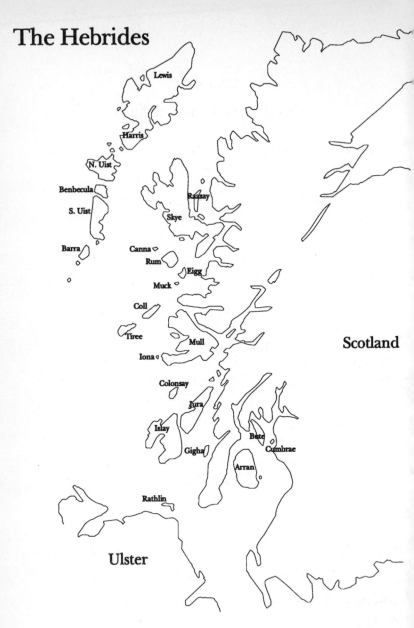

The Hebrides

Lewis

Harris

N. Uist

Benbecula

S. Uist

Raasay

Skye

Barra

Canna

Rum

Eigg

Muck

Coll

Tiree

Mull

Iona

Colonsay

Jura

Islay

Gigha

Bute

Cumbrae

Arran

Scotland

Rathlin

Ulster

Map 1

Chapter 1

Historical Antecedents

Importance of boats

HISTORY STARTS WITH GEOGRAPHY and a glance at the map should remind us that boats have always been of critical importance in the Hebrides. During the Ice Ages the sea rose and fell dramatically so the earliest settlers in our area would have found the coastline quite different. The first recorded inhabitants of Scotland are the Mesolithic families who camped at Kinloch on Rum. We know nothing about any boats they had but there can be little doubt that the sea provided the easiest and quickest method of travelling until comparatively recently. The presence of a great many prehistoric brochs and duns on the west coast prove that the sea was also a focal point for Iron Age societies. As we move into historic times this is confirmed by the voyages of the Early Christian missionaries through the Hebrides. The Irish monks came here in their skin currachs and from here to Orkney, Shetland, Faeroe and Iceland. These stalwarts of the eremitical tradition found their version of the Egyptian desert amongst remote Atlantic islands.

The obvious similarities between Highland galleys and Norse longships could lead us to overlook any naval traditions that existed in the Western seas prior to the arrival of the Scandinavians. Certainly Viking boats were technologically far superior to anything that Picts or Irish could offer but it is unlikely that native seafaring customs were completely swept away. Local conditions inform local knowledge and experience. No doubt the Vikings learned from the indigenous peoples and adapted themselves and their boats as their new environment dictated. The Iron Age and Dalriadan occupants of the west coast may have passed on widespread trading contacts.

Amalgam of cultures

What eventually transpired in the Hebrides was an amalgam of two cultures – a technologically superior caste of sea-warriors lain over a long-established native substrate. But unlike the Orkneys and Shetland, where the native Picts were completely submerged, the Hebrides saw the gradual re-emergence of indigenous tribes. What

3

will always be at issue is the relative strength and contribution of Norse and Gael. However the theme running through both cultures is an orientation to the sea. This persisted into the Middle Ages. Dozens of castles were built on islands, promontories or along the shore. Their distribution bears out their continuing political focus – Iron Age, Viking and mediaeval power was exercised by and from the sea.

Our sources for the naval history of the West of Scotland prior to the Norse are few and scanty. We have some references in Adomnan and the Irish annals, which may well incorporate entries from a lost Iona chronicle. We have a document called the *Senchus Fer n'Alban* which although tenth century in its present form may originate from the seventh century. This includes details of the levy or boat-service arrangements in Dalriada. From Ireland we also have a small gold boat model from Broighter, Co. Derry; some images on carved stones such as the eighth century stone cross-shaft from Bantry, Co. Cork; and a tradition in building skin-based currachs that has lasted into the present century. From the East of Scotland we have a stone cross-slab from Cossans, Angus, which gives us a Pictish representation of a boat.

Ireland
The Irish knew how to build in both skin and wood but the prevailing technology and economic base normally supported skin. However we should no more assume a simple monolinear development for Irish boats than we do for Viking. Boats evolved along many paths as they met needs or reflected wealth and circumstance. After the Dalriadic invasions of Argyll many of the people on the west coast of Scotland shared a common cultural base with Ireland. We can expect similar types of boat. There are a few surviving clues in West Highland place-names such as Port na Churraigh and An Curach (Iona), An Curachan (Barra), Bogh' a' Churaich (Eigg), or Curach Bheirri, (Berach's currach), a reef to the North of Kilberry Head which looks like an upturned skin boat. We must not imagine that when the Norse arrived they found a people who were ignorant of maritime matters. Nevertheless the Scandinavians possessed a simple technological superiority which had enormous military significance. In terms of naval warfare a wooden longship is far superior to a light, skin currach which could so easily be holed or upset in battle. A longship could fight at sea; a currach would be desperately vulnerable.

Early Irish boats included dugouts and reed-raft boats but skin-based currachs probably predominated. The Broighter boat model suggests a crew of about 20 whilst in 737 Abbot Failbe of Applecross and his crew of 22 were drowned in what was presumably a currach of similar size. Latterly many currachs have been small, only carrying one or two crew, but we know of a temporary one built in Ireland in 1602 which carried 30 men and measured about 7.9 metres (26 feet) by 1.8 metres (6 feet). We also have late seventeenth-century drawings by Captain Phillips which prove they could be of a very respectable proportions. The frame was traditionally of hazel rods covered with animal skin, latterly canvas or calico.

Despite their knowledge of wood the Irish preferred skin. Either this reflected an undeveloped technology for working in wood or the relative abundance and economy of hides. In the early twentieth century an Irish hide boat was one-tenth of the cost of a comparable plank boat.[1] This must have been a persuasive argument. Currachs are also light and easily carried. These simple facts explain why hide boats have always been popular in the rough seas and marginal economy of the west coast of Ireland. What they do not explain is why some Irish families, such as the O'Malleys and the O'Flaherties, adopted wooden galleys during the Middle Ages whilst others did not.

The lack of similar evidence for hide boats in the mediaeval Hebrides may be due partly to a different environment, partly to a different tradition. Journeys between the Atlantic Isles could be long and exposed; there was not always a shore to hug. Equally the Viking tradition of building in wood may have overwhelmed any earlier native tradition of building in skin. However both traditions survived on the mainland. From prehistoric times we have log-boats and canoes from a number of Scottish loch-sites and a currach survives in Elgin Museum. The dominance of galleys on the west coast between 800 and 1700 should not blind us to other Highland boat-building traditions. We just cannot specify how they survived or coexisted.

Dugouts

In the same way that crannogs (loch-houses) survived well into the Middle Ages in the Highlands so, apparently, did dugouts. They were known as 'ammir' and we have evidence from Revd Dr John Bethune in 1798 that they were still in use during the eighteenth century in Wester Ross – both for ferrying and fishing for salmon in the rivers. He mentions that he had been ferried across a river in one but adds wryly 'tho' I did not much covet the situation'.[2] Wester Ross is remote but the most compelling reason for the survival of dugouts must surely have been economic. Possibly they withstood a battering on river rapids better than a plank or skin-built boat. Certainly they would have been cheaper to manufacture and would have lasted longer. At any rate they too fell into disuse during the eighteenth century.

There is a story about a supposed exploit of Bonnie Prince Charlie in Moidart. He and his party were hoping to cross Loch Shiel but the Argyll militia had destroyed all the boats in the neighbourhood.

> *In these circumstances, the party having found a large oak-tree in a favourable position, felled it, and hollowed the trunk, partly with their axes and partly by fire, as many savage tribes are in the habit of doing, till they had produced a rude imitation of a canoe, of the kind known in America as a dug-out.*[3]

They then secretly conveyed the Prince across the loch and sank the boat until it was raised again in 1855. We should be sceptical about the detail but the principle seems credible – that dugouts could be used on west coast inland waters as late as the eighteenth century. However they were probably confined to freshwater. Despite the size of the prehistoric Loch Lotus canoe, (45 feet long, 5 feet broad at the stern), it is unlikely that such canoes were ever designed for use in the Hebrides, even if they did carry fourteen oars.

Currachs

Of greater relevance to the Hebridean situation therefore are the mainland Scottish currachs which persisted as late as the eighteenth century.[4] River-currachs are called coracles in Wales but this word does not occur in Scottish sources. In Scotland the term currach covers both the inland, one-man 'coracle' and the larger sea-going, boat-shaped 'currach'.

The river-currach was round or oval in shape, usually about four to five feet in length or diameter since this was the maximum size of boat that could be made from one animal-hide (normally ox or horse). Propulsion was by paddle and currachs were used to ferry people across rivers, to fish for salmon with spear or net, and to guide logs downstream in the timber trade. Their popularity is explained by Hector Boece, writing in 1527.[5] He marvels at the ingenuity of making a boat

> of ane bull hid, bound with na thing bot wandis. This bait is callit ane currok; with the quhilk thay fische salmond, and sum time passis ouir gret rivers thairwith; and, quhen thay have done thair fisching, thay beir it to ony place, on thair bak, quhare thay pleis.

His comments encapsulate the essentials of a currach; that it was cheap, portable and functional.

On the west coast the native tradition was completely eclipsed by the Norse as far as seagoing was concerned. However currachs survived for inland use.[6]

Scots and Picts

Scraps of literary evidence suggest that the navies of the Dalriadic Scots and Irish were not insignificant. Gildas (died *c.* 570) writes 'As the Romans went back home there emerged from the coracles that had carried them across the sea-valleys the foul hordes of the Scots and Picts . . . They came relying on their oars as wings, on the arms of their oarsmen and on the winds swelling their sails'.[7] (His image of boat as bird has parallels in Norse literature.) According to the *Annals of Ulster*, King Aidan made an expedition to the Orkneys in 580 or 581. In 719 there was a sea-battle between the Cenel Gabrain (Kintyre and Cowal) and the Cenel Loairn (Lorn). In 733 the *Annals of Tigernach* record that 'Flaithbertach led the fleet of Dalriata to Ireland, and great slaughter was made of them . . . and many were drowned in the river that is called the Bann'.

The *Annals of the Four Masters* refer to 'Flaithbertach with his mercenaries' which is uncannily prescient of the fleets of Hebridean mercenaries that used to arrive at the Bann in later times. Did they go for the river's rich salmon fishery in the eighth century as they used to 700 years later? *Grettir's Saga* informs us that about 871 the island of Barra was subject to the Irish king, Kiarval, who has been identified with Cearbhall, King of Ossory in south-east Ireland. Given that Barra is over 100 miles from Malin Head, the nearest point on the Irish coast, and perhaps 300 miles by sea from Ossory, this implies considerable naval power. Presumably the navies that these records indicate were all of skin-built currachs.

In 941 the *Annals of the Four Masters* relates 'A fleet [was led] by Muirchertach, Niall's son, and plundered and brought many spoils

from the Hebrides, after obtaining victory and triumph'. It is difficult to imagine an Irish fleet successful in the contemporary pirate's
nest of the Hebrides unless it was composed of wooden boats. Apart
from this, there is scant evidence of Irish naval power during the
Viking period and it is very likely that some of Muirchertach's boats
actually belonged to Viking mercenaries. Sea-power overturned the
political relationship between Ireland and the Hebrides. Until the
Viking invasions the Western Isles were probably in a subordinate or
tributary position. The advantage, in terms of naval technology,
which the Norse gave to the Hebrides meant that this relationship
was reversed for the next 800 years.

The Irish Scots were obviously capable sailors. How else could
they manage an effective migration from Dál Riata in Northern
Ireland to Argyll in Scotland? This is traditionally dated to *c.* AD 500
although doubtless there had been frequent maritime contact long
before that. By AD 800 the Scots were well-established in three main
groups in Argyll and their own patterns of settlement and social
organisation had taken firm root. No doubt any Picts whom they
replaced had their own boats and naval systems but sadly we shall
never know anything of these. All we have is a tantalising reference
in the *Annals of Tigernach* to a Pictish fleet that was lost in the year
729: 'A hundred and fifty Pictish ships were wrecked upon Ros-
Cuissine'. Similarly if the Pictish king, Brude, could have the
Orcadian king attendant at his court then we can presume he had
the naval strength to make his presence felt in the Northern Isles. We
have a Pictish boat on a cross-slab from Cossans, Angus, and an
ambiguous rock-carving in the Wemyss caves in Fife. This could be
Viking, Pictish or prehistoric and shows a boat with five oars (presumably each side) and a long steering-paddle or sweep.

Most interesting of all is the system of naval organisation that the
Dalriadan Scots seem to have used in Argyll. No doubt this was
brought with them from their homeland in Northern Ireland. It
appears from the *Senchus Fer n'Alban* that communities were reckoned
as fiscal units – each unit of twenty houses being required to produce
a certain number of boats of a specified size. The Norse had a
similar levying system called the leiding. It applied in Orkney,
Shetland and Norway. It may be that they tried to impose it in the
Hebrides where it would have overlaid the older Dalriadic system.
How each influenced the other we shall probably never know but it
is likely that they were complementary rather than antagonistic.

Both systems would naturally evolve in seafaring communities where people had to be organised for war in naval as well as military terms.

The Vikings

The Vikings burst onto the West Highland scene at the very end of the eighth century. Despite recent attempts to 'rehabilitate' them there is no doubt that their irruption into the Hebridean world was cataclysmic. Dalriadan society may not have been peaceful – but it was ordered. It was hierarchical, it was Christian, and Iona was the spiritual centre of their world. To the Vikings nothing was sacred. They were iconoclastic opportunists and their victims must have felt that all political and spiritual order was being challenged. Not even lip-service was paid to long-established verities. Iona was attacked in 795, 802 and 806. The monastery had to be temporarily abandoned and only a token community struggled on.

It must have been a terrifying period. The speed and ferocity of the Viking attacks militated against effective defence among the scattered island communities of the Hebrides. With their inferior boats it would have been impossible to marshal a credible naval force against an enemy who always enjoyed the critical advantage of surprise. If caught on an island the locals could not quickly summon support from another or the mainland. Islands offer excellent protection from land attacks, none from sea. Writing of King Harald's eleventh century raids on Denmark the poet Valgard gives us some striking images of the horror of such onslaughts

> *Stumbling, the survivors*
> *Scattered from the carnage,*
> *Sorrowing they fled to safety,*
> *Leaving their women captured.*
> *Maidens were dragged in shackles*
> *To your triumphant longships;*
> *Women wept as bright chains*
> *Cruelly bit their soft flesh.*   (Magnusson & Palsson)[8]

Because of the confused and sometimes contradictory chronicles of the time, it is not possible to be categoric about the process of Viking settlement in the Hebrides. Many events were catalogued and embroidered generations after their actual occurrence. Irish sources are usually hostile, Icelandic often mythic. One problem is the sheer length of the Viking period. It lasted from *c.* 795 to 1266 – a time span of over 450 years. Norse, Danes, Scots and Irish were all caught up in a bitter maelstrom. Allegiances were continually cut across by national, linguistic, family and religious differences. Out of these heterogeneous elements emerged a homogenous Hebridean society that proved remarkably resilient until after the Jacobite Risings.

There was large-scale Norse settlement in the Northern and Western Isles. The Viking tradition in Orkney and Shetland is taken for granted but it is easy to ignore their extensive settlements in the Hebrides because they were eventually submerged by the Gaelic population. Norse place-names are widespread, particularly in Lewis. They indicate that the Western Isles were not merely a convenient stopping-place on the way south to Man or Ireland; they were also settled for their own sake. The Hebrides were referred to as the Sudreys or Southern Isles and for much of the ninth and tenth centuries were controlled by semi-independent warlords.

From about 980–1065 the Isles seem to have fallen under the influence of the Earldom of Orkney. Two powerful earls, Sigurd and then Thorfinn, tried to extend Orcadian power to the west – with some success. However after Thorfinn's death the Hebrides fell back into the political orbit of Man and Dublin. From c. 1079 they were incorporated into Godred Crovan's new Kingdom of Man and the Isles. In 1098 the Norse king, Magnus Bareleg, formally wrested the Western Isles from Scotland by a violent naval expedition. This included the celebrated portage at Tarbert, Loch Fyne, when he had his boat dragged across the isthmus in an attempt to define Kintyre as an island – and so incorporate it with the Hebrides.

The Norse Kingdom of Man and the Isles remained nominally intact until 1266. In practice it suffered acute internal division from the middle of the twelfth century when Somerled's family emerged as a powerful force in Argyll. The Hebrides were split into two groups, northern and southern, with Ardnamurchan as a rough point of division. The northern group was retained by Man and governed by a son or brother of the King. The southern group was controlled by Somerled's family. The Gaelic Lordship of the Isles was the direct descendant of the Norse Kingdom of Man. The galley tradition is in some ways the most tangible part of this Norse legacy.

The Hebrides, and Hebrideans, feature regularly in the Norse sagas. At first the ship-borne invaders were pure Scandinavian but over time the two races mingled to produce a warrior caste of mixed name, mixed blood and no doubt mixed allegiance. Somerled himself, progenitor of the foremost Highland clan, the Macdonalds, had a purely Norse name. (It means 'summer warrior', a reference to the fact that the Vikings habitually went raiding in the summer season). We find warriors with Gaelic names journeying to the court of the Norwegian kings and Hebrideans were caught in a terrible conflict of loyalties during Norse expeditions such as that of 1263. Nominally their allegiance was to a distant Norse king who power was only intermittently felt. In practice they had to establish a political relationship with the kings of Scotland, who were very much closer to hand. Culturally and linguistically many of them may have felt distinct from both.

During the first half of the thirteenth century the kings of Scotland staged a series of assaults on the West Highlands and Islands. In 1263 King Hakon of Norway mounted a massive naval expedition to retain his Hebridean possessions. This ended in costly failure and in 1266 the islands were sold back to Scotland by the Treaty of Perth. Norse rule was over; the Scandinavian connection severed.

With the cession of the Hebrides to Scotland comes the ending of a 500-year Norwegian connection. No longer did letters travel east to tell of 'dispeace' in the west. No longer did Hebridean lords vie for kingship in the court at Bergen. No more were Norwegian boats sent west to plunder or impose. Political orientation changed and this had fundamental consequences for all Hebrideans. Absence of a strong central power in Edinburgh might mean relative independence for the next 250 years but the islanders were now on the periphery of a peripheral kingdom, not at the centre of a maritime trading empire. The loss was incalculable. The gravitational pull was now only east to the mainland or south to Ireland. In practice the mountains to the east proved a barrier to commerce whilst the sea to the south remained a solitary highway.

It is a sad truth that from Cape Wrath to Kintyre no commercial ports developed until comparatively recent times. It is difficult to find evidence for much trading wealth during the mediaeval period, perhaps only in south-west Argyll. Here a rich series of grave-slabs suggests either relative prosperity or conspicuous consumption during the period 1350–1500. In terms of naval development the Hebrides began to fall behind, their main contacts being with Ireland. The Islesmen took on the role of mercenaries and their galleys, which were becoming increasingly outdated, functioned as troop-transports, privateers and small fishing or trading vessels.

The European context

Galleys, and ships in many neighbouring countries, derived from the naval architecture of Scandinavia. However the Vikings burst onto the European stage at the end of the eighth century while the galleys on Highland grave-slabs date from the fourteenth to the sixteenth centuries. Scandinavian boat-building developed just as it did in the Viking colonies. Galleys, like cogs and hulcs, evolved over a period of time as part of a shared maritime tradition along the Northern seaboard of Europe. The sea was the highway of the age and we can look for clues not just to Scandinavia but also to Ireland, England and Normandy – in fact to any country with whose boats the Hebrideans would have come into contact.

The exchange of ideas between the shipwrights of different areas of N. Europe must have been of enormous importance. The sea was the prime medium of communication and the arrival of any new vessel would have generated great interest. Boats encapsulated the latest technology. It is unlikely that West Highland galleys originated from Viking longships and then pursued an independent career. It is much more likely that there was constant interaction. What relationships existed between the shipbuilders of the Hanseatic league, of Norman and Plantagenet England, Ireland, Scandinavia and the West Highlands? Were shipwrights imported, as masons or other skilled craftsmen? Were boats ordered from foreign shipyards?

While the Scandinavian connection was alive, galleys remained contemporary. After 1266 they became increasingly outmoded. The loss of political and commercial contact with the Norse empire seems to have been critical. The Gaelic Lordship of the Hebrides was doomed from the moment Scotland won sovereignty from Norway.

Chapter 2

The Early Mediaeval Period

Galleys in The Wars of Independence

THE WARS OF INDEPENDENCE saw conflict between the competing interests from the death of Alexander III in 1286 until the Irish expedition to Bute in 1335. Sea-power was an important factor in the political equation. Communication and supply by sea were crucial to the logistics and strategy of the war. The problems of transporting heavy goods any distance by land meant that Edwards I and II paid considerable attention to their fleet arrangements.

Essentially the magnates of the Highlands and Islands were engaged in their own struggles for regional supremacy against the backdrop of the larger struggle between Scotland and England. The period divides neatly into two; before and after the murder of the Red Comyn in 1306. Prior to this event the Scots were on the defensive against the military and political machine of Edward I. After 1306 the initiative moved increasingly in favour of the Scots. A decisive factor was the support Bruce enjoyed from Angus Macdonald of Islay. Angus's galleys gave Bruce a strategic advantage. They could not win the land war; but they helped Edward II to lose it.

Surviving documents demonstrate the importance of naval power. From June 1297 a letter, thought to be from Alexander Macdonald of Islay to Edward I, describes the actions taken against Edward's Highland opponents.[1] At this stage Edward was supported by the Macdonalds of Islay and opposed by the Macdougalls of Lorn and the Macruaris of Garmoran. All three families were descended from Somerled (*see* Figure 1), and linked to each other by marriage. Despite coming to the King's grace at Elgin, Alexander Macdougall of Argyll was apparently responsible for many evil actions including wasting Alexander of Islay's lands and killing his people. Equally Lochlan and Roderick Macruari had plundered the lands of Skye and Lewis, killing, burning and ravaging as they went. They even burned ships under ecclesiastical protection[2] – which implies they breached church sanctuaries.

Lochlan and Roderick Macruari were concerned to destroy boats belonging to their enemies, thus depriving them of their means to

FIGURE 1: THE HOUSE OF SOMERLED

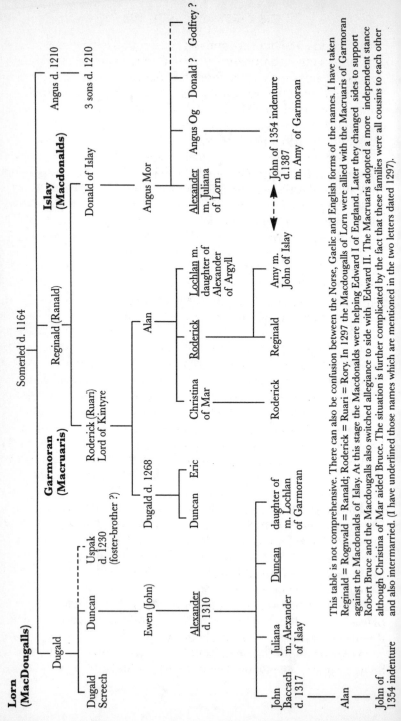

This table is not comprehensive. There can also be confusion between the Norse, Gaelic and English forms of the names. I have taken Reginald = Rognvald = Ranald; Roderick = Ruari = Rory. In 1297 the Macdougalls of Lorn were allied with the Macruaris of Garmoran against the Macdonalds of Islay. At this stage the Macdonalds were helping Edward I of England. Later they changed sides to support Robert Bruce and the Macdougalls also switched allegiance to side with Edward II. The Macruaris adopted a more independent stance although Christina of Mar aided Bruce. The situation is further complicated by the fact that these families were all cousins to each other and also intermarried. (I have underlined those names which are mentioned in the two letters dated 1297).

wage war in an island environment. The notion of church sanctuary had apparently been physically as well as metaphorically extended to include areas such as the foreshore. Sanctuary was an immensely powerful contemporary concept and its force is demonstrated by a cautionary tale in the *Chronicles of Man*. Somerled respected the sanctuary of St Machutus; Gilcolm, one of his chieftains, did not – and subsequently died a horrible death.

In Gilcolm's case it was livestock that was within the sanctuary of a church; in *Orkneyinga Saga* one of Swein Asleifson's sails was kept in the cathedral whilst he was in a spot of trouble. Taking items of value under the protection of the church, even things as valuable as boats, may have been commonplace. An entry in the Lord High Treasurer's Accounts for Scotland in 1494 refers to a payment of 2s 3d 'for beryng of the sayle and ayris to the kyrk, and for the dryen of the sayle, ii dayis'.[3] The implication here is that the church, which would normally be the largest building in a community, was the place to hang your sails to dry. Then, as now, there may have been confusion between the use of a church for sanctuary or for convenience.

At any rate Alexander of Islay would do his duty but he might need the help of the nobles of Argyll and Ross who should be instructed accordingly!

A second letter from Alexander Macdonald of Islay, is dated to the same month of June 1297 and deals more specifically with his measures against Edward's Highland opponents.[4] Lochlan Macruari in particular had ravaged the Isles and stolen goods and galleys from Alexander's men. Roderick Macruari seems to have been acting in concert with his brother Lochlan (and Alexander Macdougall of Argyll) but, after killing some 30 men, had been captured by Alexander of Islay. Lochlan himself was now being pursued by the Islay chief and his brothers.[5] It transpires that Lochlan, joined by Duncan Macdougall, a son of Alexander of Argyll, had retreated to Inverlochy Castle in Lochaber. This dates to the late thirteenth century and had probably been fairly recently constructed by John Comyn to help control his lands in the area.

In front of Inverlochy Castle lay a pair of galleys which were the biggest in the Isles.[6] These two capital ships represented a grave threat to Alexander of Islay. Should they escape to sea they could wreak havoc on his own ships and lands so it was essential that they be neutralised. The castle defenders refused to hand over the boats and prepared them for sea. Given the threat posed by these vessels and given that their neutrality could not be counted on, Alexander of Islay's men faced a critical decision. The capture of the galleys would be welcome but their proximity to the castle meant the attackers could not drag them to the water themselves. Accordingly they burnt them where they lay so that they wouldn't be a danger to Edward's subjects. The letter ends with the familiar complaint of a Highland chieftain writing to the English crown, viz. that he had not received the cash (£500) that had been promised him and reminding Edward of his current expenses.

This summary of the two letters from 1297 sheds some light on the contemporary power struggle in the Highlands and gives some hints for the future. Firstly Edward's strategic alliance with the Macdonalds of Islay must have been crucial in maintaining his position in the area. In an island theatre, ships were the principal instruments of aggression and so the capture or destruction of a rival's fleet was accorded the greatest importance. The Macruaris engaged in it, so therefore did the Macdonalds of Islay. In a relatively impoverished province the loss of such a huge capital asset as a large boat could not be easily compensated. The Macdonalds may not have been strong enough to vanquish the Macdougalls in mainland Argyll; but at sea it appears they could check the Macruaris and pursue their opponents to the head of Loch Linnhe.

The biggest Highland galleys were all based on the mainland. Inverlochy Castle represented a substantial military and economic investment and given its remote situation it would require good communications with political centres to the south. The only way to guarantee such links was to have powerful boats of your own. It is likely therefore that the castle and its navy were constructed simultaneously.[7] Just eighteen years later the largest galley documented is the 40-oared vessel which Colin Campbell was supposed to provide in return for the lands of Lochawe and Ardskeodnish. In contrast, the largest *island* galley we know of is the 34-oared Macleod boat portrayed at Rodel. These capital ships had great military and political significance. By burning two belonging to his rivals Alexander Macdonald of Islay had reinforced his military position.

At the end of the thirteenth century Edward I felt comfortably in control of the north Irish Sea. In October 1298 he issued a writ commanding the justiciary and Treasurer of Ireland 'to procure four ships of Ireland with crews of 40 good men each ready to go where

Hugh Byset, who had been appointed ... to harass the King's Scotch enemies by sea, shall direct'.[8] This cost him £160. A year later there is a further account of £175 'to pay the wages of Hugh Biset, his men and sailors of four ships going with him to attack the islands of Scotland, to repair ships for the war, and doing other necessary things'. These aggressive naval campaigns by Edward may help to explain Alexander of Islay's willingness to work with him. Equally the ability of Edward I to utilise the stores and the fighting ability of Ireland against Scotland give us a reason for Edward Bruce's invasion of Ireland in 1315. If the English could not call upon the resources of Ireland when invading Scotland then the prospects for Scottish independence would be enhanced.

By 1301 Edward I seemed to have gone a long way towards achieving his objectives. On 6 June he empowered the Admiral and Captain of his Cinque Ports fleet to receive Alexander of Argyll, his sons John and Duncan, his son-in-law Lochlan Macruari and 'all other husbandmen and middle-class people of the Isles of Scotland', to the King's peace. The Macdonalds of Islay were his allies, the Macdougalls and the Macruaris were being brought in. Any potential naval threat from Highland galleys had been negated.

An international flavour

Edward's letters paint a picture of contemporary activity in the Irish Sea. It is clear that the English king regarded Ireland as an inexhaustible granary for his Welsh castles and his campaigns in Gascony and Scotland. Ireland may then have been in the happy position of having surplus food to export. Hebrideans were not idle spectators on the fringes of this economic and military bustle; they were closely involved – in guarding, preying or conveying. The Islesmen would have first-hand knowledge of warships, supply-boats, troop-transports and fast couriers. They would have seen and noted cogs and hulcs, if not in Scottish ports then certainly in Irish ones. As practising boat-builders they would have been intrigued to see the two rival types to the Viking 'keel' tradition. They could not have remained ignorant of the latest developments in naval technology.

The foreign element in Ireland's trading community may well have rubbed off on the Islesmen. In November 1299 Edward I issued a safe-conduct to several merchants 'of the company of Friscobaldi of Florence, and their agents, [who] frequently travel to

Ireland with chattels and merchandise'. Italian merchants from the city-states of Florence and Lucca had been especially prominent and in April 1300 Alexander Normanni of Lucca was made Master of the Mint at Dublin. This is only three years after the production of the splendid boat-seal of 1297 and shows that Dublin had access to some of the finest craftsmen currently available.

For the duration of the Wars of Independence the Hebrides did not suffer by their geographic isolation. The Macdougall lords of Lorn were in London in 1309 and may have seen Mediterranean boats there. Venetian galleys were organised for the commercial run to Flanders from 1317 and five of them were in Southampton in 1323.[9]

The Macruaris

Even with the Macdonalds of Islay on his side Edward I did not have everything his own way. Other great Highland families like the Macruaris pursued an independent course of action. Warships were the only realistic instrument of control and they proved expensive to maintain and difficult to bring to bear. As both English and Scottish kings found out neither side could overawe the Hebridean lords except by a naval presence they could barely afford. Edward I, Edward II and Robert the Bruce experienced the same problems as Elizabeth and James VI. The cheapest and most effective policy was to employ one set of Highlanders against another. It was Robert the Bruce's good fortune, or perspicacity, that he secured the assistance of the Macdonalds of Islay. Throughout the mediaeval period they were the dominant naval clan. Other families, such as the Macruaris, always proved difficult to overawe. Their power expressed itself in boats, and was therefore elusive. When approached from the mainland they would retreat to the islands. Three hundred years later the Lowland Scots government was still grappling with this aspect of the Highland problem.

In about 1304 William, Earl of Ross, wrote to Edward I to the effect that since the 'foreign isles' and their chieftains were quite opposed to King John (Balliol) he had spent £1000 and more of his own money, captured 'Louwhelan and the other chieftains and brought them to King John's will'. He had also 'laboured ... to do justice' in these 'foreign isles' and had 'not yet had any allowance for himself or his servants'.[10] Evidently William was not receiving the rewards he felt commensurate with his post and due to him by virtue of his support for Balliol and Edward. 'Louwhelan' may refer to Lochlan Macruari who at this time was operating against the English king. If so, then it appears that capture by the Earl of Ross did nothing to tame him. Before his own submission to Bruce at the end of October 1308, the Earl wrote to Edward II as follows

> *We took the lands of the Isles from our lord the king, your father ... We assigned them to Lochlan Macruari to answer to us for their revenues. Since he refuses, may it please you, dear lord, to command him to answer to us as justice requires. For we have answered to your chamberlain for the revenues of those lands. But Lochlan is such a high and mighty lord, he'll not answer to anyone except under great force or through fear of you.*[11]

This was a candid assessment of Macruari power in the 'Rough Bounds' of the west. That power was exercised primarily by sea. In 1264 Lochlan's uncle, Lord Dugald Macruari, had defied a Scottish punitive expedition that seems to have reduced Caithness, Ross and Sutherland and at least threatened Skye. We can assume the Scots fleet was small and only effective close to its home bases because 'Lord Dugald defended himself in ships, and they took no hold of him'.[12] So despite the failure of Hakon's expedition in 1263 the Hebridean lords continued to enjoy a practical independence based on their galleys.

The turning point

In 1305 Wallace was executed and in February 1306 Robert Bruce murdered John (the Red) Comyn. Bruce was then crowned at Scone on 29 March 1306. There was now a radical realignment of political forces on the west coast. Angus Og Macdonald and the Campbells of Lochawe lined up behind Bruce. The Macdougalls, who had been connected by marriage to the Red Comyn, were anti-Bruce and now pro-English. Some mystery attaches to Alexander Macdonald of Islay, married to Juliana, daughter of Alexander of Lorn, who died or was displaced by his younger brother Angus Og. Angus may have derived his strength from mainland possessions in areas such as Kintyre. His support for Bruce eventually resulted in further territorial gain for his branch of the family.

From the events and correspondence of subsequent years it is plain his alliance with Angus Macdonald of Islay gave Robert the Bruce the advantage in naval terms. This had serious consequences for Edward II's logistical arrangements because Angus threatened to pick off his supply ships as they approached the West of Scotland. Angus also provided fleet-transports and supply ships for Edward Bruce's Irish campaigns. With Edward II's failure the Macdougalls went into decline and the Campbells were promoted – perhaps to balance the Macdonalds.

The Macdonalds of Islay were the regional naval power and they had no intention of letting their superiority be threatened. The Wars of Independence resulted in a fundamental shift in the political relationship between the Isles and mainland Argyll. With the weakening of the Macdougalls the island families emerged predominant. The Islay-based Lordship was established on an independent course which it successfully pursued for nearly two centuries. It was only after the rise of the Campbells that this political settlement was threatened and the mainland families returned to the fore. The pattern established by the Bruce success in the Wars of Independence leads logically to the 1354 indenture between John (Macdonald), Lord of the Isles, and John (Macdougall) of Lorn. The naval clauses in this, limiting John of Lorn to eight vessels of sixteen or twelve oars, can be seen as a conscious attempt to restrict any form of naval resurgence on the part of the Macdougalls.[13]

The changed political situation is soon apparent in the fleet dispositions of Edward I. On 29 January 1307 he wrote to the Treasurer of Ireland

> *Whereas the king has ordered Hugh Byset to cause all the shipping and all the suitable vessels that can be obtained in those parts to be furnished without delay with strong and fencible men and victuals and other necessaries and to come to the islands in the sea on the coast of Scotland, in order to set out further with John de Meneteth to repress the malice of Robert de Brus and others his accomplices, the king's rebels, who are lurking in the said islands, and to destroy the shipping of the king's said enemies.*[14]

It is clear that Edward I had the Hebrideans in mind when he dictated this. It is equally clear that he wanted to destroy the islanders' galleys. Hugh and his men were to have their wages for 40 days from the time of their leaving for Scotland.

Edward's retaliatory action makes it apparent just what the contribution of Angus Og amounted to. In 1307 he shipped Bruce from Rathlin to Carrick via Kintyre and Arran and presumably also guaranteed his retreat if things went badly. Some of the fleet of 33 galleys may have been provided by Bruce's Campbell supporters or Christina Macruari but we can suppose that many of them came from Angus's lands. This was what Edward was up against. His enemy was mobile, could strike where he wanted and retreat again as soon as necessary.

Edward's supply operation was extremely vulnerable to attack by sea, particularly when lightly-crewed merchant ships passed Man, Galloway, the Ayrshire coast or Arran. Hebridean galleys may have been too light and low to take on the larger cogs but there must have been many situations where they could pick off the smaller merchant vessels. In difficult weather, in calm or contrary winds the galleys were more versatile and easily manoeuvred. Moreover a merchant ship represented such an enormous capital asset that in dangerous times their masters probably reckoned discretion to be the better part of valour and remained close to home. As the years of warfare dragged on there is evidence that the merchant ports resisted the endless requests of the English kings. After all it was their livelihoods and their capital assets that were at stake. The Scots were also aided by the activities of French and German privateers and of course the military perspicacity of Bruce.

The less dynamic Edward II cannot be blamed for every English loss in subsequent years. We know little about Angus Og's fleet but sense its presence in the actions of Bruce and the responses of the English king. We see the shadow, but cannot tell the substance. Much as the archaeologists of Sutton Hoo reconstructed the Saxon boat from its imprint in the sand, so we can gauge the potency of galleys from the reactions to their threat.

The political situation was further transformed by the death of Edward I. From the very beginning of his reign the new king Edward II chose John Macdougall of Argyll as his lieutenant. On 2 October 1307 he appointed John as 'Sheriff of Argyll and Inchegall and guardian of these parts against the enemy'. However, as Edward was to find, Macdougall strength was primarily land-based and soon to be overwhelmed by the campaigns of Bruce. In October 1307 Bruce captured the Comyn stronghold at Inverlochy and in 1308 or 1309 he carried the attack to the Macdougalls of Lorn in their own territory. In March 1308 or 1309 John wrote to Edward II thanking him for his letter and explaining that

When it arrived I was confined to my bed with illness, and have been for six months past. Robert Bruce approached these parts by land and sea, with 10,000 men, they say, or 15,000. I have no more than 800 men, 500 in my own pay whom I keep continually to guard the borders of my territory. The barons of Argyll give me no aid ... I have three castles to keep as well as a loch twenty-four miles long, on which I keep and build galleys with trusty men to each galley. I am not sure of my neighbours in any direction. As soon as you or your army come, then, if my health permits, I shall not be found wanting where lands, ships or anything else is concerned, but will come to your service.[15]

John's men were defeated by Bruce at the pass of Brander but he seems to have escaped and from this point started a life as a mercenary in exile. On 1 April 1310 Edward ordered money for the payment of the men of Alexander and John of Argyll serving in Ireland.[16] Similar payments of 50 marks each were made to Alexander and John 'for their sustenance'. On 16 June 1310 both John and his father Alexander appear at Westminster for a Council meeting with Edward II. On 20 July 1310 Edward arranged for money and victuals for Alexander and his two sons, John and Duncan.

John Macdougall in exile

For the rest of his life John campaigned with the English against Bruce in the forlorn hope of restoring the Macdougall fortunes. Old Alexander of Lorn died *c.* December 1310 and John in September 1316. The intervening period was one of great activity. At Berwick in June 1311 he was made Admiral and Captain of the fleet destined for Argyll and Inchegall. During this month Edward tried to assemble a fleet in Northern Ireland for John to take to Scotland. Letters from seaports such as New Shoreham, Barnstaple, Weymouth, Chester, Looe, Exeter, Haverford and Sutton (Plymouth) give various excuses as to why they cannot supply ships 'at Wolrikesford [Antrim] by 25 June to go to Scotland in the company of John de Ergadia [Argyll], the king's admiral and captain'.[17]

John experienced a brief success in 1314-15 when he expelled the Scots from Man but by 1317 it seems they had regained that island. In 1315 Edward II was giving him cash 'to make good his losses from the Scots' and also for his work in expelling the Scots and 'for the support of his men keeping the Isle of Man'.[18]

Throughout 1315 and 1316 John's military opposition to the Bruces was subsidised by Edward II. In May 1316 he was granted '200 marks yearly at Exchequer for the support of himself and family'. John was now reduced to the role of pensioner although he may have supplemented his income with ransom-money. On 18 February 1315 John's men and mariners captured Moryauch Makenedy and 22 accomplices who are described as Scottish rebels.[19] John claimed that he could get a large ransom for them and the King ordered that they be taken from the Isle of Man to Dublin Castle. John must have had an independent naval capacity of his own. He had been overwhelmed by Bruce on land but had probably taken one or two galleys with him.

Nothing can disguise the fact that between 1309 and 1316 John was a beaten man, conducting a forlorn campaign to recover his position in Argyll. He lived in exile, his family and some of his friends and retainers with him. He had one or two boats of his own, but not enough, even with English and Irish reinforcements, to stop either Edward Bruce's invasion of Ireland or to carry the war to the enemy. His power-base was mainland Argyll and for Edward II he proved to be a broken reed. Either Edward totally misjudged the political balance of power in the Hebrides or he had no choice but to side with the Macdougalls. In the longer view this victory of the island-based Macdonalds of Islay against the mainland-based Macdougalls of Lorn was to consolidate the political primacy of the Lordship of the Isles for the next 200 years.

Not only did Edward II have to contend with Angus of Islay, he also faced the growing power of a Lowland Scots navy that was almost certainly made up of boats other than galleys. On 27 March 1315 Edward II wrote to John de Butetourt

> Order to take council forthwith with the men of Yarmouth and others whom he shall think fit, so that he may meet with sufficient power thirteen great cogs of the Scotch rebels and their adherents now in the port of Sluys in Flanders for the purpose of taking armour, victuals, and other goods thence to Scotland.[20]

Such a fleet was capable of doing a lot of damage. In September 1315 the Scottish navy plundered Holyhead in North Wales, carrying off the King's ship *James de Karnarvan*.[21] The names of the Scottish captains are all non-Highland and although the bigger ships were probably obtained from the Lowland merchant burghs perhaps they were supplemented by Highland galleys. In 1315 Edward Bruce invaded Ireland from Ayr with 6,000 men carried in up to 300 ships. Many of these could have been the small Hebridean galleys of Angus Og Macdonald employed purely as troop-transports.

Unsurprisingly the war had provided the impetus for building up the Scots navy, as all parties to the dispute tried to maximise their resources. At the end of the thirteenth century Edward I built about eight galleys of up to 100 oars each for his war against France. By contrast Hebridean boats appear tiny. In 1304 Lochlan Macruari ordered each davach of land to furnish a galley of twenty oars. Even Robert I's charters of the early fourteenth century mention only one galley of 40 oars, the majority having 26 oars. Robert certainly paid attention to the question of harnessing Hebridean power but he was perhaps more interested in the quantity of island soldiers than in the size of their boats. We can do no more than speculate as to whether Lowland cogs or Highland galleys were the greater threat to English vessels.

The scene of conflict was as much Ireland as it was Man or Scotland. In May 1315 Edward Bruce had invaded Ireland and Edward II of England employed John of Argyll as his admiral to harass the Scottish supply lines. He was active 'going to the Irish ports on the King's affairs' and 'on the sea-coast of Ulster' during the period March 1314 - March 1316 and we have records of payments to him of wages and provisions. The latter included 'eighteen crannocs [i.e. 36 quarters] of wheat', 'seven casks' of wine and 'twelve and a half quarters of bolted flour in two casks' which covered service for nearly eleven months. The amounts look relatively modest in relation to contemporary merchant cargoes; just a third of an average cargo between Ireland and Wales in 1296. Perhaps John had only a small force with him in exile. The items were 'delivered to . . . John de Ergadia and Dougal M'Douwylle and Doncan M'Goffry his knights, and their men-at-arms in the fleet, for wages'.

In September 1315 John wrote to Edward II from Dublin, where he was waiting for the Cinque Ports fleet, and asked for wages for his men. By the end of the same month the Cinque Ports fleet had arrived and John wrote asking if he could keep six of them with him in Ireland over the winter in order to 'harass the enemy'. His plea indicates his dependence on ships from elsewhere to prosecute the war against the Scots. However John was not powerful enough to be a decisive factor in this conflict. Not only did he need the naval support of the Cinque Ports but by December 1316 the position of the English in Ireland had become so critical that Edward was having to deal directly with a Genoese mercenary supplier. He contracted with one Sir Antoyne Pessaigne, for the supply of a huge quantity of provisions and 'also five galleys well found, each equipped with 200 men armed in plate, to be landed in Dublin for the war in Ireland'.

John could not make the military contribution of say a Somerled or Allan of Galloway. However he appears to have commanded the English Western fleet at intervals until his death in 1316. Probably John owed his position as admiral not to the number of galleys he brought with him, but out of consideration for his military experience and political status. Hebridean galleys were already outclassed in terms of naval warfare but could play an important role in piracy, harassment and the conveyance of troops.

Geoffrey Modiworthe

Of course such harassment was conducted by both sides. A certain Thomas Dun was a particular thorn in Edward II's flesh. He it was who, along with several others, had mounted the naval raid on Holyhead, North Wales in September 1315. On 9 May 1317 Edward issued a

> commission to Nicholas Dauney and Geoffrey Modiworthe to select within the ports of Exeter, Tengemuth, Dertemuth, Sutton, Plumuth, Loo and Fowy a ship and also to levy men to man her and also a 'galeye' which the said Geoffrey built, and to proceed on the king's service with the said Geoffrey against Thomas Dun, mariner, and others of his society, Scottish mariners, as the king understands that they sail up and down the Western seas, where they have committed divers piracies on merchants coming with their wares into the realm to trade.[22]

Two days later the king followed this with a writ to the southwestern ports mentioned above 'for the said Nicholas Dauney and Geoffrey Modiworthe, whom the king has appointed to levy men . . . to man two ships for two months at their cost'.

Who was Geoffrey Modiworthe? This was a few months after John of Lorn's death on pilgrimage to Canterbury and it may be that Edward had been casting about in the Highlands for a more effective replacement. Geoffrey was a galley-owner with knowledge of the west coast who would guide Nicholas and his men against Thomas Dun. It is pure speculation but the earliest references we have to Moidart are Modworth (c. 1309), Modoworthe (1372), and Mudewort (1373). The similarity is obvious. Could it be that Geoffrey was a Macruari from Moidart, named by his place of origin in much the same way as John of Lorn or Alexander of Argyll? We know nothing more of Geoffrey but Thomas Dun was captured and killed by John d'Athy, Edward's admiral, during 1317.[23]

In losing the support of the Macdonald Lords of Islay the English made a fundamental strategic error. The islanders provided a more credible fleet contingent than the mainland Lords of Lorn. The overall effect on Edward II's logistical arrangements is indicated by a mandate issued on 15 May 1322. This directed Edward's Irish officials to obtain provisions in Ireland for war in Scotland. Four days later there followed a warning to the same officials to keep the supplies in safe custody near the sea coast until the king's admiral comes to take them to Shinburness 'as the sea between the land of Man and Ireland and Skynburnesse is infested by the king's enemies with the intention of taking the victuals'.

This relative naval strength probably persisted throughout the Middle Ages. We find fewer mainland grave-slabs decorated with galley-motifs and in the sixteenth century the land-based Campbells and their associates, the Macleans of Duart, still could not compete with Clan Donald South and their allies in purely naval terms; which is why they solicited the help of the English.

Bruce's strategy

Bruce benefited from his alliance with the Macdonalds of Islay but we can also detect his caution towards a potentially overmighty subject. He bonded other western magnates by carefully-defined charters (see Figure 2). We know of at least eleven land-grants by Bruce in return for precisely-stated naval service. It has been argued that Robert drew his Highland support from Angus Og and the Macdonalds of Islay. The grants for naval service suggest the relative importance of Clan Campbell; perhaps even consciously endowed as a counterweight to the Macdonalds. Six out of eleven land-grants refer to Campbell lords. These magnates may have built up a local naval presence which they used in support of Bruce. It is ironic that in later years Clan Campbell fell back from this position of naval strength.

FIGURE 2: **ROBERT THE BRUCE'S CHARTER-GRANTS FOR NAVAL SERVICE**

Year	Grantee	Lands	No. of boats	No. of oars	Source
	Dugald Campbell	In Argyll	1	18	RMS I App 2 No 352
1329	Arthur Campbell	In Appin	1	20	Duncan p622
c. 1324	Duncan Campbell	In Argyll	1	22	RMS I App 2 No 351
1329	Duncan Campbell	Benderloch	1	26	Duncan p617
1323	John de Menteith	Kintyre etc	1	26	Duncan p508
1313	Dugall Campbell	Degnish, Kilninver	1	26	Duncan p315
	Gillespici filii Walteri	(1 ounceland)	1	26	RMS I App 1 No 107
1309 ?	Roderic filii Allani	In Moidart, Knoydart, Arisaig, Eigg, Rum etc	1	26	RMS I App 1 No 9
1314	James Macdonleavie	In Kintyre	1	26	RMS I App 1 No 105
1314/15	Colin Campbell	Of Loch Awe and Ardskeodnish	1	40	RMS I App 1 No 106
	Thomas Ranulphi	Isle of Man	6	26	RMS I App 1 No 32

From the above it emerges that the standard Hebridean warship of Bruce's day had 26 oars. 16 boats are specified; 12 have 26 oars, 1 each have 18, 20, 22 and 40 oars.

Bruce's activities at Tarbert, Loch Fyne, illustrate his long-term intention of dominating the island lords. Robert attached considerable importance to bringing the Hebrides under his sway, hence his conscious propaganda ploy at Tarbert so elaborately described by Barbour. By having his boat hauled across the isthmus he overturned the Norse claim to the Isles in psychological and mythic terms. However a stage-managed public event had to be supported by a military presence and this explains his subsequent attention to strengthening the castle at Tarbert. Some Exchequer Rolls survive for Bruce's last years. These include accounts from John de Lany, Constable of Tarbert, which cover the period April 1325 to July 1326 when substantial work was undertaken at Tarbert Castle.[24] In addition a new road was made from one Tarbert to the other (i.e. Tarbert, Loch Fyne, to West Loch Tarbert) and a new stone peel was constructed at Tarbert West.[25] Bruce regarded this strategic point as worth a good deal of investment. It controlled land access to Kintyre and commercial access to Islay, Jura and Gigha.

It is plain from the Exchequer Accounts that the area was a hive of activity. During his lifetime Bruce's western outposts were properly manned and maintained. There are payments, by 'codri' of cheese costing 7d each, to supply garrisons at the castle while boats in West Loch Tarbert had to be guarded from damage or theft. Watching a ship that had formerly belonged to Donald McGilhon cost the king 5/- for fifteen days. Such boats could carry livestock - as indicated by the payment of 10/- for 'the passage of four horses from Islay'. Islay is also mentioned as a source of victuals, a reminder of how convenient sea-freight was by comparison to land.

Watching a ship sent by Arthur Campbell cost the king 10d and a further 2/- wages for the six men who took it to the king in Arran. Is this the same Arthur Campbell to whom the king granted lands in Appin on 3 April 1329 in return for service with a 'birling of 20 oars with men and provisions'?[26] Arthur Campbell must have been one of Bruce's most reliable supporters because he features in another charter of Robert's which gave him extensive lands on both sides of Loch Etive. He was further awarded the Constabulary of Dunstaffnage, a strategic castle just north of Oban. These lands in Lorn had been forfeited by Alexander Macdougall and his son John of Lorn so Arthur Campbell was just collecting his due reward for backing the winner.

After Bruce's death no Scottish king paid much attention to the naval problem posed by the Hebrides until the time of James IV. With the Treaty of Northampton in 1328 Scottish independence was secured and events in Hebridean waters and the Irish Sea were once again of purely local significance. The island lords were not inactive, but their rivalries did not have the same international overtones and so did not register in the annals of the day. The Treaty did not abruptly end the Anglo-Scottish conflict and between 1332-1335 Edward III took the opportunity to support Edward Balliol in a renewed attempt on the Scottish throne. Edward Balliol claimed that the men of the Isles were faithful to him although it is not clear who, in particular, he was counting on. There are signs that the relations between John of the Isles and the English king were closer than those of his father Angus Og.

The fact that the Irish campaign of 1335 seems to have been directed against Bute and Arran may not have caused any problems for John of the Isles.[27] Memories of the loss, to the Scots, of these erstwhile dominions of the Norse Kingdom of the Isles may have lingered in the historical consciousness of his seannachies. Conflict between rivals for the Scottish throne could only help maintain the independence of the Hebrides. There are only sparse references to naval events in Hebridean waters for much of the fourteenth and fifteenth centuries and it is not until the 1540s that they revert to anything more than regional importance. The struggle between Crown and Lordship throughout this period did not normally involve conflict at sea.

If we exclude the Irish expedition of 1335 and the exceptional circumstances of the Wars of Independence then military traffic across the Irish Sea was overwhelmingly one way from the Viking period onwards. It took place from the Hebrides or mainland Scotland to Ireland; not the other way round.[28]

The 51-year rule of John of Islay was crucial for the development of the Lordship of the Isles.[29] By his death in 1387 John had established the pre-eminence of Clan Donald and by his judicious marriage with Amy Macruari had reunited two of the largest branches of MacSorleys. The Macruaris had been the most pro-Norse of Somerled's progeny and the marriage marks their demise as a separ-arately functioning unit. John's 1354 indenture with John of Lorn also meant he had come to a formal arrangement with his principal land-based rivals – the Macdougalls – an agreement that enshrined his own hegemony at sea.

Galleys were built in the Highlands until the early eighteenth century but from 1266 onwards they seem to have been of decreasing political importance. Technical advances in boat-building from the late thirteenth century must have left them completely outclassed by any respectable ship of the Scots or English navy. However such ships were rarely present in north-western waters and the Scottish navy had an erratic history depending on the resources made available by the king. Alexander II, Alexander III and James IV all adopted a consciously aggressive policy. At other times the Scottish naval presence in the Hebrides was patchy, negligible or non-existent. As a result of course the Hebrideans were free to pursue their old habits, albeit with increasingly outdated boats.

Trade
What of the galley's commercial function? Little is known of Hebridean trading in the Middle Ages but the contribution of the galley-fleet must be recognised. Unlike the Norse, the Hebrideans did not have the resources to build different types of vessel for different purposes. Galleys were general-purpose boats which carried freight or troops as occasion demanded. The derivation of 'birlinn' from 'byrdingr', a small Norse cargo vessel of essentially similar lines to a longship, suggests that this type of multi-purpose boat was favoured in the Sudreys from the earliest days of Norse influence. There is no evidence for the building of cogs or hulcs or any other type of mediaeval merchant-vessel in the area, though doubtless some of these ventured into Hebridean waters as advantage offered. It may be that the poverty of the region dictated against a division of functions. Highland galleys were the perfect instrument for a war-making aristocracy. Specifically merchant vessels, as knorrs, cogs and hulcs, may have been absent because the resources were not available to sustain two types of boat simultaneously. Nevertheless there remains a fundamental ambiguity as to whether the different names lymphad and birlinn distinguish two distinct types of boat or, as is implied by the Privy Council minute of 1615, they merely categorise two sizes of a boat with essentially similar lines.

Then, as now, certain economic facts must have dictated trading patterns in the Hebrides. The local market was impoverished and widely dispersed. It is difficult to believe it would have been worthwhile for merchant adventurers from elsewhere to make an expensive and dangerous trip into Hebridean waters. Equally it was probably not economic to collect the raw materials of the region unless they could be offered in large quantities. Certain products such as fish, wool, hides or wood did have value, but only if carriage charges could be kept to a minimum. We know from the sixteenth and seventeenth centuries that wood was an important commodity, but it came from the mainland Highland area rather than the Hebrides, some of which are treeless. Fish was certainly important locally but we have limited evidence of a trade in this or hides. The Highlanders probably transported their products to market themselves as the buyers were unlikely to come for them. Furthermore the Highlands maintained an essentially aristocratic society. Chieftains, bards, harpists, huntsmen, craftsmen – yes; merchants – probably not many.

In contrast, the Icelandic sagas frequently mention merchants as important and wealthy members of society. Theirs was a cosmopolitan culture. Their trading contacts gave an international dimension to what are now some of the remotest parts of Europe. In *Orkneyinga Saga* when Kali goes on a trading expedition to Grimsby in England we are told: 'There was a large gathering of people there from Orkney, Scotland and the Hebrides'. Similarly their naval capacity was considerable. In *Orkneyinga Saga* Swein Asleifson steals a boat and cargo from Knut the Wealthy at Berwick – the cargo included Knut's wife. Knut then organised a posse from Berwick which numbered fourteen ships, most of whom were merchants. There is little indication that naval capacity in the Hebrides was ever owned by merchants.[30]

There are some indications of a nascent merchant class. Islay, Gigha, Kintyre and Knapdale are all in close proximity and comparatively wealthy in Highland terms. They are rich in mediaeval grave-sculpture, particularly at the neighbouring sites of Keills and Kilmory, Knapdale. A frequent motif on these grave-slabs is a pair of small, pointed clipping-shears which suggests that wool was locally important. Two slabs bear large, square-ended cropping-shears; a hallmark of cloth-making rather than sheep-shearing. At Kilmory, Knapdale there is a three-quarter size effigy to a civilian named John. Full-size effigies to landowners or clergy usually portray them in arms or in ecclesiastical vestments. Children are often accorded a half-size grave-slab. The unusual size of this memorial and its unique style of effigy suggest someone who was not an aristocrat; perhaps a merchant who made his money from the wool trade. If so he was likely to have been a ship-owner since it is difficult to see bulky cargoes of wool, or cloth, being transported to Lowland markets any other way. There is no concrete evidence for a boat-owning merchant-class but there was plenty of precedent in the Norse heritage. It is really a question of whether such traders survived into the mediaeval Hebrides, and if they were boat-owners.

On 15 August 1275 Alexander III of Scotland wrote to Edward I in connection with the arrest of some men of Alexander of Argyll who had been seized in Bristol.[31] Men, boat and goods had all been arrested on suspicion of piracy. Edward subsequently authorised the release of this vessel whose goods were valued at 160 merks (£106-13s-4d). On 11 July 1292 Edward granted safe-conduct to Alexander of Argyll who, we are told, frequently dispatched merchants and goods to buy and sell in Ireland. Similar letters were issued to Angus Macdonald of Islay and his son Alexander.

On 20 September 1337 Edward III wrote from the Tower of London: 'The King commands Robert de Rotyngdone his bailiff of Coupeland, to release the galley, crew, and goods of John of the Isles, which had been arrested on suspicion that they were the enemy's, whereas he has always been the King's liege'.[32] On 24 May 1338 Edward gave protection and safe-conduct to three merchants (two of whom were definitely Irish) 'whom John of the Isles is sending to England and Ireland to buy victuals for himself'. A further safe-conduct was issued at John's request on 1 August 1357. It was granted to six named merchants, at least two of whom were from Ulster and only one of whom, 'Doncan', has even the semblance of a Highland name. It allowed them 'to trade in England and Ireland and the King's dominions, with their vessel and six mariners'.[33]

In July 1489 a two-year safe-conduct was issued to 'Archebald Makelar of Argile, Scottyshman' at the instance of a London merchant Thomas Grafton.[34] This permitted him to come by foot, horse or sea into the English King's dominions with 'almaner goodis and merchaundises and trade . . .' His merchandise probably consisted of wool, cloth, hides, timber or fish. When the Earl of Douglas visited the Earl of Ross in Knapdale in 1453 he was given mantles and Highland plaids. Since the sculptural evidence suggests that Knapdale was then the centre of an important cloth-making industry his presents were appropriate.

The evidence implies a reducing importance for trade in a Highland context. The Icelandic saga accounts demonstrate that the Hebrides were an integral part of an international trading network. Merchants feature nearly as regularly as aristocrats or farmers and there is no feel of a loss of status by being involved in commerce. In the later mediaeval period there is a different atmosphere. When Alexander of Argyll's boat was arrested in Bristol or when safe-conducts are issued we are given a picture of trade taking place under the protection of the great landowners. It is almost as if society is less mercantile and more aristocratic.[35]

Chapter 3

The Later Middle Ages and the Survival of Galleys

WHY DID GALLEYS SURVIVE LONG after they became technologically outdated? Because they continued to satisfy needs, because they were not challenged militarily in Hebridean waters and because they acted as troop-carriers for mercenary service in Ireland. The aristocratic society and military economy of the islands precluded the construction of anything more commercial or less functional. If a bigger boat was required then it was obtained from outside the area, not built within it.

Meeting needs

Galleys were perfectly suited to their environment. They were quick, relatively light, and easily beached. Their oarpower gave them limited independence of wind and tide. A break in the weather of just a few hours was all that was required to make the passage from one island to another or from Scotland to Ireland. There is good evidence from the English naval boats ranged against them in the North Channel that the galleys had the advantage of speed. In October 1595, despite his recent victory off the Copeland Islands, Captain George Thornton reported 'the Scottish gallies of great swiftness by oars, hardly to be followed for good service by Her Majesty's pinnaces'.[1] He attributed their speed primarily to oarpower and since he had accumulated 30 years naval service in Ulster, he knew what he was talking about. It can only have been under certain conditions of wind and tide that his boats could overtake a galley.[2]

The performance of Elizabethan and Early Stuart ships, assuming no heavy marine growth or barnacles, has been reckoned at 'two knots in a light breeze, four knots in a fresh breeze and six knots in a strong breeze'.[3] So the boats of Elizabeth's 'Ulster Patrol' could probably only overhaul a Highland galley in a fresh to strong breeze. Likewise knorrs proved faster than longships in big winds; they were built primarily for sailing whereas longships made design compromises in order to have oarpower as well. There is a story in *St Olaf's Saga* which makes this point very neatly

> *Gauti Tofason went with five warships out of the Gotha river, and when he was lying at Eker Island there came five large Danish merchant ships there. Gauti and his men immediately took four of the great vessels, and made a great booty without the loss of a man; but the fifth vessel slipped out to sea, and sailed away. Gauti gave chase with one ship, and at first came nearer to them; but as the wind increased, the Danes got away.*

Galleys could be used whilst sailing ships were becalmed. An Irish document written *c.* 1602 by Sir R Lane states that 'The lough (Lough Coan by Strangford) is within two days rowing in calm weather in a Scottish galley from Howth Head'.[4] Calm weather is fairly exceptional in the Hebrides but the ability to row against light contrary winds, even just to round a critical headland, must have given galleys a huge advantage in terms of versatility.

Galleys not only landed troops, they could be used for fishing and taking away cattle. In July 1595 Sir G Fenton reported 'I received yesterday advertisements of the landing of 1600 Scots in the North, but I think they come not to abide but to return back again with their spoil of cows'. In 1584 Hugh O' Donnell was complaining that the Scots (in this case presumably Macleans) 'have not left a cow in M'Sweeney's country'. In 1589 'four hundred Scots of the sept of the Barrones [i.e. MacNeills from Barra] invaded Erris [Mayo], killed 600 cows, freighting their galleys with the spoil, and 500 cows beside they carried to an island and there killed them and took away the hides and tallow'.[5] Unlike the Macdonalds or Macleans, who stayed to fight as mercenaries, the MacNeills lacked even this excuse – although they may have pretended otherwise to the Burkes who probably invited them. They were simply indulging in a traditional Highland 'creach' or raid, followed by an equally traditional Norse 'strand-hogg' or beach-slaughter.

The second batch of cattle were taken to an island in order to have peace to kill them uninterrupted. If their galleys carried several hundred men they would not have room for a great many carcasses so presumably these were left to rot. In 1611 the price of a hide is quoted as from 6s and since the Barra men had 1100 to dispose of we can imagine they had already secured a market with a passing merchant-ship from the Lowlands, France or Spain.[6] This was big business. The tallow would have been useful either for 'paying' their own galleys or for lighting arrangements.

In January 1630 there was a dispute between the Scottish royal burghs and the Earl of Seaforth about the introduction of strangers – presumably Dutchmen – as traders in Lewis.[7] The accusation was that there were 'great nombers of strangers in the Ile of the Lewes who daylie packes and peills, fishes, buyes talloun, butter, hydes, skinnes, plaiding and others goods of merchandice . . . not onelie in the Ile of the Lewes and adjacent yles, and in Orkney and Zetland, bot also in the mayneland' – without paying any duty! For his part the Earl of Seaforth only admitted to about ten or twelve 'strangers and fishermen' presently resident in Lewis. The Privy Council then ordered him not to let them exceed twelve until His Majesty's pleasure be known. The predecessors of these 'strangers' may well have had business contacts with the Barra-men.

If transported live, beasts would have had to be tied down since controlling frightened livestock in a rough sea could be highly dangerous. In August 1595 Captain Anthony Deringe wrote to the English Privy Council of his attempt to transport horses to Ireland in small open boats which were driven back by storm. Apparently they had 'much ado to keep their horses throats uncut'. If animals grew difficult in bad weather they might have to be slaughtered.

Clans like the MacNeills of Barra may have raided purely for economic advantage. Compared to the Macdonalds they did not have great resources of manpower but the remoteness of Barra afforded them comparative impunity. In 1593 Sir Richard Bingham reported on the 'gallies and boats of one Neale M'Barrie, a Scot that usually maketh his summer's course to steal what he can'. In this context MacNeill of Barra appears remarkably similar to the Orkney pirate, Swein Asleifson, four centuries earlier. There is a revealing quotation in a document in the *Carew Papers* entitled 'The Description and Present State of Ulster in 1586'. Writing of the O'Dohertie country between Loughs Swilly and Foyle the author remarks 'His country, lying upon the sea and open to the isles of Ila and Jura in Scotland, is almost yearly invaded by the Scots, who take the spoil of it at their pleasures'.[8]

Fishing

Galleys were also used for fishing. About 1569 one John Smyth was advising Elizabeth's government in Ireland that it should keep a pinnace or galley to prevent the Scots 'from fyshyng of the Bann and other places of the countrye wher they have suche commodytye as they can not wel live wythoute'. The commercial importance of such fisheries was well understood at the time. In a list of Irish havens or harbours made at the end of the sixteenth century there are fulsome references to the fishing riches of the Bann – 'salmons leaping and with nets taken afore they fall'. It was claimed that within two months ships of 40–60 tons could load themselves with salmon. In 1611 Sir Thomas Phillips produced a report for a proposed plantation of Londoners in Coleraine. He claimed then that the salmon fishings of Lough Foyle and the Bann were worth £800–£1000 per annum.

Hebridean involvement in the Irish fisheries may have stretched back to Norse times or even earlier. In 1557 Lord Deputy Sussex and his Council were writing to the King and Queen (Philip and Mary) that 'James M'Donnell desires peace and prays for a pardon ... Offers to permit the Deputy to enjoy the fishing of the Ban, on condition that the fishers pay him the accustomed droits'. Since the Macdonalds had married into the Bissets at the end of the fourteenth century they had held a claim on Antrim and it may be that the galleys of Islay and Kintyre regularly claimed the fruits of the Irish fisheries. Scarce resources and a relatively large population had a lot to do with Hebridean incursions into Ireland, especially for food. Annual creachs were as much an economic necessity as a proof of manhood.

Trading
Galleys were also used for trading. In March 1599 the Lord Deputy and Council issued the following instructions to Sir H Docwra, the commander at Lough Foyle

> For that some of the Scottish galleys trading with those parts bring victuals and other necessaries to the rebels, give order to your 'crompstres', barks and barges to do their best to stop these Scottish galleys and boats, making booty of them, if you find them trading with or bringing relief to the rebels; but favour and countenance those that trade with the subject.[9]

No naval challenge?
There was no concerted military effort during the sixteenth century to remove galleys altogether from Hebridean waters. Clan Campbell

were slowly encroaching on Clan Donald South in Kintyre and Islay but they were not renowned as a a naval clan and indeed seem to have looked to their sixteenth century allies, the Macleans, for assistance. (After Clan Donald South had been disposed of, the relationship of the Campbells with the Macleans would change). The English did not have the political will to send ships to the Hebrides except on occasions like Sussex's expedition to Kintyre in 1558 and when flirting with Maclean in 1595. Primarily their objective was to protect Ulster and exclude the Scots. It was not a policy of aggressive defence which is perhaps why it was so unsuccessful. On the other hand to invade the Hebrides would have involved them in political difficulties with the King of Scotland. The Scottish realm was otherwise preoccupied for much of the time and some of its work devolved onto the Argyll family who had influence if not always power over the furthest Hebrides.

The various Scottish kings approached the problem in different ways. Robert Bruce tackled it head on. He, and his supporters, had ships present on the west coast. He spent money on Tarbert Castle to ensure royal control of the harbour and portage. He also formalised the naval obligations of the Highland magnates in their charters. Of all the monarchs he seems to have adopted the most logical approach in tackling a specific local problem.

At the beginning of the sixteenth century James IV expended great effort, and more money, in creating a Scottish Navy. Whether this was well-spent is debatable since grandeur and flamboyance seem to have been more important than utility. His greatest ship, the *Michael*, had an extremely short working life as within three years of launching she was sold to the French. She cost over £30,000 to build, and reputedly carried over 300 guns and 300 crew. She was 240 feet long with a beam of 55 feet. The Hebrideans could not compete with this, but neither could the Scots afford it.

In 1540 James V toured the Hebrides with some twelve well-armed ships and, not surprisingly, met no opposition. Although the Hebridean chiefs could be brought to heel by an occasional show of force this was difficult to mount and probably not cost-effective. For real benefit such naval activity had to be constantly maintained – and that was expensive. There is no doubt that if a serious naval conflict had occurred the galleys would have been defeated. They were tiny and ill-armed compared with the bigger, heavier ships of the national navies. They had no guns mounted on board and relied on their speed to escape punitive action. They would disperse rapidly in home waters and in bad weather could hole up on almost any convenient beach. By contrast larger ships in Hebridean waters were more at mercy of wind and tide since they lacked oarpower. The destruction of such a ship represented an enormous capital loss and it is not surprising that limited attention was paid to the creation or maintenance of a naval force purely to deal with the Hebrides. It was more cost-effective to use the regional power of men like Argyll to bring the islanders under control.

Mercenary service

Hebridean involvement in Ireland has left a quantity of English and Irish evidence – particularly for the Wars of Independence and the later sixteenth century. Hebrideans had been employed as mercenaries in Ireland from at least the first half of the thirteenth century. 'Galloglaigh' or 'foreign warrior', (anglicised to 'galloglas'), is a term which first appears in 1290.[10] The Gall-Gaidhil or 'foreign Gaels' were the mixed Gaelic-Norse stock of the Hebrides and it may well be that the involvement of Hebridean mercenaries in Ireland stretches right back to the Scandinavian intrusions of the ninth century. The earliest raids may have been hit-and-run but there are clear indications in the sagas that the Scandinavians were soon working as mercenaries for Irish kings, as often as not employed to keep out other Scandinavians. After the Norman invasion of Ireland in 1169 it was inevitable that Hebridean contacts with Ulster would soon involve them with the English.

It has been debated whether mercenary service was a perennial way of life for Hebrideans or whether it was an occasional response to social disorder. There certainly are references to broken men and landless adventurers for whom the clan leaders were keen to disclaim responsibility. However in the sixteenth century much mercenary service was organised by the chiefs who called on their clansmen in the time-honoured manner. An ancient mercenary subculture and the attraction of periodic creachs or raids were what recruited Hebrideans to Irish causes. Perhaps the simplest and most obvious reason for this predation was the need for food.

Stories of raids to the Northern Isles from the Hebrides survive in the oral tradition of Barra as well as in Orkney and Shetland.[11]

Why the Northern Isles rather than Ireland? They may have been closer for the men of Lewis but they are a lot further for the men of Barra. (From Barra to Shetland is about 300 miles). Was it safer? Was there less chance of organised resistance? Was it simply because of a need for food? Was it condoned or encouraged by the Scottish government during the last years of Norse sovereignty? (Orkney and Shetland were pledged to Scotland in 1468-9). Whatever the reasons these raids provide evidence of the *reach* of Highland galleys.

Despite the bonds of kinship, language and culture most Hebrideans who fought in Ireland served as mercenaries. The fundamental reasons were always economic. The Hebrides are harsh and barren. The agricultural economy must have been under increasing strain after the decline from the climatic optimum in the eleventh or twelfth century. Most of the population struggled along at subsistence level but their advanced marine skills were adapted to a hit-and-run raiding strategy. From their Norse ancestors they had inherited a technological advantage – plank-built boats that could travel long distances relatively quickly. It is not surprising they used this naval superiority – particularly if most Irish still clung to their tradition of skin-built boats. Theirs was a paradoxical situation; a peripheral area with poor economic resources could prey upon a wealthier neighbour by virtue of the technological edge bestowed by history. (This issue of a surplus population dependent upon a fragile economic base is one of the key threads of Hebridean history. We become most acutely conscious of the problem in the clearances and emigration of the eighteenth and nineteenth centuries. It may have been part of the economic backdrop for 1,000 years previously.)

The Hebrideans were in a strong negotiating position. The Irish were always desperate for Scottish assistance, either against each other or against the English. Indeed that may have been the reason why so many of them made marriage alliances with the great Highland families. This was not confined to the chieftains. In August 1595 Sir Ralph Lane wrote of a recent landing of Scots: 'The Earl offers to give in marriage to the bachelors of them generally through the army, the daughters of his gentlemen and freeholders of Tirone, every one a wife of degree proportionable to the man that is to marry her'. The islanders' response is not recorded – but they immediately returned home.

In financial matters the Hebrideans were skilled negotiators and often secured cash in advance. Demand tended to push up the price. By the end of 1594 a messenger from O'Donnell was offering double pay to any in Argyll who would serve as mercenaries in Ireland. Donald Gorm of Sleat and Macleod of Harris spent a profitable summer in Ulster in 1594 and that winter made themselves busy arranging for a return in 1595. In the latter year messengers from Tyrone came to the Macleods with 'fyiff hunter lib starling' (i.e. £500 sterling). This was a powerful argument and the grateful chieftains of Lewis and Harris promptly raised 2,500 men. They eventually joined Donald Gorm in Kintyre where Tyrone sent another £300 with a promise of £600 more (half in armour, clothes and horses) once they landed in Ireland. To the chieftains of impoverished islands in the Outer Hebrides this was persuasive coin. Maclean on the other hand was keen to serve the English (because the Macdonalds were supporting the Irish rebels) and in 1595 he negotiated rates of pay with Captain Thornton of the English Navy. For longbowmen or halbertmen the composite pay (i.e. including food etc.) was 13s 4d, for those with firearms 16s 8d, a month.

The military evidence can tell us a good deal about the Hebrides in the later sixteenth century. Unfortunately it is a very partial view. The English were now engaged in the conquest of Ulster which was still in the hands of the Gaelic chieftains. The Hebrideans usually fought on behalf of the Irish rebels but occasionally for one Irish lord against another. There may have been numerous instances of Hebridean military involvement in the previous two centuries about which we know nothing.

Donald Dubh

The Highland rising of 1545 saw the last attempt to restore the Lordship of the Isles. Normally its Irish dimension is interpreted in terms of Donald Dubh's efforts to persuade Henry VIII's Irish government to fund his descent on Scotland. In fact there are strong signs that unless Henry had 'bought off' Donald Dubh, his 4,000 Highland troops might well have found gainful employment in Ireland fighting for Tyrone or against the English.

On 5 August 1545 Donald wrote to Henry VIII from Knockfergus. Beneath the eulogistic terms we can sense the latent threat of a man who has little to lose but 4,000 hungry mouths to feed.[12] Certainly Donald wished to untrammel the Highlands of the

meddling government of Edinburgh; certainly Lennox ought to
govern Scotland; but in the meantime here he was in Ireland with a
great many soldiers. Henry and his Irish officials must have been
anxious to expedite their return to Scotland and perhaps the most
cost-effective method was an inducement in silver. They had little
choice in the matter of Donald's arrival.

For the remainder of the sixteenth century the English State
Papers in Ireland recount a constant series of intrusions by
Hebridean mercenaries in Ulster. Whilst Hebrideans were important as a factor in the Irish land war, at no stage were their galleys a
significant factor in the naval war. They were now hopelessly outmoded as fighting ships and had been reduced to the role of troop-
carrying transports.

The table of galley numbers (*see* Figure 3) shows that, despite the
seemingly erratic estimates of individual observers, there is an overall consistency. The normal carrying capacity of a galley was
between 50 and 80 so the reckoning of Donald Dubh's contingent in
1545 either overestimates the boats or underestimates the men. The
1595 expedition may have included a number of cargo ships with
munitions etc. The functions of galleys on these expeditions were as
troop-carriers and getaway vessels. For the short crossing to Ireland
they were crowded to the point of safety and beyond. In the mass
transportations of 1545 and 1595 a lot of small eight-oared boats
were probably pressed into service.

Irish galleys

In Ireland the English faced the problem of dealing with the two
Irish clans who had a naval capacity: the O'Malleys and the
O'Flaherties. They had to devise both a high and a low-tech solution. On the one hand they overawed them with their warships, on
the other they pursued them with galleys of their own. On 18 June
1602 Sir Oliver Lambert wrote from Sligo to the Lord Deputy

> *I was proceeding to buy a galley to clear the coasts from the Flaarties and*
> *O'Malies who continually make prize of all they take. I maintain a captain*
> *in her and 50 mariners. She rows with 15 oars on a side. Sir Richard*
> *Bingham had to take this course before those islands could be brought to sub-*
> *jection and the subject go freely to sea. They have many gallies, of which they*
> *must be spoiled, for they spare none. Pray allow the expense of this galley,*
> *which is most necessary in my affairs.*

FIGURE 3: **HEBRIDEAN NAVAL INVOLVEMENT IN IRELAND IN LATTER HALF OF SIXTEENTH CENTURY**

Date	No. of galleys	No. of men	Average crew	Comment
	Scottish			
1545	180	4000	22	Donald Dubh to Ireland
1569	32 + many boats	4000	<125	
1579	16	700	43	in the Bann
1584	30	3000 or 2400	100 or 80	MacLean landings
1585	24	(2000 ?)	(83)	seen 'under Cantyre' [Kintyre]
1589	26	2000	77	under a MacLean commander
1589	7	600	86	probably MacNeills in Erris, Mayo
1591	13	700	54	MacLeans/MacNeills/MacLeods in Erris, Mayo
1593	30			belonging to MacNeills off Connaught coast
1594	34	3000	88	landed in Tirconnel
1595	up to 100	3000	30	MacDonalds, MacLeods etc
	Irish			
1591	3	200	66	Grany O'Malley's offer to serve Elizabeth
1601	1 (of 30 oars)	100	100	Grany O'Malley's – captured by Plessington

Bingham had regarded a galley as an essential weapon in his armoury, not because of its power, but because of its reach. The west coast of Ireland offered innumerable hiding-places for boats of shallow draught and driven by oars. These Irish galleys could hole up in places where Elizabethan warships could not risk pursuit. To cope in these situations Bingham required a galley.

The O'Malleys in fact behaved exactly like the Hebrideans; they fought for self-interest, not for a cultural or political cause. Sometimes they used their galleys to bring in the Scots, as apparently did the O'Flaherties, and no doubt they turned a useful extra penny this way. The O'Malleys were led by the redoubtable Grany O'Malley who had married into the O'Flaherties and so combined the naval strengths of both clans. Like the Hebrideans they were quite prepared to serve the English if necessary. Sidney wrote to Walsingham of how Grany O'Malley 'a most famous feminine sea-captain' had come to offer her service 'with three galleys and 200 fighting men, either in Scotland or Ireland'. After the invasion of Erris in 1591, and subsequent departure of the Hebrideans, Sir Richard Bingham reported

> *Grany O'Maly is preparing herself with some XXte boates in her companie to repaire after them in revendge of her countrie men, and for the spoil they committed in those partes, which I am contented to tollerate, hoping that all or the moste parte will take their journey towardes heaven.*[13]

Grany maintained herself by sea; by piracy, pilotage and the exaction of tolls. As the sixteenth century closed this became an increasingly difficult way of life in Tudor Ireland and her sons looked to the English coffers for alternative means of support.

In 1597 Clifford wrote to the Lord Deputy that he had given Tibbot, his mother (Grany) and his brother £200 worth in money and other necessaries for their valuable services by sea. Donald, also son of Grany, implied that he was short of vessels. In 1598 he offered to serve Queen Elizabeth on the following terms: 'He will take upon him to keep from the North both the Highland and Lowland succour of Scotland, if Her Majesty will build him two galleys in Wexford or Carrickfergus, the one of twenty-four oars, and the other of thirty'. Donald though may have been guilty of some special pleading. In December 1599 it was reported 'There are three very good galleys with Tibbot ne Longe [Tibbot of the boats], son to Grany O'Malley . . . These, if employed by her Majesty, would do

much good in the north and the O'Malleys are much feared everywhere by sea. There are no galleys in Ireland but these'.

What is fascinating about Donald O'Malley's offer is the size of
the proposed galleys and the sites of the shipyards. Wexford and
Carrickfergus were the two yards mentioned in 1568 with a view to
preventing the export of ship-building timber to the Earl of Argyll.
They must have been two of the most important towns in Ireland as
far as the timber trade and ship-building were concerned. Presumably the 30-oared boat was to be Donald's flagship, bigger than most
other Irish or Scottish galleys he was likely to come up against.[14] A
Scottish Privy Council minute of 1615 suggests 24 oars as the standard size of a large galley. The Hebridean fleet of the late sixteenth
century probably had few boats larger than this. The Rodel galley,
which dates to 1528, was an exceptionally large boat at 34 oars. The
sculptor may have been portraying the Macleod flagship.

Donald O'Malley was following a family pattern. His mother
Grany had also offered to serve Elizabeth. The question remains as
to why the O'Malleys and the O'Flaherties should have inherited a
plank-built tradition similar to the Hebrideans whilst other Irish
remained within a skin-built heritage? Has it to do with the nature
of Norse settlement in Ireland or Hebridean influence during the
Middle Ages? Currachs were cheaper and functionally advantageous for the Irish clans but we must also consider the role of the
Irish burghs – (for which we have no Hebridean counterparts) – in
the context of Irish boatbuilding.

English Navy (*see* Figure 4)
Apart from minor disputes during cattle-raids we have no record of
the Irish galleys offering naval opposition to the Hebrideans. What
then of the English? Elizabeth's navy was in a different league but
fortunately for the islanders was never present in great numbers.
(During this period the English faced a much more dangerous naval
threat in the form of the Spanish Armada.) That the English Navy
was reckoned a potent factor is obvious from the correspondence
and by Maclean's attempts to manoeuvre for its support against the
Macdonalds. As far as the English were concerned if they could
prevent the Scots from crossing the North Channel in large numbers
then the Irish rebels could much more easily be dealt with. The
solution was to mount a coastal patrol off Ulster and over a 50-year

period we know the names of some of the ships and commanders involved: the *Achates*, *Charles*, *Moon*, *Spy*, *Merlin*, *Foresight* and *Swiftsure*; Captains Thornton, Rigges and Moyle etc. Requests for their attendance on the Ulster patrol suggest that this was by no means permanent but they were important players in a small local conflict.[15]

FIGURE 4: The Ulster Patrol

For comparative purposes I list below *some* of the Elizabethan warships whose names appear in the Irish records. There was a huge disparity in size and armament (though not of crew) between these and Hebridean galleys. Details from Laird Clowes who warns that tonnages are only approximate. (The Royal Navy Vol. I pp 423, 425 & 588).

Name	Tons	Men	Guns
Achates	100	60	13
Charles	70	45	16
Foresight	300	150/160	37
Merlin	45/50	35	7
Moon	60	40	9
Tramontana	140/150	70	21
Spy	50	40	9
Swiftsure	400	180/200	41/42

Bingham assessed Grany O'Malley's power as follows: 'I will never aske but a boat of XXX [30] tonnes to beate her and all the boates and Galeyes belonging to the county of Mayo'.

In the Dartmouth Collection of the National Maritime Museum, Greenwich, there is a map of Kinsale in 1601 (Map 17). Three boats appear in the river, including the Moon and the Marlin (=Merlin?)

The sheer numbers of Scots who landed year after year in Ulster proved that the naval patrol was generally inadequate. However the English ships were completely effective in 1595 and subsequent Macdonald offers to serve Elizabeth were due to their new-found appreciation of her power. Undoubtedly Elizabeth's fleet faced problems of which the weather and a difficult coastline were the most severe, followed by shortages of supply and pay.

Storm damage was a major problem and naturally there would be a tendency on the part of captains not to run unnecessary risks with such huge capital assets. In November 1579 the *Handmaid* was in Dublin, 'much impaired in a storm'. Surviving repair estimates indicate the cost of maintaining such vessels in exposed waters. It also appears that the navy was plagued by the same problems of incompetence, corruption, poor supply and shortage of pay as the army. In 1595 Lord Deputy Russell reported to Burghley that 'The *Charles*, which was sent to impeach the landing of the Scots, is not furnished with victuals for more than 10 days'. In 1598 Captain Thornton of the *Popinjay* was complaining that his men were deserting for lack of pay.

However despite all the problems they experienced there is some evidence of their success against the Scottish galleys. They were not as ignorant of the coastline as might at first be thought. Captain George Thornton for instance seems to have served more or less continuously in Ireland between 1565 and 1601. In 1581 he was master of the *Handmaid* which was cruising off the north coast of Ulster to prevent any Scots coming in. In the same year he was commended to the Privy Council for his service. There were also occasional successes against galleys in action. In 1584 Sir R Byngham reported to Walsingham of the Scots 'that six of their gallies were taken or drowned by the Queen's ship' which perhaps indicates some ramming. When Rathlin was captured again by the English in March 1585 Captain Thornton's 'great and sufficient service' in transporting the troops was commended by the army leaders. Apparently he also 'took a Scottish galley' though whether at sea or ashore is not clear. By 1595 Thornton was commander of the *Popinjay* and Gregory Rigges commanded the *Charles* which were both involved in sinking galleys off the Copeland Islands at the mouth of Belfast Lough.

Copeland 1595

The skirmish off Copeland Island in 1595 is one of the few clear victories that the English enjoyed in their long campaign against the Hebrideans. In terms of subsequent Macdonald attitudes towards the English it may have been critical. On 23 July 1595 George Nicolson wrote to Bowes that 26 galleys were at sea bound for Ireland or Argyll. According to Hayes McCoy, who used George

Erskine as his source, the Hebrideans set out from Arran on 22 July in 'a hundred galleys and craft of all sizes'.[16] We can imagine a fleet composed largely of galleys, birlinns and eight-oared boats, but probably including larger cargo-vessels. They carried perhaps 3,000 troops belonging to Donald Gorm Macdonald of Sleat, a son of Angus Macdonald of Dunyveg, Macleod of Lewis and Macleod of Harris.

Judging from later events it seems the force may have partially dispersed at sea but a substantial portion came across Belfast Lough where they were met by the Queen's ships *Popinjay* and *Charles*. There are differing contemporary accounts of the battle. Rowland Strange reports 'there was six gallies that was coming after them; the Queen's ship met the five gallies and sank two of the gallies, and took two of them, and the other ran ashore and saved their men'. Mr John Morgan claimed they had 'sunk seven of their gallies' whilst an examination of two Catholic priests disclosed that 'Captain Thornton hath sunk three of the Randle's ships [Clanranald's?] with all the men and taken two others'. It seems that two or three galleys were sunk, two were captured and the rest driven ashore on the Copeland Islands.

There then followed a stand-off between the numerically inferior but relatively impregnable Elizabethan ships and the numerous but vulnerable galley fleet. The two sides negotiated and the upshot of it all was that Donald Gorm Macdonald offered to change sides and serve Queen Elizabeth! His service was not taken up and most of the Hebrideans returned home after surrendering pledges. (Maclean regarded the pledges as worthless and claimed the English had been hoodwinked.) Only two bodies of about 600 men each under the Tutor of Harris and Angus Og, son of Macdonald of Dunyveg, seem to have got through to help the Irish. In purely military terms this was a great if temporary English success. A Hebridean invasion had been prevented. The problem could recur but the naval deterrent had proved strikingly effective.

Thornton subsequently sailed to Mull to see Maclean at Duart in August 1595. He returned by October with Maclean's offer of 2,000 men in return for a salary and provided Elizabeth obtained permission from Argyll. In 1600 Thornton accompanied Docwra's expedition to Loch Foyle but in the autumn of that year was unable to pursue the Scots because his ship was in bad repair. In 1601 he died on duty off the north coast.

An effective deterrent?

Overall just how effective was this Ulster patrol? It is clear no galley could meet an Elizabethan warship in open conflict at sea. Galleys were completely outmoded as capital fighting vessels. They were caught in something of a time-warp. Hebridean galleys were still being built much as they had been in Somerled's day. They quickly fell behind the size of galleys being built in Norway where a 70-oared vessel was flagship to Hakon's fleet in 1263. Even before the end of the thirteenth century Edward of England was commissioning 120-oared galleys complete with fore, stern and top-castles. The evidence from twelfth and thirteenth-century naval battles makes it clear that critical features such as the height of the sides made the largest ships virtually impregnable. The Hebrideans had fallen behind at the first step, simply the increase in size. They never attempted to build cogs, hulcs or three-masted boats.

Three centuries later it wasn't just a matter of size and weight. West Highland galleys could not carry mounted guns. Mediterranean galleys (and some in Northern waters) could carry a single gun in the bow which fired forwards in line with the ship. Highlanders were well aware of the importance of heavy artillery on land and sea. They made use of captured Spanish ordnance after the wreck of some of the Armada fleet off the Hebrides and Ireland. Several pieces ended up in Dunluce Castle in Ulster. Nevertheless, a galley's size, its comparatively lightweight structure and its low freeboard made it unsuitable for armament.

The few boats in the Ulster patrol could not be everywhere all the time and even the best-laid plans could be disrupted by the weather. In October 1567 the Lords Justice wrote to Pers and Malbie that Captain Thornton would prevent the landing of the Scots. In November Sorley Boy landed with 600 or 700 men and in December Pers and Malbie wrote back to the Lords Justice that 'the Scots landed while the ships were driven by a tempest'; i.e. whilst the English boats had been blown out of the way. They were also not quick enough. It was a matter of luck and good judgement for an English captain to intercept a Scottish galley. In 1584 Perrot, much to his irritation, was unable to bottle them up in Lough Foyle and once on the open sea his vessels proved incapable of catching the islanders. In any pursuit the galleys could always scatter which would guarantee escape for most of them.

In 1596 the Lord Deputy and his Council proposed two small pinnaces to prevent the Scots crossing the North Channel. However they must 'be of less burthen and draw less water than the two last sent, otherwise they will do little good against the Scots galleys'. In 1599 it was proposed that the English should have two 40-oared coastal galleys with front-mounted ordnance based on Rathlin. These galleys should have a keel-length of at least 44 feet with beam of 14 feet. Attention was also directed towards preventing the Islesmen from obtaining Irish timber. The English had at last recognised the need for a 'low-tech' naval solution to the problem posed by Highland galleys. English naval superiority simply could not be brought to bear on a quick and elusive opponent. The answer was purpose-built boats. In the event English plans were overtaken by the Union of Crowns in 1603. After this James VI had a vested interest in preventing Scottish help for the Irish rebels. They were now *his* rebels.

By analogy we can understand the predicament of earlier Scottish kings who had faced exactly the same problem in the Hebrides but with slighter reserves. In both cases the royal authorities mixed occasional shows of strength with the persistent practice of divide and rule. Who can say it was not effective?

One of the few existing accounts of action between a warship and a galley actually concerns an Irish galley but gives us a vivid parallel for Hebridean vessels. In July 1601 Captain Plessington of the Tramontana cornered a galley between Teelin and Killybegs

> *where I made her run onshore amongst the rocks. Not withstanding she rowed with thirty oars and had on board ready to defend her a hundred good shots which entertained a skirmish with my boat for most of an hour and had put her to the worst. Coming up with my ship to the rescue, I quickly, with my great shot made an end to the fray. This galley comes out of Connaught and belongs to Grany O'Malley whereof a base son of hers is Captain. As I learnt since, this with one other galley was set out and manned with people called the Flahertys ... to do some spoils upon the countries ... about Lough Swilly and Sheephaven.*[17]

Here is a big Irish galley with a crew of 100 engaged on a traditional raid. They had worsted the ship's boat from the Tramontana but once Plessington could manoeuvre into position the contest was decided by his big guns. The situation is graphically displayed in John Goghe's Map of Ireland of 1567 where there is a sketch showing an exchange of fire between an English and a Scottish ship in the Irish Sea. Gunports are open and cannonballs flying. A galley simply could not cope with this. It was no longer a warship, it was merely a troop-transport.

Speed and versatility; these were the key factors. On a calm sea, on a moonlit night, or against a light contrary wind, galleys could make the short voyage to Rathlin or Ulster in a few hours. They could take advantage of any unexpected break in the weather. Whilst the majority of crossings took place in the calmer days of summer, Hebrideans went to and from Ulster even in the depths of winter. Forces arrived in January 1581 'in greate numbers' to help Turlough O'Neil. However this greatly increased the risk and in December 1582 'Captain Mynce, following after Scots that had taken a prey, compelled them to take to their galleys in a storm, whereby 140 of them were drowned'. Such setbacks did not deter them for in January 1585 it was reported that the Scots were arriving in Ulster in an 'unwonted season, manner and number'.

By contrast their very size and value meant that great care had to be taken with the deployment of the English navy. Each ship represented an enormous capital asset, one which could only be risked under certain circumstances. It was not so much the enemy that was to be feared as the weather. Damage to, or loss of, one of Elizabeth's ships could have consequences that ranged from the costly to the catastrophic. Caution must always be the order of the day, and the hierarchical structure of their navy reinforced that. Such ships could not afford to be lost in pursuit of individual galleys. Two months after his success against the Irish galley Plessington wrote describing a storm he had suffered: 'I was never so weather-beaten since I was a sailor. God save George Thorne's life for his excellent building of this ship ... I very nearly lost my masts in this storm owing to the giving way of shrouds, and lost my long boat'. The same factors applied in the Scottish expeditions to the Hebrides in the early seventeenth century. Bad weather and the risk of losing a capital ship always weighed heavily on the minds of the Scottish commanders.

These were the disadvantages, but there were corresponding advantages. The very presence of these large ships was something of a deterrent. The galleys must circumvent them at sea and avoid being trapped by them on land or in a narrow sea-loch. Beached galleys were extremely vulnerable. Were they hauled up-river, kept ashore or dispatched home with a skeleton crew against a later rendezvous? The Macdonalds may have sent their boats back to Rathlin for safe-keeping although there they ran a risk from Elizabeth's warships. In 1575 Sorley Boy could only watch in fury from the Ulster shore while Captain Norreys took Rathlin with the help of three frigates, burned eleven galleys and killed the garrison along with many wives and children of the Macdonalds. This was the most successful English action against galleys and it was presumably because they were found lying ashore and unmanned.

Elizabeth's ships were an important factor in the political equation. For years Maclean was in dispute with the Macdonalds over the Rhinns of Islay and felt inferior to them at sea. English naval help would undoubtedly swing the balance his way and he openly solicited it. In 1595 he wanted English naval protection for a joint Maclean/Campbell expedition to Ulster to help the English against the Irish rebels. He made great use of Spanish ordnance after the wreck of some Armada boats off the west coast. He had a chance to observe English naval technology closely when Captain Thornton took his ship to Duart in 1595. Maclean negotiated with a view to hiring his men to Elizabeth and it can have done his standing no harm to be able to show off such a powerful friend. However, although Maclean enjoyed the support of Argyll and links with the MacNeills of Barra, the Macdonalds maintained their superiority at sea.

The greatest danger facing the galley fleet was the weather. Elizabeth's Ulster patrol was of a limited nature and disadvantaged in respect of numbers, speed, manoeuvrability and local knowledge. If overtaken, the island galleys could scatter and disperse. They were unlikely to be met by another Hebridean fleet or indeed an Irish one. They were probably much more concerned that their homes would be raided in their absence. On arrival in Ireland they had the advantage of surprise. It might be several days before sufficient numbers of troops could be brought against them. In the meantime they could gather cattle and enjoy a strand-hogg, just as their Viking forbears had done.

Chapter 4
Ship-Service

ONE OF THE MOST INTRIGUING THEMES in the relationship between the Western chiefs and their overlords, whether Norse or Scottish, is that of ship-service. This is of great antiquity and was a continuing obligation whether the region was Dalriadic, Norse or Scottish. It may even stretch back into the Pictish or pre-Pict period.

Over the last 100 years a few brave historians have struggled their way through the tangle of land-names that burden our mediaeval charters.[1] There are davachs and tirungs, ouncelands and penny-lands, bovates and carucates, oxgangs and merklands. Each layer represents the historical deposit of Pict, Gael, Norse or Saxon. Each signifies a different fiscal or administrative structure. Each has grown into the other. In addition the place-names that embody these different patterns have themselves changed or gone out of currency depending upon the particular historical circumstances of the area concerned. By separating out these linguistic overlays, historians of land-assessment have managed to make partial sense out of an otherwise bewildering confusion.

Throughout the West Highlands, the Hebrides and Orkney the earliest traceable unit of fiscal organisation was the davach. This lingers in place names such as Davochbeg (Sutherland) and Dochcarty (Ross). It comes from the Gaelic word dabhach (vat or tub) and presumably indicated the amount of land thought neces-sary to render a davach or vat of produce as rent.[2] The davach in turn was divided into quarterlands, eighths etc., to provide a finer degree of fiscal responsibility. Such sub-units survive in place-names such as Kirriemore or Kirriedarroch (Kirkcudbright); Octofad and Octovullin (Islay).

In early Dalriada, however, a primary unit of social organisation was the 'house' which probably contained an extended family unit. This persisted at least until the twelfth century. Houses were grouped into larger units based on multiples of five, the most important being the twenty-house unit. It seems likely that in the West Highlands the house eventually evolved into the pennyland whilst the davach equated with the twenty-pennyland group. The question of the subdivision of these major units is critical because it is the subdivisions that we meet with on the ground. Pennylands, half-pennylands and farthing-lands survive as actual farm units; davachs do not. Between the major and the minor land units there was always an intermediate level, usually the five-pennyland or quarter-land. The whole subject is rich in ambiguity because of the superimposition of different systems of land-assessment over many centuries.

The Senchus Fer n'Alban is a tenth-century document with a seventh-century origin which was compiled to show how much tribute and levy could be expected from Dalriada. It contains a listing of the capacity of various areas and peoples in the new Dalriadic settlements of Argyll for military and naval service. The constantly reiterated phrase 'two seven-thwart boats to every twenty houses, for sea-campaign' indicates that this was a standard levy.[3] It seems reasonable to suppose that these seven-bench boats required fourteen oarsmen. If we add a helmsman and lookout we arrive at a crew of about sixteen per boat, a levy of 32 men for each group of twenty houses. By multiplying everything out we reach a total of 141 boats and 2,256 men from the three tribes of Dalriada – Gabran, Angus and Loarn. This looks a very large fleet but it may well be that the paper strength of Dalriada was always greater than its actual strength, much as was the case with Scandinavian levies.

A standard size of seven benches has been argued for on the basis of a rental for Lossit in Islay in 1626 which refers to a fourteen-oared boat. Since this lies in the former territory of the tribe of Angus it has been claimed as a relic of Dalriadic naval service. However it is doubtful that any one size of boat was 'standard' for a long time. In 1672 Clanranald leased Canna from Argyll on condition that he serve the Earl 'when required, with a galley of sixteen oars, sufficiently appointed with men and necessaries for thirty days yearly between the Isle of Canna and Icolmkill'. In 1590 the Earl of Argyll confirmed a grant of the lands of Kilbride for a 'birlen' of twelve oars. MacAulay has noted a 'Bagh an deich-ramhaich' (Bay of the ten-oared boat) in Grimsay. A rental of 1652 required the new MacNeill of Taynish in Knapdale to supply an eight-oared boat to Argyll. In the eighteenth century the McAlister family of Tarbert tenanted Tarbert Castle under a charter from the Campbells which included the provision of 'a boat of six oars in time of peace and war'. There is also 'Innis Sea-ramhach', or Isle of the six-oared boat, in Loch Awe. If we went on fourteenth-century charter evidence we might be tempted to settle on twenty-six oars; if we went on fifteenth-century sculptural evidence we might choose eighteen oars instead. Uniformity may simply be a projection of tidy-minded historians.

The Senchus refers to the recruiting factor amongst the peoples of Dalriada – so many men per twenty houses. Did the Dalriadic system of naval assessment articulate with any subsequent Norse expectation? What emerged in the Hebrides was very much a mixed society of Gall-Gaidhil, the proportions varying from area to area. These Hebrideans fought from Orkney to Ireland and doubtless further. Was there any form of regional levy? It looks as if Thorfinn of Orkney tried to impose one during his rule of the Hebrides. Whether it existed before, in Earl Sigurd's time, or indeed persisted after Thorfinn, is more problematic. Under the Kings of Man it was probably very localised for most of the kingdom's duration. Apart from Godred Crovan few of the Manx kings were strong enough to overcome the centrifugal tendencies of their scattered kingdom.

Houses are connected with the Dalriadic Scots; davachs are reckonings that they passed to the Picts and which had currency through much of mainland Scotland. What then of pennylands and ouncelands? Traditionally these units have been associated with areas of Scandinavian settlement but it may be that the Norse only adapted an already existing system. The late survival of the Dalriadic 'house', the ready match of 'houses' and pennylands, the perennial requirement for naval levies all suggest that we should look beyond the Norse to the Dalriadic Scots – and perhaps further.

Ouncelands are found in the Orkney Earldom but nowhere else in the Scandinavian world which suggests they were not originally a Norse device. They are scattered along the western seaboard but more in the north-western than the western Highlands. Pennylands occur in the former Orkney earldom, in Caithness and Sutherland, and throughout the West Highlands and Hebrides, particularly Mull. Both names are strikingly absent from Islay, Jura, Colonsay and Gigha. Islay was an important estate of the Kings of Man and the Isles and it later became the island home of the Macdonald Lords of the Isles with Finlaggan as their administrative base. Is the absence of a local fiscal structure due to the fact that these islands were once in the private ownership of the royal family of Man?

Whether or not they had different origins ouncelands and pennylands became bound together over time and the latter were regarded as subdivisions of the former. In the Earldom of Orkney, and its mainland possessions of Caithness and Sutherland, an ounce-land amounted to eighteen pennylands whereas in most of the Hebrides and the west coast it was reckoned as twenty pennylands.[4] (In certain Hebridean isles such as Benbecula, N. Uist and Tiree it seems to have been 24 pennylands.) It is likely that the success and longevity of the twenty-pennyland unit on the west coast was because it matched so well with the previously-existing twenty-house unit of Dalriada. Whether it evolved from it or was superimposed remains an open question.

The original land-assessments were of capacity rather than of fixed acreage. In the arable north-east davachs have been equated with fixed amounts of land but in the pastoral west they probably represented a rough-and-ready assessment of productivity. Limited surveying techniques and incomplete geographical knowledge would tend to favour fairly arbitrary methods of subdivision by a royal authority or its officers. Natural boundaries would form the basis of most early land grants. Tax-paying did not create communi-ties, it merely reinforced them and established responsibilities: 'Ouncelands defined territories, and pennylands measured shares'.[5] Early land-assessments became fiscal units, measures of ownership, military levy areas and units of ecclesiastical organisation. These multiple functions may have been originally separate but confused over time.

Ouncelands (eyrislands in Orkney) appear to have been the basic unit of assessment in those parts of Scotland most closely associated with Norse settlement. Ouncelands, like davachs, were divided into quarterlands. Due to the differing numbers of pennies reckoned to an ounce, a quarterland in the Hebrides was the equivalent of a fivepennyland, whereas in the Orkneys it equated with a four and a half pennyland. These units were not originally measures of land area, although over time they came to be treated as such; rather they were intended as a measure of the productivity of land in terms of its ability to pay tax or skat (Orkney). An ounceland was the land reckoned able to pay one ounce of silver and of course the amount of land referred to could vary with its productive capacity. Kintyre is more fertile than Lewis, Eigg than Rum.

The Norse had a well-developed system of ship-service or leiding which has been elaborated by historians like Marstrander and Marwick. It was probably first organised on a national basis by King Hakon the Good in the tenth century but is quite possibly of much greater antiquity. The country was divided into areas or shipredes, each of which was responsible for providing, equipping and manning a vessel. The longboats started at 26 oars (the smallest permitted size according to the Gulathing Law) and could go up to 50 oars or more. Norway is thought to have been capable of a war-fleet of about 300 vessels in the thirteenth century although this full muster was never raised.[6] As with the Highland magnates and the Barons of the Cinque Ports, a Norse war-fleet summoned by the king was only liable for a period of time. The half-levy was for external adventures; the full levy for national defence.

This is how it worked in Norway; we simply do not know what happened in the Hebrides. We could expect Hebrideans to be cul-turally attuned to naval service. Both Scot and Norse had originally arrived by boat and it was only to be expected that they would retain their naval capacity over the generations. Most Hebridean islands are too small for anyone to avoid seafaring and the mainland west coast has always looked to the sea for livelihood. Boats answered a psychological as well as a physical need. The Norse maintained galleys as expressions of power, security and cultural display. In their relationship with the Scottish realm we should expect Hebrideans to serve by sea. In some respects this tradition has continued into the twentieth century through service in the Royal or Merchant Navy.

There may well have been differences based on different social structures. The peasant farmer levies of Norway may not have found a parallel in the Hebrides where such farmers did not constitute a numerous or independent class. However in the late sixteenth century island warriors enjoyed high social status

> in raising or furthbringing of thair men ony time of yeir to quhatsumevir cuntrie or weiris, na labourers of the ground are permittit to steir furth of the cuntrie quhatevir thair maister have ado, except only gentlemen quhilk labouris not, that the labour belonging to the teiling of the ground and wynning of thair corns may not be left undone.[7]

In order to pressurise their tenants, authorities everywhere set muster figures higher than they could reasonably expect to call out. There is a telling sentence in *Orkneyinga Saga* of Earl Einar's desire to levy ships from his share of Orkney in the years after 1016. The Orcadian farmers persuaded a man called Thorkel to speak for them against Earl Einar's harsh scale of levy. Einar replied: 'I had intended to have out from land six ships; but now I shall have no more than three'. When the situation repeated itself the following spring Thorkel again pleaded for leniency towards the farmers. Einar was so enraged that Thorkel had to go into voluntary exile in Caithness. Einar controlled two-thirds of Orkney and the relative success of an earl in raising a levy must always have been a reflection of his political strength. In the preceding narrative the saga-writer makes this clear: 'Einar ... was a strong ruler and his following was a large one. The levies he used to impose were severe'.

Such a system gave the central authority significant power, if only for a limited period and for defence rather than aggression. Further recruits were attracted by personal ties or the lure of booty. The business of levying was always a compound of tenant obligation, personal loyalty, kinship and greed – sometimes one aspect more important, sometimes another. It operated at every level from king down to petty local magnate. The power, prestige and military ability of the levying authority, whether monarch or earl, would dictate levels of turnout.

Marwick's estimate of the Orkney fleet at about seventeen boats is supported by the evidence.[8] When Hakon sailed to meet (St) Magnus on Egilsay he took eight warships from his half of the islands. Similarly in a night sea-battle by Knarston, Earl Erlend, earl of half Orkney, had seven ships whilst Rognvald, earl of the other half, probably had eight. We know that in 1066 seventeen ships from Orkney joined Earl Tostig in the invasion of Northern England. The total number and relative sizes of these boats varied over the years but we can expect the Earl's boat to have been one of the biggest, perhaps even a 25-bencher. Levying was a fairly erratic affair depending on the overall political situation. Like all forms of taxation it was avoided as much as possible, especially after a few years of peace.

There is a telling hint in *Orkneyinga Saga* about a raiding trip planned by Somerled. One of his ship's captains 'had sailed into the lochs looking for people who had not yet turned up'. This is probably less of a comment on West Highland timekeeping than a reflection on the universal desire to avoid risking life and limb unnecessarily. Another interesting passage in the same saga suggests that levy duties were taken particularly seriously in the immediate aftermath of the battle of Tankerness in 1136

> *Then people were appointed to raise levies in different parts of Orkney. Thorstein, son of Havard Gunnason, was in charge of North Ronaldsay. His brother Magnus had Sanday, Kugi had Westray and Sigurd of Westness, Rousay. Olaf Hrolfsson went across to Duncansby in Caithness and was in charge there . . . Earl Paul presented his friends with gifts, and all of them promised him their undying friendship. He kept a large force together throughout the autumn until he heard that Rognvald and his men had cleared out of Shetland.*

This passage may reflect the fact that Earl Paul had only managed to levy seven ships from Orkney, despite the fact that he was sole ruler. In addition two of the ships had not arrived until *after* the battle and his narrow margin of victory no doubt made him keen to ensure a better turnout in any sequel.

By comparing Man with Orkney in terms of estimated productivity and population Marwick reckoned Man could furnish perhaps twelve vessels.[9] When the King of Man surrendered in 1264 to preempt a Scottish invasion he offered ten ships, (5 each of 24 and 12 oars). In 1310 Bruce gave Man to the Count of Moray for the service of six boats and some cash.[10]

We could also apply the Orkney formula to the Hebrides since the only difference we know of was the number of pennylands reckoned to an ounceland. Davachs and ouncelands were divided into quarterlands and these were the equivalent of Orkney skatlands. It seems reasonable to assume that the same system of ship-service applied; particularly from about 980-1065 when the Orkney Earls Sigurd and Thorfinn extracted rents and recruits from the Hebrides. Alternatively this fiscal and administrative substructure could have existed from the first days that the Norse kings took an interest in their overseas colonies. Early raiders were just concerned with tribute or protection money. Once the land itself was claimed, which it seems to have been from the early ninth century, there may always have existed the idea of a fiscal or military obligation to superior authority. It was just a question of whether that authority was seen to reside locally in each island, or in Man, or Orkney, or even in the Norse King.

The concept of a regular Norse system of taxation and military obligation could have been present in the Hebrides from the latter half of the ninth century; it is very likely that it was already familiar to Hebrideans from their previous Dalriadic and Pictish overlords – whether on a local or regional basis. Distance and weakness may have made it a system that was irregularly applied but no doubt both the Earls of Orkney and the Kings of Man tried to reinforce or re-establish it from time to time.

Taking the Orkney skat as a starting-point we can estimate ship-service along the west coast. Kintyre comprised about 42 ouncelands.[11] This would give 168 men or 4 x 40-oar (6 x 26-oar) longboats at one man per oar. Kintyre though was rich and productive. Glenelg was reckoned at twelve davachs or ouncelands (48 men) while Eigg and Rum together made six (24 men). Sunart and Knoydart counted as only three ouncelands or twelve quarterlands each and so would have provided merely twelve men apiece, not even one boat-crew. Both areas were presumably regarded as relatively impoverished.

The basis of the levy principle was that each unit of land, whether house, pennyland, quarter or davach should supply so many men towards a boat. The questions remain – what were the units of reckoning and was there a standard rate we can establish retrospectively?[12] (*See* Figure 5.) From the surviving data we cannot establish a fixed rate of taxation, or even an approximation to one. The ratios varied widely and we can say little other than that a 26-oared boat is a common unit. This had been a standard size for the smallest Norse longships and evidently it was the size best suited to Hebridean conditions and the prevailing economic base.

There is an interesting reference in *Hakon Hakonsson's Saga* about the billeting arrangements in Orkney during King Hakon's expedition of 1263. After his return from the Hebrides 'He had a list made of the ounce-lands, for the barons and heads of companies, for the purpose of billeting'. Ouncelands are again the unit of assessment, but here not for raising levies, rather for accommodating levies raised elsewhere.

Hakon's saga also gives us two indirect references to the obligations of sea-service which the Hebridean chiefs owed to the King of Norway. When John of Lorn came to Hakon at Gigha 'The king asked [John] to accompany him, as he was bound to do'. Again when Angus and Murchaid surrendered Islay 'the king gave the

This table shows documentary evidence of ship-service in terms of a ratio of oarsmen to land area – where that can be established. Since more than oarsmen would be supplied for each boat the total crew would be slightly higher.

Date	Granted by ... to ...	Area	Source	Qty of land (ouncelands)	No. of Ships	Oars	Ratio of oars to land area Oars/pennyland
1264	Surrender of Man to Scotland	Man	E.S. II 653	c. 216	5 / 5	24 / 12	180/4320 = .04
1325	Robert 1 to Count of Moray	Man	RMS 1 App 1 No 32	c. 216	6	26	156/4320 = .036
1304	Order by Lochlan MacRuari ?	Garmoran	CDS II No 1633	per davach/ounceland	1	20	20/20 = 1
1309	Robert 1 to Roderick MacRuari	Garmoran	RMS 1 App 1 No 9	17.75 +	1	26	26/355 = .07
1306-29	Robert 1 to Gillespie, son of Walter	(Cowal)	RMS 1 App 1 No 107	1	1	26	26/20 = 1.3
1343	David II to Malcolm MacLeod of Glenelg	Glenelg	APS 12; Suppl. p 7	8.25	1	26	26/165 = .16
1343	David II to Torquil MacLeod of Lewis	Assynt	RRS VI 487	4	1	20	20/80 = .25
1429/30	Act of Parliament		APS II p19	per 4 merks=8 pennylands ?		1	1/8 = .125
1463/4	Confirmation of John of Isles' Charter	Sleat	RMS II p173	28 merks=2.8 ouncelands ?	1	18	18/56 = .32
1498	Alexander Macleod	Harris/Skye	RMS II p514	c. 22	1 / 2	26 / 16	58/440= .13
1508	Eugene of Kilmallie	Morvern	RMS II No 3284	1.9	1	22	22/38 = .58
1510	Sir D. Campbell to Archibald, his son	Kilbride, Lorn	OPS II p103	16 merks=1.6 ouncelands ?	1	8	8/32 = .25

Three documents are in terms of merks, which were changing units of value, whereas pennylands were fixed areas of land. McKerral found that valuations of ouncelands in merks varied considerably but I have settled on his ratio of ten marks to the ounceland for the purposes of this table.

island of Islay to Angus, [on the same terms] as the other chiefs of the Hebrides held [their territories] of him'. We can presume these terms included so many days galley-service.

Ship-service to the Scottish kings

The most frequent *official* reference to galleys comes in the form of ship-service. Throughout the mediaeval period we have charters granting somebody so much land in return for service with a boat of a specific size with so many men for so many days per year. No doubt with the passage of time this was honoured more in the breach than in the observance but it illustrates an accepted pattern of land-tenure and indicates what certain land-holdings sustained by way of tax or public service.

Robert I, when issuing charters to his western magnates, stipulated ship-service instead of man-service.[13] In doing so he was perpetuating a system already well-established rather than making special arrangements for chiefs for whom knight-service was not convenient. Boat-service was practised from the days of Dalriada. It may be that when the Norse arrived they merely imposed their system on top of a native Scottish one. In turn Robert I utilised an existing practice for his own advantage. He did not try and impose a completely alien form on his (comparatively recent) subjects in the Isles. As Barrow says

> In the West the typical unit of military service was not the mounted knight nor the bowman but the 'birling' or galley of 20, 22, 26 or 40 oars ... Robert I brought many (perhaps all) of these men into a direct feudal relationship with the Crown by confirming or regranting their estates as fiefs in return either for fixed numbers of birlings of a stated capacity, or else (but much more rarely) for knight service.[14]

In terms of obligations felt by the chiefs, the Scottish system was probably more important in form than substance. The Norwegian king Olaf had made similar claims of superiority over Orkney when Thorfinn and Brusi quarrelled after 1020. For the most part though, Norwegian authority had been distant and preoccupied. Under Bruce a new legal framework was laid so that over the years, and as the Scottish kingdom grew more powerful, so the western chiefs could be brought into line. After all, what the king had given, the king could also take away. The charters may only have been pieces of sheepskin but they came to acquire enormous symbolic power, granting legitimacy to their holders. It was a system the Lords of the Isles themselves took up as they granted and regranted to their subordinates in turn.

There is one certain conclusion to draw from the fragmented documentary evidence: military service was a continuing obligation, only its degree or kind might alter. The critical question is whether or not there was, for any length of time, a standard rate of obligation such as one man per pennyland or quarterland. The evidence suggests the latter but perhaps it was an expression of an ideal, honoured as often in the breach as in the observance. There was no central organisation for levying; the system was enforced locally by landowners. At a regional or national level it was formalised by earls or kings who wished to incorporate these independent local fiefdoms.

The precise rate, so many men for so many days from so much land, probably fluctuated, depending on the relative strength of royal or local authority and the political exigencies of the day. In practice, as in Norway, this area levy was always supplemented by support from those who had more personal motives. These could be ties of obligation or family, political convenience, opportunism, fear or simply greed. Local sea-captains and their crews would attach themselves to a powerful force, whether local or national, as they saw it advantageous. Such support of course has always been notoriously fickle. Magnus Bareleg found he lost recruits in 1098 when he decided to spend the winter in the Hebrides: 'Kali advised him to call his troops together for a roll-call and, when the King did so, he found there were a good many absentees'. King Hakon experienced exactly the same problem in 1263: 'But while King Hakon lay in the Orkneys, the greater part of the army had then sailed for Norway; some, with the king's leave; but many gave themselves leave'. For the same reasons Alan of Galloway's personal power secured him a massive fleet of 150–200 boats in 1230; but it was a power that died with him.

Whatever the tidy administrative theory behind ship-levies the practice was always compounded by ambition, avarice, economic necessity or the cult of war. Some of the earliest Vikings may have been invited as mercenaries (e.g. to Man) just as the earliest Saxons to England. Eyvind was given the 'land-defence' of Ireland in the ninth century and there is no doubt that Man, the Hebrides and the Northern Isles provided men and ships at frequent intervals throughout the early mediaeval period.

Chapter 5

Numbers and Sizes of Boats

THERE ARE MANY LOOSE REFERENCES to boats in the documentary sources. In 1230 Alan of Galloway was credited with having 150–200 boats. Probably nearly all of these would have been owned by Galwegian, Manx or Hebridean chiefs who were attracted to the service of a successful war-lord by the promise of booty and the spoils of war. Their loyalty might only have been as long as a summer-raiding season or the period of their success. One defeat or the death of their leader and the fellow-travellers would steal away in the night. The indiscipline associated with such self-interest has bedevilled all non-professional armies and navies. It is a theme which recurs throughout Highland history. In this respect the Highland host was like a Dark Age barbarian horde, where the leadership of one man was critical; without him everything fell apart.

We have erratic references to other large fleets such as the 'three-score long-ships' which accompanied John of Islay to the Clyde on his marriage to Margaret, daughter of Robert Stewart, future King of Scotland.[1] In 1545 Donald Dubh is reported to have crossed to Ireland with 4,000 men in 180 galleys. The carrying ratio here seems to be just over 22 men per boat so possibly many of these 180 galleys were small – which is as we have come to expect in a Hebridean context. Nevertheless it is a large fleet and must have appeared very impressive.

Can we construct any sort of pattern which will give us a clearer idea of numbers of boats and their likely sizes? We are dealing with a period of nearly 500 years and sources of variable quality. Both aggressors and victims exaggerated – and not a single boat survives. The best we can do is 'guestimate' from the sources we have and draw analogies. (*See* Figure 6.)

Fleets of all kinds are encompassed here. At the one extreme there are great national invasions, by Norse, Danes or English, where hundreds of boats might be assembled. At the other there are small raiding parties where a few dozen adventurers coalesce around a successful war-captain. In between lie all the claimants and usurpers who struggled over Man, Orkney or the larger kingdoms.

FIGURE 6: **FLEETS**

Date	Commander/Nationality	From	To	No of Boats	Purpose	Source
729	Pictish			150		ES I 226
849	Scandinavian	Scandinavia	Ireland	140		ES I 279
871	Olaf & Ivar	Dumbarton	Dublin	200	War v Strathclyde	ES I 302
874	Vethorm	Scandinavia	Hebrides	18	Plunder	ES I 318
937	King Olaf (Ireland)	Ireland	England	615		ES I 429
1066	Harald	Norway	England	200–300	Invasion	Harald's saga (p.139)
1098	Magnus Bareleg	Norway	Hebrides	160	Conquest	ES II 102
c. 1143	Swein Aslefison	Orkney	Hebrides	5	Plunder	ES II 194
1151	Ronald	Orkney	Holy Land	15	Crusade	ES II 214
1154–6	Somerled	Hebrides	Islay	80		ES II 231
1158	Somerled	Hebrides	Man	53		ES II 239
1164	Somerled	Hebrides	Scotland	160	Invasion	ES II 255
1171	King Henry (England)	England	Ireland	240	Invasion	ES II 270
1191	King of England	England	Holy Land	181	Crusade	ES II 326
1210	Norse	Norway	Hebrides	12	Piracy	ES II 379
1210	King John (England)	England	Ireland	500	Invasion	ES II 388
1212	Hebrideans	Hebrides	Ireland	76		ES II 393
1224	Olaf	Hebrides	Man	32		ES II 459
1230	Allan of Galloway			150–200		ES II 476
1263	King Hakon	Norway	Hebrides	100–200		ES II 617
c. 1350	John of the Isles	Hebrides	Glasgow	60	Marriage	Rel. Cel. II p. 159
1545	Donald Dubh	Hebrides	Ireland	180	Rebellion	Gregory p. 170
1595	Macdonalds & Macleods etc	Hebrides	Ireland	c. 100	Mercenary service	Hayes McCoy pp250-1

However there are enough references for us to begin to get an idea of the scale involved. At any stage between 800 and 1266 an invasion could mount in excess of 100 ships; whereas a raiding party was more likely to be between five and twenty. Even a regional war-captain like Somerled or Alan of Galloway could periodically collect over 150 ships about him.

Native Hebridean boats were probably smaller than those belonging to Norse or Orcadian visitors. On the basis of the Bayeux Tapestry and the archaeological finds in Norway we can speculate that the earliest Viking raiders had boats averaging between 32 and 38 oars. Over time the average size increased so that boats from Norway or Orkney probably came up to a standard of at least 40 oars. According to the Gulathing Law the smallest ship that could be 'counted by benches' was a 13-bench or 26-oared vessel. The standard size of muster ship in eleventh and twelfth century Norway is thought to be 20 or 25 thwarts (i.e. 40 or 50 oars). The larger Skuldelev longship is estimated to have had 20–25 pairs of oars with an overall length of about 29 metres. The smaller warship was 17.4 metres long with probably twelve pairs of oars set 90–95 centimetres apart. The latter wreck is thought to be a particularly Danish type, long and low and well-suited to flat Danish beaches. A frequent galley-size at the time of the Wars of Independence is 26 oars which may have been 18.5-19.5 metres long. A 40-oar galley such as belonged to Colin Campbell in 1315 would have been in the region of 26 metres.

The average size, if not the number, of boats declined slowly from the thirteenth century onwards. The indenture between John of Islay, Lord of the Isles and John Macdougall of Lorn, dated 1354, permitted the latter to build eight ships of sixteen or twelve oars each. This was a deliberately restrictive condition for such a fleet could pose no challenge to John of Islay's own forces. Considering that the Lord of Lorn was one of the greatest magnates of the west coast it points to his relatively limited resources and power. By 1615 the official expedition to deal with Sir James Macdonald and Coll McGillespic could only call on six galleys, fourteen birlinns and some eight-oared boats from the most powerful western chieftains who included Argyll, Clanranald and Macleod of Harris. Since galleys, the largest of the vessels, were reckoned to have between 18 and 24 oars such a force was impoverished by Norse standards, or even those of Somerled or Allan of Galloway.

The only surviving boats from this period are to be found in Norway and Denmark. There are complete vessels from the Oseberg and Gokstad ship-burials in Norway and from 1957–1962 a series of five Viking-period boats was excavated off Roskilde in Denmark. These last are known as the Skuldelev boats. We do also have some documentary references to size but these surviving boats are our best evidence. (*See* Figure 7.)

Number of crew

A boat, of any size, always needs a minimum crew but there must have been great variation beyond this base level. Vikings were ever alive to the potential of a well-manned boat. It was a much more attractive and formidable proposition than a poorly-manned one. The poetic euphemism they employed was to refer to its shield-rack, the display of shields along the gunwale of a boat as it entered or exited port. A glance at the shield-rack indicated a boat's military potential and so this highly visible display of plumage could both deter and impress. According to *Njal's Saga*: 'There was shield touching shield' whilst in the Gaelic poem on the expedition to Castle Sween in 1310 we are told that 'shields hang from the long sides of the ships'.[2] (*See* Figure 8.)

In the merchant-ships propulsion was by sail and the oars were mainly for manoeuvring. Crew numbers could be reduced to those required to cope with mast, tackle and rigging, plus a helmsman. Depending on the size of vessel and the length of journey the crew could number as few as five or six. Whilst longships are the boats associated with the Vikings in the popular imagination it was in fact the beamier knorrs or merchant-ships that were the primary vehicles of exploration and colonisation. It was the knorrs that plied between Norway, Iceland, Greenland and Vinland. The longships were long and narrow with little freeboard which meant they were unsuitable for long-distance ocean crossings. They were primarily troop-transports and rapid deployment vessels. Knorrs could of course carry larger crews if required. The boats that explored the North American coastline had crews of 30 or 35.

There was a wide variety of size and name for early boats. This is the case in both Irish and Norse terminology and it survives still in the Northern Isles with words such as 'sixareen' or six-oared boat.

FIGURE 7: **BOAT SIZES**

Source	Length (m)	Beam (m)	Depth (m)	Draught (m)	Oars	Type	Date	Proportions Length/Beam
Sogn	5.25				4		800/900	
Faering from Gokstad boat	6.5	1.4			4	Ship's boat	850/900	4.6
Spinnoway (Shetland)	9.14	2.46	1.27		6	Sixareen	1889	3.7
Seksaeringur (Faroese)	9.3	2.28	.8	.71	12			4.1
Wreck 6 (Roskilde)	11.6	2.5				Fishing	1000	4.6
Aileach	12.1	3.05		.61	16	Replica	1991	4
Rong	13.5	2.8			16		900	4.8
Wreck 3 (Roskilde)	13.8	3.4	1.3		7	Trading	1000	4.1
Wreck 1 (Roskilde)	16.3	4.5	2.1			Trading	1000	3.6
Wreck 5 (Roskilde)	17.4	2.6	1.1	<.5	24	Warship	1000	6.7
Flatoy Book	18.5				26			
Tune	19.3	4.35	1.2		22/24			4.4
Oseberg	21.44	5.1	.85	.75	30		800	4.2
Gokstad	23.3	5.3	1.95	.85	32		850/900	4.4
Flatoy Book	28				40			
Wreck 2 (Roskilde)	29	3.5/4			40/52	Longship	1000	7.3/8.3
Flatoy Book	52				60			

As oars gave way to sail so the length of the ships was reduced in proportion to beam; perhaps down to about 3:1. Laird Clowes also reckoned that for decked vessels a proportion of depth-in-hold to breadth of 1:2 was established fairly early. For these boatbuilders **proportions** may have been more essential than measurements. We know the overall length of the Gokstad boat and we know the distance between the rowing-spaces. By deducting the total of the latter from the former we know how much extra to allow at either end. If we make similar allowances for boas with differing numbers of oars we can deduce figures which match well with those in the table:

A **13**-bench boat (26 oars) c. **19.35m** or c. **63' 6"** LOA. A **17**-bench boat (34 oars) c. **24.48m** or c. **80'** LOA — (The Rodel boat has 34 oars.)

FIGURE 8: **BOAT CREWS**

This table, which is by no means comprehensive, shows some documented crew numbers over the centuries.

Date	Description	Type of Boat	Crew per boat	No of Boats	Source
737	Abbot of Applecross drowned	Currach ?	22	(1)	ES I p.236
986	Danes hung by Scots		c.50	3	ES I p.489
c.1000	Earl Erling of Norway	Longship (32 benches)	200 +	1	Heimskringla
1016	Merchant-ship, Caithness	Merchant-ship	18	1	ES I p.541
1034	Monk(s) drowned from Scotland to Ireland		30	(1)	ES I p.578
c.1047	Thorfinn to Norway	20-benchers (40 oars)	50 or 60	2	O.S. ch.31
1098	Hebrideans killed by Ulstermen		c.40 +	3	ES II p.114
c.1110	Emissary of King Sigurd of Norway		nearly 60	1	ES II p.158
1151	Earl Harold	40 or 50 or 60 oar	80	1	ES II p.215/Marwick (1935)
1194	Battle of Floruvagar	Longship	90/100	1	ES II p.340
1238	Lochlann - off Welsh coast		c.80	1	ES II p.509
1263	Hakon's flagship : Kristsuden	27 or 37 bench (54/74 oars)	c.300	1	ES II p.610
1357	Safe-conduct for merchants of Isles	Merchant-ship	6 + 6 traders	1	Bain : CDS III No 1639
1601	Tramontana's capture of Irish galley	30-oared galley	100 +	1	W Clark p.81

In a Norse context boats are described in terms of the number of oars or, alternatively, the number of benches. At what point was it necessary for the crew to take one oar each, not two? Since a 'tolfaeringr' or twelve-oared boat is the largest to be named by *number* of oars this perhaps represents a cut-off point. In a boat of less than twelve oars each crew member could theoretically take two oars; above that it was one man per oar. Naturally in a small boat the oars were neither long or heavy. As boat-size increased so did oar-size and weight.

Like all tidy theories this glosses over an enormous variety of practical arrangements depending principally on just how many crew were available. We find a good instance in *Grettir's Saga*: 'So the three set out in a ten-oared boat . . . Thormod taking the bow-oars with Thorgeir amidships and Grettir in the stern'. When the rowlocks broke they bored holes in the gunwale. Admittedly part of the point of the story is to demonstrate Grettir's strength but we are dealing here with practical men making do with the resources they have. In the case of a problem they improvised with a jury-rig. Whatever the theory, men crewed boats according to the circumstances of the time. In *Orkneyinga Saga* we learn that Svein 'was with three others in an eight-oared boat' or that 'Uni chose three young Shetlanders to come with him in a six-oared boat'. There is a picture of a sixareen from Fair Isle being rowed by five men, the aft rower managing two oars.

In the longships minimum manning-levels depended primarily on the number of oars. As boat size and oar-length increase so does the workload for each crew-member. What we cannot be sure of is the point at which a second oarsman becomes an advantage or even a necessity. Moreover, making room for him requires a beamier boat. In some of the very biggest Norwegian boats there may have been more than one bank of oars. For long and heavy oars (particularly in the upper bank) more than one rower per oar would have been essential. After *c.* 1206 in Tunsberg we learn that King Erling Stonewall, Reidar the Messenger and Philip commissioned three great ships: 'They had two rows of oar-holes between the well-rooms and among them there were 24 oars in the lower bank and 48 in the upper. The oars in the upper bank were 20 ells long' (i.e. about eleven metres). Nothing more is heard of these boats so we can assume they were an unsuccessful experiment. Oars this length must have required several oarsmen to pull.

The Norse ran into the design limitations of their tradition comparatively early. In 995 Olaf Trygvason built the *Crane* at 30 rooms (60 oars). From then until 1262–3 when Hakon built the *Kristsuden* at 37 rooms (74 oars) there was only a slight increase in the size of longships. Extra size (and oarsmen) meant extra power; hence the experiment with banked rowers as in Classical times. However increasing the length also meant extra keel-scarfs and an element of structural weakness. In the second half of the thirteenth century there seems to have been a dramatic increase in the number of rowers. Edward I built galleys of up to 120 oars for his French wars. There are difficulties in fitting a known number of oars into an estimated length and yet leave adequate room for each rower. It may be that Edward's boat-builders came up with another type of rowing arrangement.

Even in boats with only one bank of oars it seems the crew often enjoyed a greater than one-to-one ratio. The space between each set of oar-ports was known as a room. In larger vessels where the thwart did not run across the whole width of the boat the space on one side was known as a half-room. On Norwegian levy ships the standard was three men per half-room, sometimes four or five or more.[3] The high sides of the 'great ships' meant that their oars were particularly long and heavy. Rowing such vessels over any distance would have been exhausting and it may have been a practical necessity to provide more than one rower per oar, or have the men work in relays. The biggest longships, like merchant vessels, depended on sail and were probably rowed infrequently.

The best clue to crew-sizes comes from the minute of a Privy Council meeting of 1615 concerning a punitive naval expedition to the Highlands.[4] The members of the Council had been at pains to seek exact information about naval matters in the west and after detailing the relative sizes of galleys and birlinns they went on: 'The complement of a galley or birlinn and the number of men of war they are able to carry is calculated according to the number of oars, counting three men to every oar'. This is not a statement to the effect that each oar required three men. Boats as small as these could easily be worked with one oarsman per oar. Instead it was given as a rule of thumb to reckon the carrying capacity of each boat. It was also an allocation factor. Soldiers, like cargo, had to be distributed evenly and the rough-and-ready formula for West Highland galleys was three men to each half-room.

As far as the smaller vessels were concerned a glance at the *Aileach*, a reconstruction of a sixteen-oar birlinn, leads one to doubt that they could comfortably carry 48 crew with weapons and oars. One would be inclined to apply the three-man-per-oar crewing ratio to the larger, longer boats, and then only occasionally. However there is a story that in 1616 Malcolm Macleod and 40 men armed with muskets and targes joined fifteen Harrismen in an eight-oared boat for a bit of piracy in Lewis!   Practice probably varied enormously.   When the hero of *Egil's Saga* is fleeing King Eirik: 'Those who rowed after Egil pursued him vigorously, two men to an oar'. An early seventeenth-century iorram or boat-song from Lewis describes a Morrison chief urging his boatman to row hard to escape pursuit

> 'I will have two row together,
> if I must, then three together'.[5]

The 1615 minute reveals the existence of at least three classes of boat. All three types were rowing-vessels and the only classification factor is number of oars. At the bottom of the scale are eight-oared boats, a class that was still popular in the eighteenth century. The next group are birlinns which have twelve to eighteen oars and then galleys which have 18–24 oars. The Privy Council only distinguishes them by number of oars and name. There remains the underlying question of whether these distinctive names concealed differences of line as well as number of oars.

The Gokstad ship had 32 oars and was found with 64 shields which suggests a crew of about 70 and a crewing factor of two to each half-room. Later Scandinavian boats could have four, five or more men to each half-room but they were correspondingly bigger. Nevertheless, ships with over 30 rooms were exceptional, even in Norway, and we only know of about sixteen in a period of nearly 300 years.   Unless, like Hakon's flagship, they were part of an invasion fleet no such boats plied or were built in the Hebrides. They were instruments of state for Scandinavian waters.

More common in Norway were the boats of between 20 and 30 rooms, popular with the magnate class. These would have travelled west although we know of only one 40-oared boat in Highland charters. Some Hebridean chiefs visited Norway, particularly during the troubled first half of the thirteenth century, and it is perfectly possible that they brought back the occasional Norwegian vessel.

However, in West Highland galleys the normal crew-factor was one to three men per oar, (only one being strictly necessary) and most boats were of the nine to twenty room size. Speed, manoeuvrability and adaptability were the primary concerns in the Hebrides. It was also advantageous if boats could be 'portaged', or carried across land, which dictated against great size and weight. They were beached to unload their cargoes since jetties and harbours were almost non-existent. They carried animals so either their sides had to be low for easy disembarkation or they used a system of gangplanks.[6]

We know the sizes of the Hebridean fleets that gathered round great chiefs like Somerled or Donald Dubh but we have no idea of their personal naval strength. In *Egil's Saga*, Arinbjorn, one of Norway's principal nobles, had three big longships. In *Harald's Saga* (dated to *c.* 1230) the formidable Einar Paunch-Shaker had 'eight or nine longships and almost five hundred men'. In 1615 the Privy Council is informed that Maclean has two galleys and eight birlinns. None of the other chiefs mentioned has more than one galley and two birlinns.

There are no direct comparisons between Norse and Hebridean boats but some of Hakon's dispositions in his campaign of 1263 hint at the differences within his fleet. The boats that were portaged to Loch Lomond included virtually all his major Hebridean supporters and quite probably their boats were lighter and therefore more suitable. Again, although Hakon was delayed for some time in Gigha by contrary winds he 'sent a light ship south'. Evidently this boat was not delayed by the wind which suggests that it was more manoeuvrable and perhaps more easily rowed than Hakon's heavy Norwegian boats.

This question of size and weight was critical with regard to a boat's speed and versatility. If oarpower was requisite, either because the wind was light or contrary, then you needed a light longship. We know that such were specifically built. Around 1150 King Ingi of Norway gave Earl Rognvald of Orkney 'a pair of longships, rather small, but very handsome and fast, designed more for rowing'. The larger, heavier boats required a breeze for sailing, and a stiff breeze was preferable to a light one. This paradox is perfectly illustrated by another passage in *Orkneyinga Saga* which describes Earl Rognvald's voyage from Norway to Orkney on the first leg of his journey to the Holy Land

There came a day when they appeared to have a fair wind, so they left the harbour and hoisted sail. But the breeze was in fact very light, and the Earl's ship made poor headway, needing as it did a strong wind. The other captains lowered their sails, not wanting to sail ahead of the Earl, but once they got out beyond the islands the wind grew stronger and began to blow so fresh that they had to reef sail on the smaller ships while the Earl's ship raced ahead.

They eventually 'sailed from Orkney with a fleet of fifteen large ships'.

There is good, 'negative' evidence for a major difference in boat-size between Scandinavia and the Hebrides. In Scandinavia a 26-oared boat was regarded as about the minimum size for a longship and they often had 40, 50 or more oars. These larger boats could be 90 feet long. Now we have no early evidence of the relative size of Hebridean boats but only one is cited in the mediaeval charters as having 40 oars. Apart from this, and a reference in 1512 to a galley of 36 oars, all the others in the documentary record have 26 oars or less. At least 80 stones in the West Highland series of crosses and graveslabs bear representations of galleys. Of these the largest has 34 oars and only about three others have more than twenty. Even the rich island of Man, seat of the Kingdom of the Isles, only produced boats of 24 or 26 oars for ship-service to Scotland in 1264.

Boats in the Northern Isles

There are indications, particularly in *Orkneyinga Saga*, that boats in the Northern Isles kept up with Scandinavian standards rather more closely than did Hebridean boats. This is readily explicable if we assume that boats in the treeless Northern Isles were often built in Norway and then exported.

Around 1047 Thorfinn sailed for Norway with two ships of twenty benches each and a crew of 50 or 60 per boat. About 1150 Earl Harald Maddadarson went to Caithness 'in a boat with twenty benches and a crew of eighty'. At about the same time Earl Rognvald set off for the Holy Land accompanied by a group of wealthy magnates, some from Norway. During the preparations

it was stipulated that none of them, apart from the Earl, should have a ship with more than thirty oars, and that his would be the only one to be orna-mented. This was to ensure that no one would envy anyone else for having more men or a better-equipped vessel.

Earl Rognvald commissioned Jon Foot to build him a suitable boat.

Its great size may have dictated that it be built in a Norwegian rather than an Orcadian shipyard. When Rognvald returned to Norway two years later to collect his vessel 'Lying at the quayside was the ship Jon Foot had built for the Earl, with thirty-five rowing benches. It was magnificently constructed, everywhere carved and inlaid with gold upon prow and stern, wind-vanes and so on'. Again, after his return from the Holy Land it is said of Rognvald that he 'had no ships at his disposal, so he went and asked his kinsmen and friends to build him a longship in the winter' (i.e. in Norway). In the meantime he took passage in a merchant ship to return to Orkney. After his arrival home the saga says 'At the time Earl Rognvald was without ships and had none till the following summer when his ships came west from Norway'.

Sverre's Saga tells us that before the Battle of Floruvagar in 1194 King Sverre collected ships from northern Norway. 'He had no ship larger than a twenty-bencher, and from that downwards. He ... had twenty ships, rather small; while the Islanders [from Orkney & Shetland] had fourteen ships, most of them large'. The boats from Orkney and Shetland must have had at least 40 oars and were presumably based on models from southern Norway.

Until the nineteenth century boats were often exported in kit-form from Scandinavia to the relatively treeless Northern Isles.[7] This may have been the case, particularly with smaller boats, in earlier periods as well. In this event we should expect Orcadian boats to match Norwegian boats in both size and line. A graffito from Jarlshof, Shetland, shows a longship with steering board and 24 oars on one side. This implies a ship of 48 oars altogether, further evidence of the large size of boats in the Northern Isles as opposed to the Hebrides.[8]

The Hebrides

The Hebrides were much more open to influences from mainland Scotland, Ireland and England. Some of the more exposed islands were probably treeless but there was any amount of native pine available on the mainland. This had been used as a resource for building wooden boats from Adomnan's time. The earliest Viking boats came from Norway, but as the Norse settled and a mixed Gall-Gaidhil society emerged so local copies of the Viking longships came to be made. Suitable tall oaks were probably scarce but pine was plentiful and a native tradition developed. Boats, in both skin and wood, had always been made locally but no doubt the Norse wrought a qualitative revolution.

Conditions and resources in the Hebrides have always favoured small boats. A term commonly used in the past was 'naibheag' or little ship. *Orkneyinga Saga* shows that when Olvir and Thorfinn recruited in the Isles their boats were distinctly small. Scattered island communities in a materially poor environment did not have resources comparable to mainland Norway, even in a kinder climatic period. They simply could not support 40 or 50 oared boats. Instead, according to the Privy Council minute of 1615, three smaller classes of boat emerged, although we have no idea when or how.

What size then were these navies? In a 40-oared boat the crew could number from about 45 to 160. A hundred-boat invasion meant an army of at least 4,500 men, a ten-boat raiding-party a battalion of 450. Hebridean fleets with an average size of 26 oars and crews from about 30 to 80 were correspondingly smaller. A useful parallel is found in a raid made by the Wendish fleet of Duke Ratibor in 1135 with, reputedly, some 660 'snekkja'. (A 'snekkja' seems to have been a small warship of about 40 oars.) Each of these boats carried 44 men and two horses which gives a very plausible ratio of one man per oar, one helmsman, two lookouts[9] and a captain. The fleet total may be an overestimate but the carrying capacity seems convincing.

The figures for Viking and even West Highland fleets seem excessively high if we consider that the Battle of Bloody Bay in the 1480s may have involved no more than a dozen boats, or that the planned punitive expedition of 1615 would only comprise twenty boats of any consequence. Was there was a reduction in both the size and number of West Highland galleys as the Middle Ages advanced?

Dalriadic society could support lots of currachs. They were cheap to build and raw materials were easily obtained. To build a longboat was far more costly. Pine was plentiful but not necessarily oak. Whilst the Hebrides or Sudreys were tied politically to Norway it may have been the case that boats tended to gravitate westwards from Norwegian and Orcadian shipyards. Once the Norwegian link was broken more boats would have to be produced locally. Those figures we have of boat-numbers suggest large quantities of smallish skin-built boats until the Viking invasions; then substantial numbers of larger wooden boats until the end of the Norse period in 1266. By this stage the cost, in money and wood, of boat-building must have been putting a severe strain on both Norwegian and Highland economies. In addition the climatic optimum of the earlier period had passed and from the thirteenth century there was a return to cooler, wetter weather with all the economic consequences this entailed.

We should then expect a long slow decline in both the number and size of galleys as the Hebrides languished on the periphery of Scotland. They were no longer at the centre of a commercial network between Norway, Dublin and Iceland. They were an impoverished appendage to a kingdom that looked south and east for trading contacts. They lacked urban centres, markets and good quality agricultural land. And yet the strange thing is that boat-building did not decline quite as we might imagine. As late as 1545 the Hebrideans could launch a fleet of 180 boats and at the end of the same century another that was still of respectable size.

Galleys played a crucial role in Highland economic life. They were the basis of all inter-island communication, all trade and all warfare. Galleys may have become smaller but it was unthinkable not to build them. They also had their life prolonged by Hebridean mercenary service in Ireland. This may have continued more or less uninterrupted from the first Viking invasions c. 800 until the Union of Crowns in 1603. It helped subsidise life in the barren islands. Mercenary service and the galley economy were inextricably inter-twined. Galleys carried the clansmen to Ulster and spirited them away again at the end of the season. They also carried the spoils of war; some coin no doubt, but substantially cattle, hides, corn and fish.

Between 1266 and 1603 there may have been a steady decline in the average size of Hebridean galleys. These had been smaller than their Norwegian counterparts from the earliest days of local manufacture. After 1603 this was accompanied by a marked decline in their number. Government hostility may have been partially responsible but the decline in mercenary service in Ireland was the prime cause. By the nineteenth century there were few large boats in the Highlands. There were no political interests left to serve. Instead innumerable small boats met local and domestic economic needs as best they could. There was not even the capital available to build decent fishing boats.   However it may be that research into eighteenth and nineteenth-century boat-building can shed light on the proportions of boats from earlier periods. There is a good deal of evidence from the Northern Isles and also in the Forfeited Estates Papers.[10]

Chapter 6
Naval Battles

SEA-POWER WAS ALWAYS OF paramount importance in the Hebrides and as rivalries developed so these were tested in battle. We know little of Dalriadic or early Viking conflicts apart from their dates. In 719 the *Annals of Tigernach* refer to 'the battle of Ardde-anesbi, on the sea, between Duncan Bec, with the tribe of Gabran, and Selbach with the tribe of Loarn; and Selbach was defeated'.

At times there were acute divisions between Norse and Danes. (White-Foreigners and Black-Foreigners as the Irish chroniclers put it.) This resulted in naval clashes in 852 and 914. As the *Annals of Ulster* laconically state for the former year: 'The crews of eight-score ships of the White-gentiles went to battle with the Black-gentiles at Snam-aignech. They fought for three days and three nights, but the rout was before the Black-gentiles and their opponents abandoned their ships to them'.

From accounts of naval battles in the Northern Isles and Scandinavia we can draw analogies for likely procedures in the Hebrides. However the longships of 800 were different to those of the thirteenth century and by the 1260s Hebridean boats were generally much smaller than Scandinavian vessels. The size of fleets also reduced. In 1156 Somerled's battle off Islay could have involved up to 100 boats. In 1230 Alan of Galloway was credited with up to 200 ships. The battle of Bloody Bay in the 1480s may have involved less than a dozen. By the early sixteenth century Hebridean naval power had been completely eroded by gunpowder. Galleys had declined from capital ships to troop-transports. Scottish expeditions to the Western Isles demonstrated the effectiveness of the new weapons by reducing hitherto impregnable castles such as Cairnburgh. The relative poverty of the region now left it fatally handicapped. In 1264 Dugald Macruari had 'defended himself with ships' and the Scots punitive expedition probably got no further than Skye. In 1506 Macleod was not even safe in Stornoway Castle which fell to Huntly and gunpowder.

From descriptions in the sagas we can glean some ideas about what naval warfare involved. It does not seem to have been a Viking tactic to ram the opposition. There was always the risk of damage to one's own boat and no doubt boats were regarded as amongst the most valuable prizes of war. There was no point in spoiling an enemy ship if you hoped to acquire it. Viking longships were not designed to give battle in mid-ocean, they were more in the nature of troop transports. Battles on water did occur but more often in sheltered stretches than the open sea. Norse and Orcadians roped their ships together before battle and this would have been impossible unless the waters were reasonably calm. This raft gave a composite fighting platform. The whole became stronger than the sum of the parts and any point that was growing weak could be reinforced quickly. Such a defensive raft also exposed fewer angles to enemy attack.

In *Orkneyinga Saga* it is said of Earl Erlend's men 'in the evening they would rope their ships together and slept on board at night'. This tactic was in preparedness for battle. Swein Asleifson's success was partly due to his perpetual wariness. During one troubled period it is said 'but at night he stayed aboard ship, always on guard against his enemies'. Swein's ship was his castle.

Victory was achieved not by sinking the enemy but by clearing his deck of defenders. This entailed shooting, grappling and boarding, followed by hand-to-hand fighting. Despite claims to the contrary, fighting took place at night in at least three major battles: Nissa, Sweden; Floruvagar, Norway; and Somerled's battle of January 1156.

Battle often started with an exchange at distance. If you could pick off some of your enemy's crew before you closed with him this was worthwhile. Vikings were keen bowmen and skill at archery was regarded as a worthy accomplishment right up to the level of king. In *Orkneyinga Saga* Earl Rognvald writes of himself

> *Expert am I on the snow-shoes,*
> *With the bow, and pull an oar well;*
> *And, besides, I am an adept*
> *At the harp, and making verses.*[1]

The history of the 'galloglaich', or foreign mercenaries, in Ulster suggests a strong Norse heritage.[2] Gerald of Wales comments on 'the affinity in language and culture, as well as in weapons and customs' between the Scots and Irish. He also discusses Irish weapons which include 'big axes well and carefully forged, which they have taken over from the Norwegians and the Ostmen'. Once boats had drawn together the weapons for close-quarter fighting included spears, axes, iron-covered stakes, swords and stones.

One way to shorten the odds was by surprise, a tactic the sea has always favoured. In the winter of 1228-9 King Reginald unexpectedly came to Man in the middle of the night and 'set fire to all the ships of his brother King Olaf, and of all the nobles of Man, at St Patrick's Isle'. Burning an enemy's boats struck him a grievous blow financially as well as militarily.

Despite the shortage of harbours in northern and western waters boats were not always beached. John of Lorn invaded Man in 1250 and landed armed men on St Michael's Isle. The *Chronicles of Man* describe the situation: 'While the tide of the sea was going out, by which the approach to the island was being cut off, the aforesaid John and those who had been with him re-embarked on board their ships. However many were still wandering throughout the island, while others were preparing the provisions'. In the late afternoon the Manx staged a counter-attack and 'killed a number of men'. 'Many fled to the ships and drowned while swimming out'.

John and his forces had decided not to expose their boats to attack by beaching them. Instead they let them lie offshore. This gave them the option of re-embarking before the tide had gone out too far – which John did – or staying ashore. It rather sounds as if those who remained ashore were either cooking food or involved in a strand-hogg. The problem for the invaders was that with the tide well out those on board ship could not readily come to the aid of their friends who were, quite literally, stranded on the beach. The Manxmen chose precisely this moment to attack – when the tide was lowest in late afternoon.

Methods

The normal Norse tactic was not to fight running battles at sea but to lash one's own boats together in a sort of impregnable raft. It made your own boats much more difficult to board because only the ends could be approached. Since the vessels were sometimes of very unequal size the smaller boats would be left unattached so that they could skirmish round the flanks or go to the aid of any particular section of one's line that needed support. It was hand-to-hand fighting that then decided the engagement. The most important factor was the size of the boats and the relative height of the decks. This was critical in a sea-battle; ships with high sides had an overwhelming advantage.

Stones frequently feature as naval ammunition in the sagas. In *Arrow-Odd's Saga* Hjalmar and his crew prepare for battle 'loading their ship with stones'; while in *Egil's Saga* 'they attacked them immediately hurling both stones and weapons'. In *King Harald's Saga* the poet Stein Herdisarson comments that at the Battle of Nissa 'Stones and arrows were flying'. They were also used on land. Gerald of Wales says of the Irish 'They are quicker and more expert than any other people in throwing, when everything else fails, stones as missiles, and such stones do great damage to the enemy in an engagement'. Why were stones so popular?

They were cheap and expendable, whereas good iron weapons which ended up in the sea were irrecoverable. If they were of any size and weight they threatened to damage or destabilise the enemy boat and therefore its ability to continue the fight. In the Battle of Tankerness (Orkney 1136), Svein Breast-Rope altered the course of the struggle at a critical moment. Olvir had just struck down Earl Paul with a spear-blow

> There was a lot of shouting and just at that moment Svein Breast-Rope picked up a large piece of rock. He flung it at Olvir, hitting him such a blow on the chest that he was knocked overboard into the sea. His men managed to get hold of him and pulled him back aboard but he had been knocked unconscious and nobody knew whether he was alive or dead.

How did Hebridean galleys fight? We have nothing but the odd literary comment and the evidence from grave-slabs to help us. Poems demonstrate that bows and arrows were favoured here long after they became outmoded elsewhere – partly due to the Highlander's difficulty in keeping up with the costs of warfare in an age of gunpowder.[3] Closing with another boat took time and archers were the only soldiers who could prove useful at a distance. From a sea-captain's point of view men were more expendable than boats and quite possibly a good deal of skirmishing took place before engagement. Grave-slabs suggest that bows, axes, spears and long daggers were all used – but that it was the sword which had most status.

Pentland Firth

The *Orkneyinga Saga* describes a sea battle in the Pentland Firth between Earl Rognvald of Orkney and his uncle Thorfinn in about 1046. Rognvald had support from Norway, Shetland and Orkney whereas Thorfinn's men came from Caithness, Scotland and the Hebrides. This may explain the difference in the sizes of the boats. Rognvald had 30 large ships, some of them Norwegian, whereas Thorfinn had 60 ships 'most of them quite small'. The importance of this factor is reinforced by the role given to Kalf Arnason, who joined Thorfinn at a critical point in the battle. The timing may be an example of poetic licence but Kalf's role was decisive because he had 'six large ships'. Kalf was himself a refugee from Norway so presumably his ships came from there also. The boats were lashed together in traditional Scandinavian fashion and the commentary makes clear that the height of the gunwale was critical

> *Each of the Earls encouraged his men as the fighting grew fierce, but soon Thorfinn began to suffer heavy losses, mostly because the ships in the two fleets differed so much in size. He himself had a big ship, well fitted-out, and he used it vigorously in attack, but once his smaller ships had been put out of action, his own was flanked by the enemy and his crew placed in a dangerous situation, many of them being killed and others badly wounded.*

Thorfinn cut the grappling ropes, broke off from the battle and disembarked his dead and wounded. He then managed to persuade the watching Kalf to enter the fray on his side. They rejoined at a critical phase of the conflict

> *Kalf attacked the smaller ships of Rognvald's fleet and it did not take him long to clear their decks, since his own stood so much higher. When the troops levied in Norway saw the ships next to them being put out of action, they loosed their ships from the ropes that had been holding them together and took to flight, leaving only a few in support of Rognvald's ship. That was the turning-point of the battle.*
>
> (Palsson & Edwards)

Tankerness, Orkney

In 1136 there was a challenge to the rule of Earl Paul of Orkney, son of the Earl Hakon who had murdered (St) Magnus. King Harald of Norway had given Orkney to Magnus's nephew, Rognvald, who had helped him in the recent civil war in Norway. Rognvald's party recognised that they would have to fight Paul for their claim and recruited Frakokk and her grandson Olvir in return for a promise of half of Orkney.[4]

Olvir recruited in Scotland and the Hebrides and set out to join Rognvald who had meanwhile landed in Shetland. 'As for Frakokk, she had set out from the Hebrides in the spring, she and Olvir having got together a number of men and about a dozen ships, mostly small and poorly manned. Around midsummer they headed for Orkney and their agreed appointment with Earl Rognvald.'[5] In the meantime Earl Paul was collecting his forces and

> as they were rowing east of Tankerness, twelve longships came sailing towards them east from Mull Head, so the earl and his men roped their ships together. Then the farmer Erling of Tankerness and his sons came to Earl Paul and offered to help, but the ships were so crowded, they thought they couldn't pack any more aboard. So the Earl asked Erling and his men to spend the time, while there was no risk, in collecting rocks for them. Just as everything was ready, Olvir's fleet came up and attacked them with a larger number of ships, though they were smaller ones. But Olvir himself commanded a large ship, which he sailed right up to the Earl's, and a fierce battle began. Olaf Hrolfsson moved his ship towards the smaller craft of Olvir, and his stood so much higher that it took him very little time to clear three ships. Olvir laid so hard against the Earl's ship that the men in the bows were forced back behind the mast and, urging his men to board the ship, he was the first man himself to do so.

At this critical stage in the battle Olvir was knocked overboard.

> Then some of Olvir's men ran to cut the grappling ropes and get away, and every single one of them was driven off the Earl's ship. They started rowing away and, though Olvir came to and ordered them not to run, nobody took any notice of what he was saying. The Earl chased after them east of Mainland, then all the way beyond Ronaldsay into the Pentland Firth, but when the gap between them began to widen the Earl turned back. Five of Olvir's ships were left deserted at the place of battle and these the Earl took, putting his own crews aboard ... then a large number of men came to join him with two longships, so that by the morning he had twelve, all of them well-manned. (Palsson & Edwards)

Earl Paul's levying system did not work as well as it should have done. He had no lack of men, but he did lack ships, to the extent that he couldn't even make use of all the men he had. Two boats arrived too late to be any use in the battle and Paul tightened up the levy procedures immediately thereafter. It may be that the levy ships had to stop frequently to pick up crew from all the small settlements *en route*. Five large and well-manned Orkney boats saw off some eleven small and poorly-manned Hebridean boats and one large vessel of Olvir's which presumably came from Sutherland. It was fortunate for Paul that he only met one fleet in this battle. Rognvald was still in Shetland with five or six ships. If he had managed to combine forces with Olvir the outcome might have been different. As it was, five of the Hebridean boats were captured.

Floruvagar[6]

During the twelfth century Norway was wracked by civil war. In the 1190s one of the claimants, Sigurd, won substantial support from Orkney and Shetland. A fleet from there sailed East to Norway in 1193 in a kind of reverse 'viking' or pirate expedition. These men were nicknamed 'The Islanders' in opposition to King Sverre's supporters who were 'The Birchlegs'. The Islanders wintered in Norway and in spring 1194 King Sverre moved swiftly against them. He caught them with their forces partially dispersed since at least nine of their boats were elsewhere. Sverre's force consisted of only smallish ships.[7] The battle took place in early April 1194.

> *'This is my advice,' said Hallkell (of the Islanders), 'that we should tie our boats together; then will our host keep together best. Let us give them first a shower of stones, and next let off our arrows; and then let each do his manliest; and then may God defend us'.*

King Sverre advised his men to

> *mark all our ships, [and] bind linen bands about the prows, in case we set on them before it is light. We must also protect ourselves in the grappling, which we shall have to take part in against the superior height of their gunwales: let us keep our ships free at first, while they are most vehement; look to yourselves at first, and protect yourselves; let then their weapons drive overboard. Let men look to their oars; we shall need them whichever side conquers.*

King Sverre had twenty ships, rather small; while the Islanders had fourteen ships, most of them large.

> *In the morning, at dawn, the Islanders lay tent-less; and next they loosed their cables, and rowed out from the bay. They laid cords between their ships, both fore and aft, and rowed all in line, and intended to look then for King Sverre. But because it was dark, they did not see anything before King Sverre's ships*

were running at them; and both sides raised the war-cry. Then the Islanders seized the cords and pulled the ships together. But the ships were running without sail; and each ran upon the other's oars and broke them across. They drew all their ships into the ropes. Then the Birchlegs' ships ran against them: the battle began then at once. The Islanders attacked vigorously while the Birchlegs put their shields above them so closely that they were nowhere visible uncovered. They let their ships move about, and made feints also; it was evident that they were accustomed to this work, so skilfully did they go about it . . . Then they [the Birchlegs] rose up under their shields, and made a second affray; some threw stones, some shot [arrows]; and they laid their ships so close that some thrust, and some hewed. The Islanders received them manfully; they had now the advantage of their higher gunwales. They came with grappling-hooks against the king's ship; and they slew the forecastlemen, and took the standard, and cleared very nearly all the ships, to the front of the mast. But when they began to board, the king urged on his men. Then the Birchlegs pressed forward against them so boldly that the Islanders drew back; some were slain and some betook themselves back to their ships. Then the Birchlegs got their ship free. The same thing happened to all those who had laid in so close to the large ships, and with whom the Islanders had come to grips; so that they cleared some ships of the Birchlegs. And this encounter was deadly to both sides, but by far the more fell on the king's side.

At this stage the Birchlegs drew off their ships and the Islanders, thinking they had won, cut their ropes and broke ranks to go into pursuit.

But when the ships were loosed asunder, and they were to begin rowing forward, they missed the oars; then the ships drifted before the stream. Then the Birchlegs rowed against them, and laid two ships or three to one.

At that moment the fortress-men came out from the town; and they had a long-ship, with a hundred men on board; and they all had coats of ring-mail: that force came well at need. Then the ships of the Islanders were cleared; and as each was cleared, the Birchlegs went from their small skiffs and into the larger ships . . . It is the talk of men that the battle has never been, in which men have conquered against so great gunwale-odds as there were in Floruvagar.

Islay and Man

In 1156 and again in 1158 Somerled fought full-scale naval battles against Godred of Man. The *Chronicles of Man* give few details

In the year 1156 a naval battle was fought on the night of the Epiphany between Godred and Somerled and there was much slaughter on both sides . . .

In the year 1158 Somerled came to Man with fifty-three ships and joined battle with Godred and put him to flight. He ravaged the whole island and went away.

Bloody Bay

The Battle of Bloody Bay was fought sometime in the 1480s between Angus Og Macdonald and forces loyal to his father John.[8]

Angus Og's boats were delayed on the north side of Ardnamurchan for five weeks by contrary weather. When they rounded the point and made their way up Loch Sunart they spotted a galley of the Laird of Ardgour and sped to attack it, mistaking its colours for Maclean's. Other vessels opposed to Angus Og came out to help Ardgour, principally those of Maclean of Duart, William Macleod of Harris and MacNeill of Barra. It seems that others still returned to the safety of Tobermory harbour, fearful of losing their galleys. Angus Og had at least four boats – his own, one of Donald Gallich of Sleat's, one of Clanranald's and one of Clanranald's son. Against him were at least five, the four mentioned above and one belonging to 'the heir of Torkill of the Lewis'.

Maclean of Duart was taken prisoner, as was Macleod of Harris who lost many of his men. Macneill of Barra, who seemingly had only one galley, escaped round Coll, three galleys in pursuit.

Archery was an important skill: 'the heir of Torkill of the Lewis . . . was . . . mortally wounded with two arrows, whereof he died soon after' and galleys were regarded as a valuable prize. Discussing those of Lord John's forces who did not venture to do battle Hugh Macdonald says 'the rest of the faction, seeing themselves in danger at least of losing their galleys, thought best to enter their harbour' and further 'the galley of the heir of Torkill of the Lewis, with all his men, was taken'.

We have a very practical example of their battle-tactics: 'Ranald Bain, Laird of Mudort's eldest son, grappled side to side with Macleod of Harris's galley. There was one called Edmond More Obrian along with Ranald Bain, who thrust the blade of an oar in below the stern-post of Macleod's galley, between it and the rudder, which prevented the galley from being steered'. The Laird of

Ardgour had 'displayed his colours in his galley' – presumably a standard method of identification at sea.

Battle site by Kentra, Ardnamurchan.

There are few clues to battle-sites in Highland waters. Both Islay (1156) and Bloody Bay (1480s) prove elusive. However, among the strands between Gortenfern and Sgeir a Chaolais by Kentra, Ardnamurchan, is the traditional site of at least two battles, one of them supposedly involving Scandinavians. These beautiful bays are remote by land but from the sea their golden sands are visible miles away. It is the northernmost beach, Cul na Croise, which has proved most productive. Finds include a silver penny of Edward I, ten to eleven daggers or knives, two to three spears, six arrow-heads and a great many clinch-nails. The quantity of clinch-nails and some vitrified material suggest that boats were burned on the sand. Whatever really happened the Wars of Independence saw a good deal of Highland involvement on both sides.[9]

Tall men?

A report to Henry VIII about Donald Dubh's Highlanders in 1545 comments: 'three thousand of them very tall men, clothed for the most part in habergeons of mail, armed with long swords and long bows, but with few guns; the other thousand, tall mariners that rowed in galleys'. The observer was struck by the stature of Highlanders whose favoured weapons seem to have been the bow and claymore. Racially Hebrideans owed much to the Vikings who were traditionally tall. At first glance this might suggest that the Viking stock of the islands persisted in naval service – in much the same way that the armies of some countries are largely drawn from one particular tribe or national group. We also have a poem of 1310 about an abortive attempt to regain Castle Sween, Knapdale, which refers to 'tall men . . . arraying the fleet . . . Norsemen – nobles at that'.

On the other hand the comments about height may simply imply approval of the fighting qualities of the men concerned. Stature was regarded by Irish observers as a key qualification for military prowess and they were anxious that any Highland mercenaries they enlisted should be tall. Dr Johnson's common-sense approach offers the most likely explanation by relating stature to diet. Referring to the people of the Hebrides he wrote: 'The tallest men that I saw are among those of higher rank'. The average height of people in Britain has increased over the last century because of better living standards and we know that galley-crews were not low-born men. Nothing can be founded on chance historical comments but they prompt some interesting speculations. We also have to bear such factors in mind when considering distances between oar-ports. Tall men need more space, as the crew of the *Aileach* found out in 1991.

Chapter 7

Decline and Demise

THE SCOTTISH GOVERNMENT HAS been held responsible for the destruction of Highland galleys on the basis of decisions such as that reached by the Privy Council in July 1598. The evidence though is contradictory and it seems likely that whatever the proclamations in Edinburgh they were seldom translated into action on the ground.[1]

Seen from a Lowland standpoint the Highland problem was an irritant. Why not remove the source of a Highlander's maritime mobility by destroying his galley? In the days of Bruce this had not been possible but he had tried to incorporate Hebridean power into the body-politic by insisting on naval as well as military service. In later times it became possible, but not practical. From the early fourteenth century Highland galleys were outclassed by Lowland boats. Since they dare not risk conflict at sea it became less of a military struggle and more a war of attrition. It took energy and resources to daunt the Isles and these were not always available. However, if goaded into action, the Stewart kings could usually summon the means to bring the Hebrides to heel. In 1504 the royal fleet bombarded Cairnburgh in the Treshnish Isles until it surrendered. In 1506 Huntly took Stornoway Castle with guns brought from Edinburgh Castle. In 1540 King James V cruised down the west coast and kidnapped several chiefs. The problem was that military action alone was no solution. The Highland galleys would never risk battle and their obedience only lasted as long as the presence of the royal fleet.

In the summer of 1598 James VI supported the Fife Adventurers' plans for a plantation in Lewis because he dreamed of opening up the fabulous resources of the area. His belief in the economic prospects of the islands was a current misapprehension fuelled by ignorance, propaganda and greed. In the Articles of July 1598 a charge was to be given to the principal men of the Isles to assemble together and demolish and destroy all their birlinns and lymphads – within fifteen days of being told so to do.[2] As far as mainland Highlanders were concerned they had to deliver their vessels for the use of the Fife Adventurers. The only exception, both in the Isles

90

and on the mainland, was for six-oared boats or less – 'all sic boittis as rowis with thrie airis in the syde'. No new vessels were to be built for three years. The reason for such drastic military and economic action was to prevent galleys being used as troop-transports by the local opponents of the gentlemen adventurers. The violent language of the Council Registers reveals a brutal quality in this government-backed onslaught on the troublesome islanders.

The Adventurers ran into fierce local opposition. In December 1598 Murdoch Macleod attacked and captured James Leirmont of Balcomie, one of the Fifeshire lairds, off the north-west coast. Balcomie was ransomed for 3,000 marks (£2,000) but died subsequent to his release. A year later the tables had been turned and Murdoch Macleod was tried for his exploit in Fife before being executed at St Andrews. During his detention in January 1600 Macleod signed documents which give some details about his kidnap of Leirmont.[3] Murdoch's force consisted of one galley, two birlinns and one smaller boat (perhaps eight-oared?).

The various government attempts to bring the Islesmen into line can be followed in the splendid Jacobean prose of the Privy Council Registers. By July 1605 the Council was waxing indignant over

the barbarous and deteastable murthers, slaughters, and others insolencies comittit be the rebellious theives and lymmers, violent possessers and inhabitants of the Lewis ... [whose] only delyte is in blude, reift and oppression, they being altogither voyd of the knawledge and feir of God, and having na regaird of our Soveraine Lords authoritie, royall power, and laws; and, [here we come to the point] besydes thair barbarous and lawles forme of living, they are avowed enemies to all lawful trafficque and handling in these bounds, and the maist profitable and commodious trade of fishing [4]

James and his Council then appointed three Justices and Commissioners with virtual *carte blanche* for Lewis. Among the measures that followed was a charge for rendering the boats of the isles and adjacent mainland to Loch Broom. The Council had considered King James VI's efforts towards Lewis

for reducing of the rebellious inhabitants thairof to obedience, planting of answerable people thairintill, and establishing of peace, justice and quietnes within the same, and seing ane of the cheife and principall causses quhich procurit the rebellion and disobedience of the Ilismen is the number of galleyes, limfadis, boitis, and birlings within the Ilis, quhairby the rebellious theives and limmaris, inhabitants thairof, hes the commoditie at all tymes to be

transportit to and fra, alsweill for eschewing of apprehension quhen thai are
persewit as for mutuall concurring and assisting ilk ane with others against
his Hienes and his authoritie, ... And thairfoir the saids Lordis ... comand
and charge the masters, awners, havers and possessors of quhatsomever gal-
leyis, limfadis, boitis and birlings within the Ilis and continent nixt adjacent,
... that thai and every ane of thaim ... bring thair saids galeyis, limfadis,
boits, and birlings to Lochbrume, and thair delyver the same to the persons ...
quhom his Majestie hes appointit to ressave thaim, to be keipit be thaim for
his Majesties service sa lang as the necessitie of the said service sall require.

Given that seven years had elapsed since the declaration of 1598 it
is obvious that the latter had enjoyed little success. Equally there is
now no talk of the islanders boats being destroyed – unless they
failed to hand them over.[5] The implication is that they would only be
kept by His Majesty's forces as long as they were required. Just as in
1598, this edict had little effect.

In 1608 Ochiltree was in charge of an expedition to Islay and
Mull and part of his task was to destroy Hebridean boats. He set off
from Ayr for Islay on 30 July.[6] His fleet consisted of two English
ships, two ships of his own and ten 'barkis' which presumably acted
as troop-transports for his force of almost 900 men. He arrived
between Texa and Dunyveg on 2 August and the castle was delivered up to him. He set off for Duart in Mull on the afternoon of 14
August and that night suffered a severe tempest which cost him one
of the masts of his own ship. On his way from Islay he met with the
promised reinforcement of an English 'gallay' and another ship
carrying munitions and ordnance. It was immediately obvious to
Ochiltree, and Captain Bingley of the English galley, that the latter
was totally unsuitable for Hebridean waters. They resolved to dispense with her services if the Privy Council approved – which they
subsequently did. The munitions and ordnance were requisitioned
from the accompanying freight ship and she too was sent back.

Maclean of Duart surrendered his house and Ochiltree arranged
a court for later that month 'to tak ordour with that Yland'. He pro-
fessed great difficulty 'in executing of that parte of my commissioun,
in destroying of lumfaddis, birlingis and heyland gallayis'. He then
gave a lengthy excuse on the unfairness of following this course of
action in the islands and not along the mainland shore. Obviously
the islanders had 'nobbled' him and persuaded him to leave them
their galleys in opposition to those of the mainland lairds. Ochiltree

wrote to the Privy Council on 18 August pointing out the anomaly.
The islanders had persuaded him that they would be at the mercy of
the 'grite nomber of those vashellis quhilkis ar intertenyit upoun the
mayne shoir' unless he took like action on the mainland. He therefore sought additional powers to destroy galleys in both places.

On 1 September the Privy Council met in Edinburgh and
approved a commission to Ochiltree for 'breaking the lumfads,
galleys and birlings on the mainland'. Allowing for time for the
document to reach him and given that Ochiltree kidnapped a group
of chiefs and was back in Edinburgh by 5 October it is doubtful that
he completed this part of his commission very thoroughly. Perhaps
Ochiltree did not want to take too much upon himself because of the
anomalies and contradictions of the government position. His
slightly legalistic concern for impartiality may just have been a
convenient excuse – as well as a delaying tactic. (Letters took about
five to seven days to travel between Ochiltree and Edinburgh). He
would have been aware that to destroy island boats alone would alter
the political balance between mainland lairds and Hebrideans – a
consequence he may not have favoured. The claim that there
was a 'grite nomber' of galleys on the mainland may have been a
misrepresentation.[7]

By July 1610 the Privy Council was expressing itself satisfied with
most of the islands except Lewis.[8] It felt that the work of Ochiltree
and Bishop Knox in 1608–9 had largely brought the Hebrides into
civilised society. However they were still vexed by those who 'haif
maid the trade of fischeing in the Lewes, whiche wes most proffitable
for the haill cuntrey, to become alwyse unproffitable, to the grite
hurte of the commounwele'. There was considerable piracy during
this period and the government was keen to protect fishing-boats
from local abuse. Accordingly Lord Kintail was given a two-year
commission as Justiciary over Lewis. The Privy Council granted

> *pouer lykwyse to oure saide justice, for the bettir executioun of this commis-
> sioun to tak the lumfadis, gaylayis, birlingis and boitis in the nixt adjacent
> yllis and in the Lewis for the furtherance of thame in thair service, the said
> justice being alwyse ansuerable to the awnaris of the saidis lumfaddis,
> gaylayis, birlingis and boitis for redelyverie of the same at the finisehing of his
> Majesteis service.*

In the twelve years since 1598 the Privy Council's stance *vis-à-vis*
Hebridean boats had modified considerably. First they issued orders

for destruction, then threats, now it was an enforced loan with the promise of return. By June 1615 the Council had shifted further still – to actually commissioning the Hebridean lairds to use their naval forces on the government's behalf. The Council's previous threats had met with a complete lack of success and it was now attempting to utilise amenable islanders against the rest – the classic policy of divide and rule.

In October 1614 the Privy Council issued a proclamation which covered the West Highland area between Kintyre and Lochaber and charged all between sixteen and sixty to prepare themselves and be in readiness with 'thair lumfadis, boitis, gaylayis, scoutis, and birlingis' to help Campbell of Caddell in crushing the Islay rebellion, 'both with thair personis and with thair boitis'.[9] The owners, masters and boatmen of these vessels were also strictly charged not to go to or from Islay without permission – under pain of destruction of their vessels. It is plain that the government only really felt antagonistic about such boats when they were used in opposition.

The islanders were also capable of putting up legalistic arguments against the destruction of their vessels. During October 1614 the Privy Council were dealing with the rebellion in Islay and were concerned with what weapons and boats the islanders should be allowed. 'Hagbuttis' and 'pistolettis' were completely banned but: 'Anent the discharge of having and keiping within the Ile of galayis and birlingis, that poynt was thocht unreasonable becaus it is understand that divers within the Ile are obleist be thair infeftmentis to have galayis and birlingis'. So the wheel had turned full circle. Bruce and his successors had used galley-service as a way of absorbing a threat. Obedience to these or similar charter-clauses was now quoted as a reason against removing that threat!

At the end of 1614 and the beginning of 1615 Archibald Campbell of Glencarradale was present at the siege of Dunyveg. Angus Og Macdonald surrendered on 2 February 1615 between five and six p.m. just as it was getting dark. In his account Campbell makes some interesting comments on the continuing efficiency of Highland boats. After Angus Og's surrender the besiegers were keen not to let any of the remaining Highlanders escape the castle. However the rebels tried to steal away in the gathering dark 'in a boat whiche yei had fittit for ye purpos'.[10] There was an exchange of fire between the rebels and the besiegers who launched their own boats in pursuit. The rebels also had to run under the fire of some musketeers stationed on a rock near to the castle. However 'the rebellis boat being moire swift than the boats yat were apoyntit to wache them that night did ower rowe them and the rebellis boatte being sum what onthight althoghe werrie swift yei were forcit to drawe to the narrest shoire yei culd cum att and landit in the Od of Illa where yair boate was sunk'.

The crucial factor in this escape was the relative speed of the rebels' boat. Sir John Campbell of Calder, who commanded the besieging forces, had his own galley, but his troops comprised a mixture of Campbells, Irish and the Royal Navy so the types of their boats must remain uncertain. Fear and desperation lent wing to the rebel oars. Campbell of Cawdor pursued them 'and causit brek all the boatts of the Ille so as yei can not eshaipe'.

In the troubles with Coll McGillespic and Sir James Macdonald in the summer of 1615 it becomes obvious that what was at issue as far as central government was concerned was not power but parsimony. In June information came from Glasgow that 'Coill Makgillespik with four score broken hieland men assisted with a bark and some birlinges had taken the seas' intent on robbing boats travelling between Scotland and Ireland. Sir James Macdonald is described as getting a big boat in Sleat (Skye) 'with oars, saile, and taikleing'. They met on Eigg and according to Sir Rory Macleod their combined forces numbered some 140-160 men who took to sea 'in two barkes and sindrie other boats'.[11] By the time the Privy Council considered the matter on 20 June the rebels were thought to number 300 men. At least 500 men were required to proceed against them by sea 'with galayes, birlingis and such lyk veshelles of this birth or there abouttes'.

There was no threat to James VI with the combined kingdoms of Scotland and England behind him. Instead the rebellion was an irritant on the west coast that threatened to become something larger if the Irish became involved. The Earl of Argyll was slow to take the matter in hand whilst the west coast burghs were reluctant to shoulder the financial burdens of an expedition that the government wanted them to take part in. Instead they pointed out that they already paid customs dues and recommended that the Council fit out one of His Majesty's ships and call upon the mainland lairds to provide 'gallayis' and 'birlingis'.

At their meeting on 25 June 1615 the Privy Council laid down detailed measures for an expedition.[12] Their minute outlined the naval forces then thought to be available in the islands. The Privy Council also had to write to the King on 30 June requesting one of his ships to transport artillery to Islay – further proof of the relatively small size of galleys. The west coast was expected to provide ground-troops and ships for their transport. On the same day the Council sent out a proclamation to all between sixteen and sixty in the Sheriffdoms of Argyll and Tarbert to 'be in reddyness with all warreelyk provision and furnitour, and with gallayis and birlinges'.

Once Argyll had finally bestirred himself in October 1615 the rebellion collapsed. Sir James Macdonald escaped to Ireland, Coll McGillespic surrendered Dunyveg. The ensuing correspondence from the royal forces are full of concern for the safety of the King's ships in the coming winter. The writers were well aware of the treacherous and dangerous nature of west coast weather – as well as the continuing drain on His Majesty's purse. A letter to Archibald Campbell dated 25 October makes the issues very plain.[13] Argyll should dismiss the royal forces before the end of the month and do anything else needful out of his own pocket

> So unles his Lo. [Lordship] be able to qualifie just and necessar causes of keiping men under pay I hartlie wishe that his Majestie may be fred of that neidles burdene; it is also expedient that so sone as the necessitie of the service may permit the returne of his Majesties schippes that my Lord consent to it and urge it, for besydes the great cost thair stay thair bringis to his Majestie, thair danger upon that stormie cost in this winter season is greatlie to be con-siderit and ffar as may be eschewed.

That the winter storms were regarded as perilous is proven in an account by Campbell of Carradale for January 1615

> On the fyft of Januar the liwtenant [Campbell of Calder] met with Sir Oliver Lambert at the whit foirland of Jura, being fowrtein or fyftein dayis afoir stayit by contrarie wynds and wehemet stormes, such as Captane Buttone, caiptane of his Majesties ship calit the Phoenix, a worthie gentelman na thing inferior in knowledge of sea fearing matteris to any in his Majesties dominions, afirmis that he newer endurit the lyk nor vas newer in a moir dangerous place.[14]

The reaction of the government in Scotland to the Islay rebellion reveals the inherent contradictions of its position. On the one hand

Courtesy of Manx National Heritage

Plate 1 (*above*): Hedin cross-slab, Maughold, Isle of Man

Plate 2 (*below*): Graffiti, Kilchattan, Luing

D Rixson

Detached Seal XLVII – 1145 – The British Library   *Detached Seal XLVII – 1128 – The British Library*

Plate 3a *(left)*:
Seal of Angus Mor of Islay – 1292

Plate 3b *(right)*:
Seal of Alexander of Argyll – 1292

Plate 4 *(below)*: Seal of Dublin 1297

Natinal Museum of Ireland

J Paul Getty, K.B.E., Wormsley Library

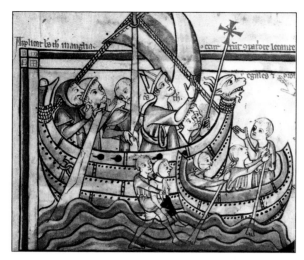

Plate 5 (*above*): Scene from the Becket Leaves *c.* 1220–1240

Plate 6 (*below*): Matthew Paris: The King returns from France – September 1243

The Master and Fellows of Corpus Christi College, Cambridge

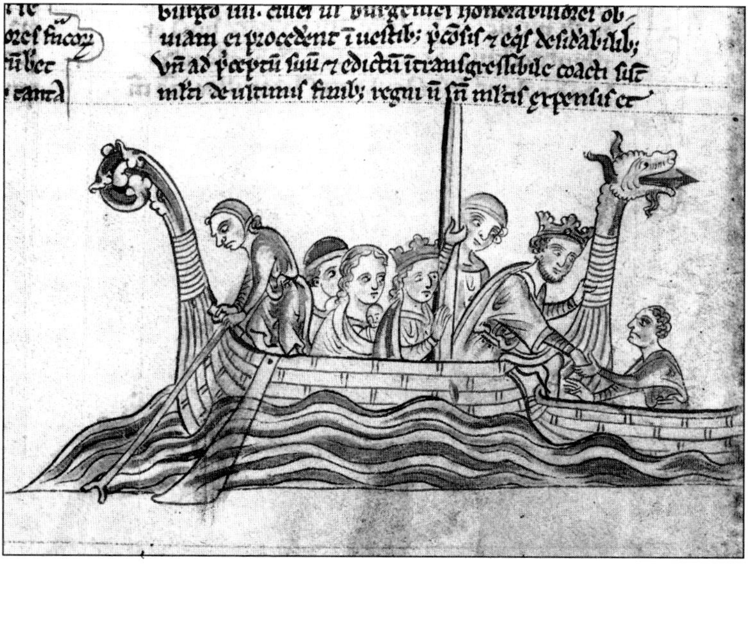

Plate 7 (*above*): Boat-building in the Bayeux Tapestry – 11th century

Plate 8 (*below*): Boat-builder's grave-slab? Inishail, Loch Awe

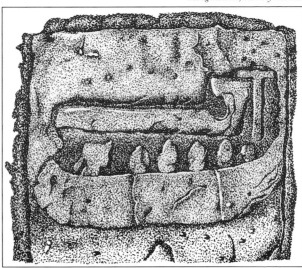

Plate 9 (*above*): Detail from Abbot Mackinnon's cross, Iona

Plate 10 (*below*): Detail from mediaeval grave-slab, Iona

Plate 11 (*above*): Detail from mediaeval grave-slab, Kilmory, Knapdale

Plate 12 (*below*): Detail from MacLeod wall-tomb, St Clement's, Rodel, Harris

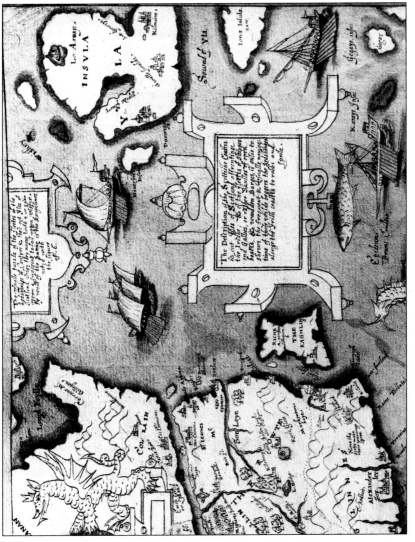

The Description of the Scottishe Castes & out Iles of Scotland affronting the Irishe, & of the Forthes of Shippes and Gullies, or Crawlen Barges is entire to succees the Frequent & Gullies woyages of being restile baggers the Redshanks along the Irish coastes to robbe and Spoile.

National Maritime Museum, London

Plate 13: Detail from map of Ulster *c.* 1602

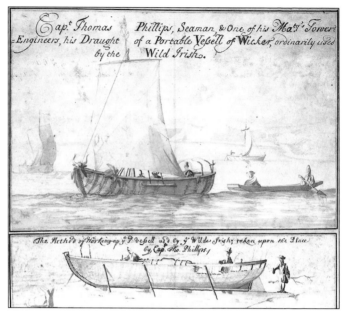

Plate 14 (*above*): Irish currach – late seventeenth century

Plate 15 (*below*): Galley on armorial panel, Kilmory, Arisaig – 1641

it wanted to dispense with the threat posed by Highland galleys; on the other it wished to take advantage of them as troop-transports should the need occur. In June 1615 the Privy Council had decided that a naval force was essential to deal with the rebellion in order to allow pursuit by sea. It resolved that the force should largely be drawn from the island clans – putting the onus on them to solve an island problem. It also stated that service for the government by these islanders 'sall liberat the personis foirsaid and thair cuntreyis frome all forder service be sea'. The government, when it chose to, regarded naval service with galleys as an obligation on the land-owners in the west. To save itself expense it would invoke this obligation.

Further evidence that governmental measures against galleys were not seen as formally restrictive comes in a marriage contract dated February 1613 between John Moidart, son of Clanranald, and Moir, daughter of Rory Macleod of Dunvegan.[15] Clanranald gives his son and future daughter-in-law lands in Arisaig and in return Rory Macleod undertakes to deliver to John Moidart 'in name of tochyr' (i.e. dowry), either 180 or 200 cattle 'and ane gaillay of twentie foure airis with her sailling and rowing gear gud and sufficient within ye spaice of ane zeir eftir ye compleition of ye said mariage'. From the time-clause it rather looks as if the galley had not yet been built but the parties cannot have been worried about government disapproval because they agreed that the contract be inserted and registered 'in ye buikis of counsale'.

There was no concerted government attempt to destroy the naval strength of the west coast. When deliberate destruction of Highland boats was required, as in Lewis in the 1590s or Islay in 1615, it was carried out in a haphazard and piecemeal manner, if at all. Contemporary documents reveal a continuing concern with the Highland problem and an understanding that galleys provided the means for Highland mobility and incursion. Equally there was a reluctance to undertake a wholesale military solution and a continuing dependence on some Highlanders, such as Argyll and his Campbells, against others, such as the Macdonalds. As a result there was no strategy, just a series of temporary, tactical responses. It was a form of crisis management. However to have done any more would have involved an enormous outlay of resources, for dubious advantage. There was a gradual but perceptible shift in government attitude – from outright antipathy in 1598, through persuasion, to toleration and even usage.

There is also evidence of strong pressure from the government to extract promises from Highlanders whose loyalty they doubted. On 26 July 1616 a bond was entered into by five Hebridean chiefs which limited them to one birlinn each.[16] Macleod of Harris, Mackinnon of Strathordale, Maclean of Coll, Maclean of Lochbuy and Clanranald were the leaders affected in what was basically an agreement, made under duress, to clip their wings

> *And that the saidis personis ... sall haif or keepe ony ma birlingis of xvi or xviii airis bot everyone of thame ane; and that, quhen thay travell athorte the Ilis with thair birlingis and comes on land, that thay nor nane in companie with thame in thair birlingis sall not sorne upoun the cuntrey.*

They were forbidden to 'sorn' or live off their tenants and the standard size of a birlinn was by now reduced to sixteen or eighteen oars – perhaps only 40-50 feet in length. Like other types of central government edict we can doubt that this bond was, by itself, very effective; but a combination of factors, including the removal of mercenary service and slow insistent economic pressure, probably did the government's work for it.

Piracy

In troubled times, and the aristocratic society of the Hebrides was habitually troubled by family dispute, each chieftain had to rely on his own strong arm. Doubtless some lairds entertained retinues far beyond their means for purely military purposes. Such men had to be provisioned by regular creachs. There is a story in the Old Statistical Account about John Macleod of Handa which could have sprung straight from an Icelandic saga if it did not refer to north-west Scotland in the days of James VI. 'He was low of stature, but of matchless strength and skill in arms; kept always a bierlin or galley in this place with 12 or 10 armed men ready for any enterprise. Some alledge he practised piracy, but of this there is no certainty.' No certainty – but every likelihood!

A good example of contemporary piracy is furnished in the complaint made in 1616 by Isobel Mackenzie, widow of John Mackenzie, and various skippers from 'Bruntiland' and 'King-horne'.[17] These people had suffered in Lewis at the hands of some of the Islay rebels who had become pirates

*Having taken a French bark which they furnished and armed, and obtaining
the assistance of a number of fugitive thieves of the Isles, they resolved to make
an attempt against the merchants and fishers in the North Isles, and especially in the Lewis. They were assured of friendship and resset among the men of
McCleud of Hereis.*

The Privy Council register gives the names of fifteen of Macleod of
Harris's men who took an eight-oared boat to the rebels and offered
to guide them to capture the ship of Robert Alexander, 'skipper in
Bruntiland'. The chief of the pirates, 'Malcome McRorie McCleud'
then took another 40 men, armed with muskets and targes, into the
eight-oared boat. It seems scarcely credible that there were now 56
men aboard this little vessel. Anyway they travelled up the coast of
Lewis and captured Robert Alexander's ship. Malcolm Macleod
then went ashore with twenty men in the eight-oared boat and slew
John Mackenzie at his house in Lewis. They returned to Robert
Alexander's ship and 'towed hir to thair bark' where they divided up
the spoils. Macleod of Harris's men took off their booty of 'wyn and
merchandice, with thame in thair awne boit' to Dunvegan where
they openly sold it.

There are other instances of piracy in the late sixteenth and early
seventeenth century. In 1604 Rory Macleod of Dunvegan had to pay
£500 for goods taken 'from a bark in Loch Hourn' in 1587. Hugh
MacGillespic Clerich of Trotternish raided fishermen and traders
alike. In 1600 he seized a ship belonging to Thomas Inglis, merchant
of Edinburgh, in Loch Sheil, Lewis. In the 1620s Clanranald took
the contents of a ship from Leith and in 1636 of the English barque
Susannah – both off Barra. Previously Clanranald had been
in trouble for seizing a fishing-boat and then compelling the
owner to buy the contents back. It seems this was not an infrequent
occurrence.

In the seventeenth century large wooden boats in the Highlands
came from outside the area. It was said of Clanranald in 1648 that
'he set off from Uist in a rigged low-country frigate which he had,
and in a Highland galley, with about 300 soldiers'. In May 1653 he
was on the Commonwealth side and asked for a commission to use
a small frigate he owned as a privateer against the Dutch. In 1685
the most valuable single item stolen in the Duke of Atholl's punitive
expedition against the Argyll estates was a three-masted boat from
Campbeltown. The disparity between Highland and Lowland naval

strength is demonstrated by the Book of Clanranald's description of Alasdair MacColla's expedition in 1644: 'At that time, three large ships of war belonging to the Scottish Parliament sailed round from Leith, and came to the mouth of Loch Eiseord, while Alaster's ships lay in the loch; they fought them, but Alaster's ships were taken'.

Galleys carried thousands of mercenaries to and from Ireland in a lucrative trade which ended with the accession of James VI to the English throne in 1603. Galleys declined thereafter because of the economic impoverishment of the area, and because the society and economy that maintained them underwent radical change. With the removal of mercenary service as a form of support, financial pressures slowly and insidiously reduced their numbers and size. They reflected the power of a chief and his clan at a time when these were no longer allowed independent expression.

A change in galley design?

There is a problem with galley-design during the sixteenth century. The latest galley-slab for which we have a firm date was carved in 1539. This, and other early sixteenth-century carvings such as Rodel (1528), all show the same type of boat; i.e. the traditional Viking model with high endposts and no superstructure. The problem arises from the fact that there is evidence for a change in design from the mid-sixteenth century. What does this amount to?

Much of our evidence for the traditional model of Highland galley comes from the rich series of West Highland grave-carvings between 1350 and 1550. After the Reformation this art went into rapid decline although this may have owed as much to the loss of the Lordship and the absence of patronage as to new religious values. We have no comparable series of monuments for the period after 1550 but we have isolated examples which give us some clues. We have a trio of stones, presumably commissioned by Clanranald in 1641, and found on his estates in Arisaig, Eigg and Uist. The Arisaig slab shows a marked change in boat-design. There only seem to be six oar-ports but we can probably ignore this since it is unlikely the sculptor was attempting to portray a boat of any particular size. However neither stem nor stern are as high as they used to be and there is a pronounced tiller at the stern. The stem too has changed in shape. Instead of curving up it now projects forward.

In the Dartmouth Collection of the National Maritime Museum,

Greenwich, there is a fascinating map of north-eastern Ireland. We have no author or date but a reference in the text to 'Her Majesty' proves it was executed before Elizabeth's death in 1603. This may be a map referred to in the Calendar of State Papers for Ireland in 1602. It formed part of Sir Rafe Lane's submission for a plantation in the area known as the 'Duffrinne' and is listed as missing. The dates and subject matter match well; both documents are concerned about the incursions of 'redshanks' or Scottish Highlanders, and both stress the historic role of the de Courcy family.

The map formed part of what was essentially an investment prospectus. This would have been presented in the highest circles of government, perhaps even to the Queen herself. No expense would have been spared and a well-known artist would have been commissioned to create the cartographic centrepiece. The text suggests that the author was familiar with the area and the annual invasions of 'redshanks'. However the map that survives may be the work of a copyist rather than the original cartographer. Unfortunately we do not yet know his identity.[18] The map gives copious information about the annual descent of Scottish galleys on Northern Ireland

The Description of the Scottishe coastes and out Isles of Scotland affrontinge the Irishe; and of the fleetes of Shippes and Gallies, or rather Skulles of open boates, and woodden Barges, is onlie to shewe the frequent and usualle navigations of those wilde beggers the Redshankes alonge the Irish coastes to robbe and spoile ...

The usualle parada of the fleetes of the Redshankes of Cantyre and those out Iles of Scotland when they meane with 2 or 3000 uppon a suddeine to fall uppon Ulster by west of the Banne is the Raughlines ... The usualle Parada of the Redshankes fleetes when they designe to fall uppon the Clandeboyes is the Mulle of Gallowaye or the Isles of Arranne ...

In other words, if the Highlanders were raiding west of the River Bann they assembled at Rathlin, if they were going down the east coast to Clandeboyes then they collected at the Mull of Galloway or Arran. The blank areas of sea are filled with galleys on their way to Ireland, a visual reinforcement of a theme well rehearsed in the text. At first glance this appears like a wonderful body of new evidence. The trouble is that none of the galleys look anything like the carvings in the West Highland series of grave-slabs. They are one-masted, but the sail, although square (i.e. set athwartships), is given the feel of a lateen/fore-and-aft rig by being consistently set with a sloping yard-arm. They all have a little cabin on the stern – which projects aft, as does the stem forward. This gives an overall shape that is quite different to the traditional West Highland galley where stem and stern usually end in a steep upward curve.

In his *Supplemental Descriptive Catalogue of Ancient Scottish Seals* Laing illustrates two seals belonging to John Moidartach, Captain of Clanranald, and his son Allan, which are attached to a document dated 1572. The seals incorporate heraldic designs where the galley is indisputably of a new type with raised decks at stem and stern. Both ends now lack the steep upward curve characteristic of the grave-slab birlinns. Numbers of later heraldic devices incorporate this new galley-type.[19]

There is a complete disjunction between the traditional Highland galley and this new vessel. It is undoubtedly drawn from Mediterranean models but not necessarily by direct input. The English, Irish and Lowland Scots all had their own galleys and it may be that the new design had been mediated through their ship-wrights. We do not know the extent to which old and new models coexisted or in what proportions they were built. It is perfectly possible that the new type was championed by the wealthier chiefs whilst the old survived in remote island backwaters. It is also possible that the new galleys were built by means of skeleton rather than shell-construction. Since it was a comparatively short-lived import I shall not examine it further. Unfortunately historians have sometimes confused the native and foreign designs.

Demise

The early seventeenth century seems a good point at which to draw this historical survey to a close. Galleys were built for at least another century[20]; but fewer in number and smaller in size. In the eighteenth century the eight-oared boat was still a practical unit but anything larger was probably an import or along different lines. Certainly there was no Highland naval force by the time of Bonnie Prince Charlie. Alasdair Macdonald's poem 'The Birlinn of Clan Ranald' is not only a monument to these boats but also an epitaph. His description gives invaluable detail of a type that must have been archaic by 1743. We should also be cautious about assuming that the term galley described the same boat in the eighteenth century as in the sixteenth.[21] It is impossible to know if the seventeenth century saw *gradual* decline or whether the political upheavals of 1615-1616 had dramatic repercussions in terms of the destruction of numbers of boats which were never replaced. There are several factors to consider.

Economic

We can suggest economic causes for their disappearance. Was it simply that Highland incomes could not keep pace with the spiralling costs of boat-building or were the Highlands getting poorer? The period saw climatic changes that led to it being christened the 'Little Ice Age'. Average temperatures dropped, the Thames froze over and there was a series of disastrous harvests in Scotland at the end of the seventeenth century during the so-called 'ill years'. Did agriculture, the mainstay of the Highland economy, suffer serious setback? Did rents and disposable income decline in real terms? Or was it because the Union of Crowns prevented Highland chiefs from earning Spanish coin in Ulster to finance the building and upkeep of galleys?

Bigger ships were not so manoeuvrable in treacherous Highland waters. They could not be beached so easily or portaged at all. They required harbours, which the Highlanders did not have and could not afford to build. Galleys had the advantage in these respects but could only be maintained by warfare or raiding. As these opportunities were restricted so they became liabilities rather than assets. Galley-service was part of the culture of Hebridean life and the population of the Hebrides had been dependent on the fruits of that service for the previous 800 years. With its erosion came all sorts of economic consequences. Those once entertained as mercenaries in Ireland now found employment as soldiers – in the Civil Wars of the seventeenth century, in the Jacobite Risings from 1689–1745, and in the British Army in the late eighteenth century. When all these avenues were closed they then became the subjects of clearance and emigration in the eighteenth and nineteenth centuries.

The galley-economy was essentially mercenary. It depended on a subsidy – money in return for the supply of troops. Alternatively the crew just helped themselves to provisions, as happened so often in Ireland. This exchange supported the economy of the Hebrides from Viking times to *c.* 1603. During this period commercial activity does not seem to have flourished for long enough to sustain the creation of an alternative economic model. There is some evidence for trade and prosperity in mid-Argyll and Kintyre in the fourteenth and fifteenth centuries – probably based on wool. Unfortunately this did not survive. When other resources such as fish were exploited in a later period such trade was usually in the hands of outsiders. The Highlands were always impoverished, always on the periphery, but until 1603 they could subsidise themselves by force of arms. After 1603 the galley-type decayed and no functional alternative appeared. Imprisoned by their poverty the Highlanders could not invest in new forms and their boat-building techniques became entrapped by tradition.[22]

Timber

Another factor is shortage of timber or difficulty in obtaining it. Sails could be made from wool, plant fibre or skin; ropes from tree-fibre, skin or heather roots. Iron nails and rivets could be partially replaced by tree-nails. Anchors could be of wood and stone rather than metal. Timber, though, was indispensable.

Woodland management is not a new theme even if the concerns of our predecessors were based on practical common sense and self-interest rather than informed by any ethical imperatives. Conservation ran close behind exploitation. Its political profile depended on the extent of local woodland and whether or not this was being irrecoverably damaged by usage.[23]

Hewn boards are much more wasteful than sawn in that fewer planks can be taken from the same tree. In the dense forests of Scandinavia during the Dark Ages this may not have been a problem and waste chippings would do for fuel. Nevertheless, in some Norse colonies such as Iceland, Shetland and Orkney, trees were scarce and precious. The sagas suggest that Icelanders quickly developed a responsible conservation policy to any woodland they owned. In the case of both Iceland and the Northern Isles there were extensive timber imports from Norway. In ninth-century Orkney the Vikings themselves used peat as fuel, hence the nickname for Earl 'Torf-Einar'.

The situation in the Highlands and Hebrides was complex and diverse. Some islands in the windswept Outer Isles may have been perennially short of timber. In the Inner Hebrides and the mainland things were different. Writing of the Calf of Mull in 1549 Dean

Munro says that it is 'full of woods' and pertains to Maclean of Duart. An account written in 1577 for James VI says: 'There is many woods in all parts of Skye, specially birkis [birch] and orne [oak] but the most wood is in Slait and Trotternish. There is ane wood in Slait 8 miles long'. It is puzzling therefore why in 1553 the government had been compelled to issue an injunction preventing Donald Gormson of Sleat, 'ane broken Hielandman', from taking timber out of MacKenzie's territory 'for making of langfaddis [lymphads]'. Whilst there were considerable oak woodlands on the west coast it may be that much of this was not sufficiently good quality for boat-building. Short curved pieces would do for knees but keel and strakes needed long straight-grained planks. Donald Gormson may simply have preferred MacKenzie timber to his own.

James VI was aware of the fragile economic resources of his native country and determined that if anyone was going to exploit them it should be he. In 1609 he issued instructions towards preserving Scottish timber for domestic consumption, not for export. He wanted to safeguard the forests against the possibility of building ships for the Navy. They were not to be sold off to foreigners.

Macleod records indicate that wood was plentiful in Glenelg. Mainland areas of Argyll and Lochaber were densely forested in places. Indeed this was one of the attractions for English and Lowland ironmasters who set up charcoal furnaces in the eighteenth century – at Furnace, Bonawe and Invergarry. The Forfeited Estates Papers make it clear that woodland was a valued resource for timber, for bark, and for charcoal-burning. A letter dated 1770 maintains that the woods in Stratherrick have been badly damaged 'by the tenants cutting what quantities they please – pealing thousands of fine young Oaks, which die when stript of the Bark – that the practice of keeping Goats is likewise very destructive to the woods there'. Goats also caused considerable destruction in Knoydart – as did the fishermen pursuing the herring in Loch Hourn. In 1791 there were regulations in force at Dunvegan and Glenelg forbidding goats on account of the damage they did to wood.

From mediaeval times woodland has been a managed resource on the Clanranald Estates.[24] It was plentiful on the mainland and so wattle, not stone, was the predominant material in the manufacture of the 'creel huts' which were then the norm for houses in the Rough Bounds. Eighteenth-century evidence makes it obvious that timber was still abundant, although not always as well maintained as was desirable. The managers of the Forfeited Estates had a strong sense of responsibility for the woodland in their care and intervened as they saw fit. In the Barrisdale Estate a 'Firr Park' was intended which would bring in £6-5s-6d per annum. On the Lochiel Estate the fir woods were leased for three years in 1768 at a fixed extraction rate of either 200 or 250 tons of timber at 12/- a ton. 'At the expiry of that Lease the woods were judged too young for Cutting, and no new lease was granted'.

As the eighteenth century continued the woods came under increasing pressure, particularly from ironworks such as Bonawe. Cheape has suggested that they may have stripped some of the woodland from Loch Shielside. Glenfinnan was apparently a centre for charcoal collection at the very end of the eighteenth century 'when timber and charcoal were transported up the Loch and then overland and by sea through Loch Eil to Bonawe'. In his little tale 'The buried pot of silver at Bracara', published in 1907, James Macdonald wrote: 'Angus, along with many others, was engaged in carrying wood down to Loch Morar, which, at that time, was the scene of a stirring industry, for both sides of the loch being thickly wooded could afford to export no slight quantity to the southern markets . . . which . . . gave employment to several of the natives. One day, however, Angus . . . was drowned while engaged in raft-making upon the loch.'25

It appears that, given a smaller population and a less exploitative economy, the Highlands had plenty of woodland before the eighteenth century. Trees may have been absent from certain areas and particular types of tree, such as tall, straight-grown forest oaks, may have been scarce, but trees there undoubtedly were – despite the recurrent myth of destruction by Scandinavians. Cheape has shown that on the Clanranald Estates in Uist and the mainland the Danes were held responsible. There is a similar tradition with regard to the Norsemen in Skye. These myths reveal a sense of loss and a desire to blame somebody for it. There could have been continual erosion of woodland in the Highlands and Hebrides throughout the mediaeval period. This may have been perceived and understood by the inhabitants of the area. It may also be that from their first arrival the Norse were heavy exploiters of wood for houses, boats and fuel. Or it may be that they proved a convenient retrospective scapegoat.

Woodland in Lochaber

Some of our earliest evidence for timber in Lochaber comes from the manuscript maps of Timothy Pont who did his fieldwork during the period 1583–96. On the south shore of Loch Leven Pont writes 'Many Fyrre Woods heir alongs'. Blaeu, following Pont, shows thick and extensive woodland beside both Loch Eil and Loch Arkaig. Lochaber must have been well-known for its timber because Nicolson quotes the Gaelic proverb "B'e sin fiodh a chur do Loch Abar" (i.e. 'That were sending wood to Lochaber', which has a similar meaning to the English saying about sending coals to Newcastle).

In the seventeenth century we find more evidence that wood was locally abundant. In Macfarlane's *Geographical Collections* there survives a description of parts of the Highlands written *c.* 1630 by an unknown author. Describing Locheil (Loghyeld) he writes 'There is a great number of Oaktrees, and one bigg wood of Oak at the Northsyde of Loghyeld at the head of the said Logh ... And they wont to build shipps of the said Oakin wood'. Further on when writing of Glen Scaddle he says 'There is a great number of fir trees in this glen, and easlie to be transported to the seasyde. There uses manie shipps to come to that Countrie of Ardgoure, and to be loadned with firr Jests, Masts and Cutts'. Here we have proof of the use of oak and fir for shipbuilding in the Highlands in the later mediaeval period.

These woods survived into the eighteenth century although we cannot tell if this was by chance or because they were managed as a sustainable resource. In 1772 William Morison made frequent comments about former woodland on the Lochiel estate and in one instance wrote 'there are numbers of the roots of old oak scattered here and there on the face of the hill but no fresh shoots'. It is perfectly possible that some of these ancient woods died out, not because they were cut down, but because they did not naturally regenerate.[26]

Norse in Lochaber?

It is a received truth that the Vikings were not present in the Great Glen. Nevertheless there is a scatter of names along the shores of Loch Linnhe which suggest a one-time Norse colony or trading-post. We have Glen Scaddle which may contain the Norse element

'-dalr' (valley). We also find Eilean nan Gall at Glen Scaddle itself with Camusnagaul along the shore to the north opposite Inverlochy. Both these names contain the element 'gall' for stranger or foreigner and mean Foreigners' Isle and Foreigners' Bay respectively. These names could of course refer to much later 'Strangers' than the Vikings because Loch Linnhe forms the southern routeway to the Great Glen. Nevertheless it seems perfectly reasonable to suppose that Loch Linnhe and Loch Eil were exploited for their timber resources from the earliest times. We know that Adomnan and the monks of Iona came to mainland Argyll for wood. The Norse were equally capable of setting up a timber trading-post near Inverlochy.

Furthermore Hugh Macdonald informs us that, just before the Battle of Inverlochy in 1431, Donald Balloch and his allies selected 600 of their best men 'and came in their galleys to Invershippinish, two miles south of Inverlochy'.[27] Now 'shippinish' is just another version of Skipness, a place-name meaning 'ship-point' in which both elements are Norse. The same name occurs in Kintyre, Colonsay and Tiree. Skipness by Inverlochy does not survive on today's maps but was presumably at the 'inbhir' or junction of the River Lochy and the River Nevis with Loch Linnhe.[28]

Norse expansion into Ross was closely related to the need of the Orkney Earls to control the timber resources of the mainland.[29] Crawford contends that the establishment of Dingwall was an important element in this expansionist policy and draws on local place-names as evidence. She points to a number of 'dale'-names which include Norse words for particular types of tree (e.g. Eskadale=Ash-dale, Alladale=Alder-dale). Her arguments can be extended to the west coast where, as she recognises, oak was an important resource. On Loch Shiel in Moidart we find Glenaladale just north of Gaskan which, Cheape records, is associated with a boat-building site for Clanranald.[30] Carriage was a significant element in the overall cost of constructing a ship and the logical answer was to build your boat where wood was plentiful – even if that meant a remote location. Craftsmen could always be imported.

Before she emigrated to Iceland, Aud the Deep-Minded, daughter of Ketil, Lord of the Hebrides, built a ship secretly in the woods of Caithness. In the closing chapters of *Njal's Saga* we meet Skeggi of Freswick in Caithness who must have been something of a shipping magnate. He provided Kari with a fully-manned longship and, two years later, a cargo-boat for sailing to Iceland. In 1249 a boat was prepared in Inverness for the French Count, Hugh de Chatillon. The Latin descriptive term which Matthew Paris uses for this vessel has been variously translated as 'handsome', 'wonderful' and 'splendid'. Perhaps the reason the French crusader chose Inverness was as much to do with an abundance of cheap timber as it was with any particular skill of the local shipwrights.

James Fraser comments that in 1643 Captain George Scot built a ship in Inverness 'of a prodigious bignes ... The carpenters he brought with him north, and my Lord Lovat gave him wood, firr and oake, in Dulcattack woods [in Glenmoriston]'.[31] These boat-building ventures were all entrepreneurial attempts to exploit local timber resources.

Timber from Ireland?

Timber and fish were two commodities mentioned as plentiful in some of the 'economic' reports compiled on Ulster and the Hebrides during the late sixteenth and early seventeenth centuries. Such reports were by no means impartial. They should be read like an investment prospectus, which is what they amounted to. They were written in terms which the author supposed would appear most attractive to the speculator. Nevertheless we can assume that the truth was stretched rather than disregarded altogether. Writing of Ireland c. 1185 Gerald of Wales had said 'Even to this day the plains here are few in proportion to the woods'.

In 1611 Sir Thomas Phillips wrote on a proposed plantation of Londoners in Ulster.[32] He paid great attention to the potential of Irish timber and was principally concerned to see off the Dutch competition. He thought

profit is to be made by joists and other sorts of timber which the Scots buy for building and other uses .... all sorts of timber, as joists, clapboards, wainscots, barrel boards, hogshead boards, oaken planks for shipping, and other uses. These kinds of commodites I hope in time may be afforded here cheaper than the boards and timber which the Dutchmen bring hither.

He implies therefore that a supply of oak boards for shipping already derived from Ireland. He adds 'for masts, I hear there are very fair ones to be had out of the Isle of Scotland'. He may have meant the Hebrides or mainland for this supply of masts but at any rate the islanders also had access to tall straight timbers for masts. His view of the Hebrides was rosy: 'the Isles of Scotland where there are great fishings, and yield great store of other commodites as cattle, hides, wool etc'.

In the Irish State Papers there is a little document called 'Remedies and the Benefits which will accrue from them' which dates to the reign of James VI & I.[33] Item number six reads

> *The Scots, if unable to support themselves in their own country, come over here and disturb the peace of Ireland, encouraging those that are willing to rebel. The timber of which their gallies are made comes chiefly from Wexford, Wicklow and Arklow. The men of these places either sell their timber directly to the Scottish merchants, or, if they fail, sell to merchants in Dublin, who 'trock' the same to the Scottish merchants for Scotland. Some timber is sent to Carlingford and Carrickfergus to be sold, but not so much as in Dublin. It is easier for the Scots to get timber from Ireland than from their own isles.*

Item seven then details a licensing system 'to prevent the exportation of corn and of timber except for the making of fishing boats on the coasts'. The implication is that the timber was exported and the galleys built in Scotland.

The supply of mercenary pay and timber from Ireland were very probably twin buttresses of the military economy of galleys. The pay gave out from 1603 and no doubt the export of timber also suffered; less from government diktat than a lack of cash and demand from the Highlanders.

Economic blockade/Restrictions on wood imports?

In July 1568 Argyle issued a proclamation at Largs 'boding fear of war' and in favour of Mary Queen of Scots. He was soon asking the Spanish for men and munitions and taking a very anti-Elizabethan stance. By the end of the year he was threatening to invade Ireland if Elizabeth didn't help the Queen of Scots. On 4 August 1568 Edward Waterhous reported from Chester to the Lords Justice in Dublin that the Earl of Argyle was 'diligent in making galleys'. On 11 August 1568 the Lords Justice wrote to Pers and Malbie, Commissioners in the North, sent them a copy of Waterhous's letter and told them 'to stay wood and boards from passing out of Knockfergus'. On 28 August 1568 the Lords Justice wrote from Dublin to the Queen that they 'have restrained the export of boards from Carrickfergus and Wexford, to impede the Earl of Argyle in making galleys'.

About 1609 a complaint was made by Maclean of Duart, Macdonald of Islay and others against a proclamation preventing the mainland inhabitants of Argyll from buying cattle, horses or other goods in the Western Isles.[34] This primitive form of economic blockade was immediately annulled by the Privy Council but it gives rise to the speculation that trade embargoes were used as weapons in certain clan conflicts. There is nothing new in this and burghs in Ireland could be jealously restrictive against the 'wild Irish'. Municipal laws in Galway and Waterford forbade boat-building materials to be sold to the Irish – the O'Malleys and the O'Driscolls respectively.

Did Campbell control of the woods of mainland Argyll prevent timber from reaching some of the island lords? That export restrictions occasionally existed is suggested by an Act of the Privy Council in 1575 against Hugh Fraser, Lord Lovat. Glengarry had complained that Lovat was preventing him, 'his freindis kin and commonis of his landis, to bring and cary wod and tymmer doun in bottis to the burgh of Inverness, throw the water of Lochnes'.[35] An act was duly passed prohibiting Lovat from impeding the Glengarry men.

Craft decline

Decline in a craft such as shipbuilding feeds on itself and amplifies the ill effects. Building large wooden boats requires ample resources, raw materials and skilled craftsmen. If, during the seventeenth century, the number of galleys went into irreversible decline so too would the number of yards, the number of skilled shipwrights and, eventually, the ability to build the boats at all. Such a decline would have been compounded by the climatic, and economic, effects of the so-called 'Little Ice Age' in the last years of the seventeenth century. Highland shipyard practice may have been relatively uneconomic in a country that was beginning to move from labour-intensive to capital-intensive forms of production. Traditional Viking craft were made from hewn planks but from the thirteenth century sawn boards gradually became the norm. Hewing timber was horrendously wasteful both of wood and human energy but the practice lasted longer in the Highlands where both these natural resources were plentiful.[36]

Political decline

Political decline must also be added. Somerled and his descendants provided a Gaelic dynastic settlement that lasted between *c.* 1150 and 1545. The Lordship of the Isles was forfeited *c.* 1493 and for the next 250 years there was turmoil and increasing fragmentation in the Highland area. The Campbells were the principal agents of the Scottish kings in their desire to bring the Hebrides within the Scottish realm. It was a long, fraught and bloody process but was eventually successful. The Highland chiefs could never unite for long enough to mount an effective opposition and after the collapse of Donald Dubh's rising in 1545 it was all downhill. Throughout the mediaeval period they had made several agreements with England but these came to nothing and after the Union of Crowns this avenue too was closed.[37] The building of large wooden boats depended on aristocratic or commercial patronage. After 1603 this could not be sustained in a Hebridean environment.

Part II

The Evidence

Chapter 8
The Shared Tradition

The Scandinavian legacy

THE ARCHAEOLOGICAL EVIDENCE is very largely Scandinavian. There are no Scottish finds comparable to the ship burials of Gokstad or Oseberg in Norway or the wrecks found in the fjord off Roskilde in Denmark. One day the remains of a galley may come to light but currently only a few fragments survive. We have two endposts buried in Eigg and other items like clinch-nails from the battle-site at Cul-na-Croise, Ardnamurchan.

The Vikings occupy an important place in the national histories of Scandinavia and so their boats have been well-researched. The time-scale is enormous. The Viking expansion started prior to AD 800 and by the 1260s enormous flagships like the *Kristsuden* were being built, again for a Scottish expedition. The demands of commerce and war meant there was constant evolution and development over the years. Equally there were regional variations between the Eastern and Western Baltic and between boats for the deep fjords of Norway or the shallow shores of Denmark. There was a great variety of Scandinavian boats and surviving Norse names include: skuta, karfi, langskip, snekkja, skeid, drekki, knorr, byrdingr, buza and hafskip.

Karfi and skuta seem to describe light coastal vessels with speed being the particular hallmark of the skuta. In *Egil's Saga* Egil and his men escape from one particular scrape by taking their skuta into shallow water where a snekkja could not follow.[1] The differences, or similarities, between 'skuta' and 'karfi' have implications for the Hebrides since these smaller, lighter warships may have been the types favoured in an island environment. Although crew numbers varied enormously on Viking ships a skuta often had about 30 men. In *Egil's Saga* one is described as short-handed with only eighteen men on board. In *Grettir's Saga* we read of a 'large sixteen-oared boat' with about 31 crew. If, typically, a 'skuta' had about 16 oars and 30 crew then we may be looking at the ancestor of vessels like the *Aileach*.

Langskip, snekkja, skeid and drekki are all warship names. Langskip is the general term for longship, snekkja's characteristically have about twenty benches and are associated with Sweden whilst skeid's are perhaps rather bigger or faster. The biggest warships became drekki or dragon-ships if they carried dragon endposts; possibly there was some notional cut-off point above which a boat was held to qualify.

The image of a dragon became a very powerful metaphor in the Norse linguistic set. Coupled with this was the idea of flight; the raising of the oars appeared like the lifting of wings. It was an ideal; a boat that was at home on the sea but skimmed the waves so lightly she had almost mastered the element of air. Such thoughts are voiced by Thjodolf in *Harald's Saga* where the image of oars being raised and lowered prompts the poet with the simile of a great bird

> *Above the prow, the dragon*
> *Rears its glowing head ...*
> *Norwegian arms are driving*
> *This iron-studded dragon*
> *Down the storm-tossed river*
> *Like an eagle with wings flapping.*
>
> (Magnusson & Palsson)

Longships normally had lower freeboard than merchant-ships such as knorrs. Of Olaf Trygvason's great ship *Ormen Lange* it was said that 'the freeboard was as great as in ocean-going ships'. Theoretically longships could always be rowed although in the case of the biggest ships this was infrequent. Trading-ships had few oars and these were probably used mainly for manoeuvring. Large fleets, at any period, probably consisted of a motley collection of whatever was available.

Trading vessels included knorrs, byrdingr and buza; hafskip being the general term for large ocean-going vessels. Knorrs were big and beamy with a high freeboard, byrdingr rather smaller. Buza may be a name imported from the Mediterranean via Viking employment in the Byzantine navy and seem to have replaced knorrs by the early fourteenth century. Both knorrs and buza were sometimes used as warships whilst byrdingr could, if necessary, be lengthened into warships.

Boats could also be distinguished by name. *Visundr* (Bison), *Trani* (Crane), *Stigandi* (Strider), *Ormen Lange* (Great Serpent) all suggest distinctive qualities in a vessel. By the thirteenth century, saint and personal-names were becoming increasingly popular although to a certain extent these overlooked the individual characteristics of each boat. The Gokstad and Oseberg grave-ships are atypical; they represent something like royal yachts.

The Skuldelev boats are much more typical but presumably the Danes chose to sink their oldest and least useful vessels when blocking the fjord channel. Some of the Roskilde boats were built for the tideless Baltic rather than the Atlantic. The small warship, (Wreck 5), had a low freeboard and shallow draught which made it light and relatively easy to portage. It differs from the type of boat you would expect on the exposed coasts of Norway or the Hebrides. The more we know about Scandinavian boats the greater seems to be the variety of form and function.

A Viking ship-type, a 'keel', had a design fundamentally different to that of a currach, a cog or a hulc. This type formed the basis of most North European boats for perhaps 300 years. From about the twelfth century it seems to have been gradually replaced by forms such as the cog, which offered a better cargo-carrying ship for a changing economic and political environment. Nevertheless the Viking design persisted for hundreds of years afterwards, particularly in the construction of small boats. Aspects of its design remain useful; when drifting or rolling a clinker-built boat grips the water better than a rounded hull and this fact is still reflected in the designs for small fibre-glass boats used in freshwater or inshore fishing.

The 'keel' tradition

What were the essential features of a Viking boat? Firstly it had a hull that was symmetrical at both ends. The lines of planking curved up to give a pronounced sheer at stem and stern. The ship was essentially built around the keel, stem and stern-posts. (English boats built in the Viking tradition were long known as 'keels'.) Once the keel and endposts had been laid a shell of thin planking was built up strake by strake, each slightly overlapping the one beneath. These planks were fastened together by iron clinch-nails and roves, hence the name clinker-built. Internal timbers such as ribs and crossbeams were only fitted afterwards and *to* the lines of planking which were formed intuitively by the eye of the boatbuilder. This is the opposite method to a carvel-built boat where the basic design can be mapped out, a framework built and then the planking attached to the frame as if to seal out the water. These two models, shell or skeleton, and their associated methods, clinker or carvel, are fundamentally different.

There was a strong keel and the first strake or two was angled steeply to give the boat more 'bite' in the water and so ensure she did not drift too much to windward. The end result was a boat that was enormously supple and flexible. It was quick and rode the water well. It was of shallow draught, could be easily beached, go up-river and could be rowed or sailed. They were built by craftsmen and every little detail was attended to. Oar-ports could have little shutters to keep out the sea and slits for withdrawing the blade of the oar. Such slits weren't just cut anywhere, but at the point of least friction. Plank-scarfs or joins faced aft so that minimum water found its way into the wood. There was a single mast stepped amidships and a rectangular sail carried from a yard. Steering was by a robust steering-board attached to the right or starboard side of the boat. Normally there was no decking which gave rise to two problems. The boat had to be baled manually which could be a desperate task in heavy seas. Secondly the crew were very exposed to the rigours of the weather, especially on cold nights. To give some shelter the mast was lowered and laid horizontally on vertical supports; the sail could then be draped over to make a tent-like cover or 'mast-tent'.

Characteristic features of Viking longships were the decorative figureheads on stem and stern-posts. These elaborate wooden carvings were removable and could be attached to either or both ends. They were often of terrifying appearance and could be painted or gilt. We know of dragon's heads, beaked heads, bearded men and oxen. We find prehistoric parallels in the apparent animal-head of a boat from Loch Arthur, Kirkcudbright, and also the boat associated with the Roos Carr figures from Humberside. Warrior societies were, and still are, keen on weapon-display. No doubt on the return of a successful raiding-party the shields and trophies were hung out along the sides of the boat. The figureheads would be put in position, flags flown, victory songs sung.

It is unlikely these figureheads were kept in position all the time. Norse accounts talk of setting up the dragons' heads and the display of such heads could be forbidden in home waters. Their purpose was evidently symbolic, to strike terror in the enemy and create a show. A carved stem-post would have been far too fragile and valuable to risk in normal use. Similarly shields would quickly have been ruined if hung along the gunwale out at sea. Rather these were the attributes of a Viking boat as it set off in swagger or returned in triumph.

It is extraordinary how long-lived is this tradition of symbolic figureheads on boats. After the mediaeval period the figures were often transformed from animal to human designs and reached extraordinary elaboration and personification. Other symbols could be used to invite good fortune. In the absence of a carved figure a natural substitute would do. Leafy branches appear on some mediaeval boats and Captain Phillips's drawing of a seventeenth-century Irish currach shows both greenery at the top of the mast and a large bull's head mounted on the prow. Today's fishing boats are often seen with a creel or basket near the stem.

Boats were cultural artefacts which indicated power and status. In *Egil's Saga* it is said of Thorolf: 'In the spring he had a big long-ship built, with a dragon prow, [and] had it equipped as splendidly as possible. ... He became powerful and spent a lot of thought on the display of his ships and weapons'. Again: 'Thorolf owned a large ship. It was built for the open sea, as good as it could be in every respect, with much paint-work above the water-line, and a sail coloured in blue and red stripes. All the equipment for the ship was most carefully made'. Similarly when King Harald Hardradi built an enormous new warship his saga describes it as 'most carefully built in every detail . . . The King had all the fittings of the ship made with the utmost care, the sails and rigging as well as the anchor and ropes'.

A boat represented a capital investment. It was an expression of wealth but also a means to accumulate further wealth, either by raiding or trading. In the story of Helgi Thorisson: 'Helgi had had a dragon-head fitted on to their ship's prow, and the whole stem was decorated above the sea-line. This is how Helgi had invested part of the money Ingibjorg had given him, but some of it he'd locked in the neck of the dragon'.[2]

Boats were maintained carefully not just because life and limb depended on them but because they were an enormous capital asset whose depreciation should be deferred as long as possible. How long a boat lasted depended of course on its maintenance and usage. Leif the Lucky used Bjarni Herjolfsson's boat when he tried to repeat Bjarni's exploit of finding North America. By this time the ship was at least fifteen years old.

Trading ships were built rather beamier and sometimes with a stepped gunwale to facilitate loading. There was a part deck fore and aft but otherwise they offered little protection to cargo or crew. There were fewer oars which were used primarily for manoeuvring. Longships could cross the North Sea and raid through the Hebrides but their low freeboard would have made them too risky for a long ocean voyage. The voyage from Norway to Shetland could be completed in 48 hours; the minimum to Iceland was about eight days, and more usually between twelve and twenty. Both longships and trading vessels could carry small ship's boats; in fact three were found in the Gokstad boat though it is unlikely she ever carried more than one. These ship's boats could be used to ferry men ashore and as lifeboats.

Stern-rudders

The most significant change for boats of Scandinavian origin was the moving of the steering-oar from the starboard (or 'steering-board') side of the boat to the stern where it became transformed into a rudder with a tiller arm. This process started in the late twelfth century. One of the main reasons was functional – against a quay or jetty the steering-board was inconveniently placed and risked damage. Boats would have to be presented port-side on for loading and this might not always be opportune. (The old name for the port side of the boat was larboard or ladeboard, i.e. the loading side of the boat.) Boats were increasing in size, weight and draught and becoming more dependent on sail rather than oars. A stern-rudder offered a slightly greater turning moment whilst retaining some purchase on the water when the boat heeled dramatically.[3]

In Highland tradition Somerled has been credited with the innovation but it undoubtedly came from outwith the area and probably after his time. There can have been few quays or jetties anywhere in the Hebrides but the new style was adopted here as elsewhere in north-western Europe. As seals demonstrate both styles existed side-by-side for a number of years but the starboard rudder seems to have been ousted as the thirteenth century progressed. Hebridean chiefs were not behindhand during this period.

Improvements in naval architecture would have quickly reached every part of the Scandinavian world. Boats brought news of themselves.

The only evidence for starboard-rudders in the Kingdom of the Hebrides is on two carved stones, both belonging to the Viking period. One on Man, known as the Hedin cross, is perhaps late twelfth-century and carries the inscription 'Hedin set this cross to the memory of his daughter [H]lif'. (The starboard-rudder as shown was not part of the original design but a stern-rudder is conspicuously absent.) The second, the so-called Sigurd stone on Iona, shows no rudder at all. It is probably tenth or eleventh-century so we can presume a starboard-rudder. Our earliest West Highland carvings date to the fourteenth century and without exception show a stern-rudder. From the intervening period the only evidence we have are the church-wall graffiti at Kilchattan, Luing, and the seal of Angus Mor of Islay dating from 1292.[4]

The boats surviving in their former colonies give clues to the original Scandinavian boat-types. This is an immense and complex subject, not least because Scandinavians differed among themselves. The Norse boats found at Gokstad and Oseberg are different to the Danish vessels sunk at Roskilde. Boat-building evolved continually throughout Northern Europe. It is true that the keel tradition passed to the Norse colonies in Britain but after direct Norse control ended, so each colonial outpost developed distinctive forms within the context of its environment. Even within the Northern Isles differences have been noted between the boat-styles of Orkney and Shetland.

The sea was the common highway for commerce until at least the early nineteenth century. With every voyage there was venture and return, exchange of ideas and practice. Shared words did not necessarily bear identical meanings. Terms like galley, yole and skiff could cover a multitude of boat-types. For the future we can hope that research into prehistoric, dark age and mediaeval boats in neighbouring countries will shed light on the evolution of boat design in Scandinavia and so Scotland.

Galley-building in England and Scotland

Another source of information is galley-building elsewhere in the British Isles during the thirteenth and fourteenth centuries.[5] In 1294 Edward I sent word to a number of towns around England to build twenty galleys of 120 oars each and we have more or less detailed accounts for eight of these. With the possible exception of one built in London they all seem to have been smaller than 120 oars which suggests that Edward's plans were scaled down for reasons of economy. We also have an account for *La Phelipe*, built at Lynn in 1336, an account for a galley at Winchelsea in 1347, some repair bills for two English boats, (the *St George* and *St Edward*), at Bayonne *c*. 1350 and an inventory for the *Paul* of London in 1373.

There must have been frequent contact between seafarers in all the English ports and it is unlikely there were strong regional differences in building procedure. Such valuable royal orders would have been met with the best marine technology of the day; a technology which had long since enjoyed an international dimension.[6] A master-builder from Bayonne was imported to oversee the building at Southampton, presumably in order to access his knowledge and expertise.

In the earliest Viking period all planks had been hewn but sawn timber was now in general use. In the Ipswich accounts 32 logs were sawn into planks for 9s. Returns for August 1306 show 4d per day was paid to sawyers sawing timber for boats that were being carried to Loch Doon, Carrick. Presumably they were needed for the siege of the island castle on Loch Doon. Given the contacts between the English and the Macdougalls during this period it is certain that Hebrideans would know of the practice.

Keel-scarfs

The massive size of Edward's galleys meant that their keels needed to be made from more than one piece of timber. One galley, built in London, may have had four or five timbers joined for her keel. The keels at Southampton and Newcastle each consisted of two pieces, the latter being scarfed together with five bolts. This gives us a clue to an otherwise enigmatic phrase in the *Chronicles of Man* referring to Godred Crovan, first King of Man and the Isles. Apparently 'he so tamed the Scots that no-one who built a ship or boat dared use more than three iron bolts'. Presumably these 'Scots' were the mainland magnates of the west coast though whether of Galloway, Ayrshire or Argyll must remain speculative. The first and last in particular could have threatened his position in the Kingdom of the Isles by cutting his lines of communication.

These bolts were somehow necessary to strengthen or fix a ship's timbers and the bigger the boat the more bolts were required. Perhaps the bolts were needed for keel-scarfs, the number of which affected the overall size of the vessel. With boats above a certain size no single tree could provide a long-enough timber so the keel had to be composed of two or more sections 'scarfed' together. A scarf was a weak point in the boat's structure and much attention was paid to securing the timbers effectively. A minimum of three bolts might be required for one scarf so perhaps this restriction prevented the launching of any over-large vessels that might challenge Godred's hegemony.[7]

Edward I's galleys were certainly big but we have little idea of their precise dimensions. The keel at Newcastle was composed of two pieces of timber 56 feet and 52 feet long respectively. Assuming a scarf overlap of 3 feet we arrive at a keel length of 105 feet plus an allowance for rake fore and aft. Given the traditionally steep sheer of endposts in the Viking tradition, we can estimate an overall length of 120 feet. We do not know the number of oars on the Newcastle galley but if we assume 100 then the problem arises of how to fit 50 oarsmen a side and also leave a few feet at bow and stern where the boat narrows. Allowing an optimum of nearly 3 feet between oarsmen the boats become unrealistically long.[8] If, however, we only allow 2 feet between rowers they could not sit in the same alignment or they would be forever knocking into the backs of the men in front.

In 1991 the crew of the reconstructed galley, the *Aileach*, found this a particular problem. With an overall length of 39 feet 9 inches (12.2 metres) they felt the boat was over-oared at sixteen and should have been fourteen instead.[9] The spaces between thwarts would then have increased from 2 feet 11 inches to 3 feet 3 inches. Admittedly average size has increased with better diet but we know from a contemporary commentator that Donald Dubh's Hebridean mariners in 1545 were all 'tall men'. If rowers were sitting in the same alignment they would need at least 2 feet 9 inches between benches. This question of space is critical since comfort and efficiency are closely linked in a strenuous and repetitive job like rowing. In *King Harald's Saga* there is an account of the king building a new warship at Eyrar: 'It had thirty-five pairs of rowing-benches, with plenty of space between each'. This phrase suggests that the perennial compromise between numbers and comfort was usually weighted against the latter.

One solution is an arrangement known in the Mediterranean as 'alla sensile'. Here the rowing benches are set at a slant and those men who sit on the same bench use oars of a different length. There is a reference *c.* 1206 to the Norwegians building three galleys with oarports at different heights. There is also a poem by Einar Helgason quoted in both *Egil's Saga* and *Jomsvikinga Saga* which includes the following line: 'I shall line with ring-shields Sigvaldi's ship which has double rows of oars'. Any such boat was in the nature of an experiment and neither Norwegians nor English built Mediterranean-style biremes. They would have heard about, possibly even seen, Mediterranean galleys but it is unlikely that Northern imitations were built in the thirteenth century. Highland galleys were too small to require exotic rowing arrangements.

The size of each English galley is borne out by the height of mast and quantity of sail. Mast sizes have been estimated at between 70–120 feet, of which at least 10 feet may have been within the depth of the boat. The figures for sail cloths suggest sail areas of between 2,400 and 6,450 square feet. In 1991 the *Aileach* had a sail area of 360 square feet. *Aileach* was under-sailed and theoretically might have carried up to 532 square feet but given the English galleys were also single-masted there is a huge difference in scale.[10]

The enormous sail areas could be reduced by reefing in an over-strong wind. Froissart reports an English fleet running before a storm in 1342 on one-eighth normal sail. Reefing was normally from the bottom up and the yard was lowered so that there was no dangerous work in the rigging during high winds. Reef points were arranged in rows, possibly more frequently in the lower sections of sail. There seem to have been considerable numbers of them. The English galleys usually had an awning or 'tilt' in the waist of the ship which protected the crew at night. This is reminiscent of the Viking mast-tent. The only possible parallel in the West Highlands is amongst the graffiti at Kilchattan.

The English boats had up to three castles – fore, stern and top. There is absolutely no evidence for these in the West Highlands, not even on the seal of Angus Mor of Islay for which a top-castle is sometimes claimed. Edward's galleys also mark an intermediate stage as far as rudders were concerned. The accounts suggest that his galleys were equipped with *both* types, sometimes even carrying spare side-rudders. Such extravagance could not last and early in the

fourteenth century side-rudders seem to have given way completely
to stern-rudders. *La Phelipe* (1336) and the *Paul* (1373) had stern-
rudders only.[11]

The galleys were well payed with grease, pitch and tar and subsequently painted. It was not only the superstructure and castles that
were painted, sometimes also the hull – as is implied by the *Becket
Leaves* and a fourteenth-century ceiling-painting at Skamstrup
Church in Denmark. *Egil's Saga* refers to a karfi 'painted all above
the waterline'. In *Grettir's Saga* Grettir noticed 'a ship rowing up to
the island . . . painted above the waterline'. Intriguingly the painter's
assistant at Newcastle carries the Scottish name of Duncan. The sail
of the Dunwich galley was 'dyed in various colours' which is reminiscent of the Bayeux Tapestry and the *Becket Leaves*.

Once complete the boats were launched with the help of rollers
which may also have been made into a type of cradle to support the
massive structure. Sometimes a ditch was dug to the water.[12]
Haulage could also be by the laborious method of wetting and so
shrinking taut ropes. This is possibly portrayed by a scene in the
Bayeux Tapestry where men are shown attaching ropes to a tree
after building William's invasion fleet.

What is remarkable is that until the mid-thirteenth century West
Highland galleys were right up-to-date. Angus Mor's seal of 1292
indicates a stern rudder only – at a time when English boats were
still carrying both types. From then on it is as if the West Highland
boat-building tradition stood still for 250 years. They had no stern
or forecastles, no windlass or capstan, no extra masts. They stuck
with oars and sail, not sail alone. They never accommodated more
than 40 oars and any larger boats in Hebridean waters seem to have
been captured or imported, not built locally. Hebrideans continued
to build boats, and lots of them, but of local materials, with local
knowledge and for local needs.

Gunn has drawn attention to the Scottish evidence in the Lord
High Treasurer's accounts for the end of the fifteenth and beginning
of the sixteenth century.[13] It appears that one or two galleys were
built in Glasgow and Ayr by men like David Lindsey and John
Broun. Gunn has wisely cautioned against the assumption that these
were necessarily of West Highland type. Nevertheless there is a payment of 14s on 1 May 1512 'to ane Ersche rynnar to feche ane
wricht out of Arrane to the King to mak ane galay'; (to an Irish

[Gaelic] runner to fetch a wright from Arran to the King to make a galley).

It is not wholly coincidental that in July 1512 the King gave Duncan Stewart of Appin a life-rent of lands round Inverlochy in Lochaber for his good service and 'for his gift to the king of a galley of 36 oars'. It sounds as if James was building up a fleet suitable to deal with any Highland difficulties. After all it was not that long since the final forfeiture of the Lordship of the Isles. These accounts, and other surviving mediaeval ledgers, give us copious information about wages, prices, inflation and boat-building practice.

In October 1512 32d was paid for 'ii stane of mos' – presumably for caulking. Between then and January 1513 tallow varied between 58s and 50s per barrel. In November 1512 'dowbill naill' were 40d per 100; 'singile' were half that. In January 1513 we find four dozen of 'tymmer' at 4s 6d per plank. Twelve knees[14] for the galley being built at Newhaven, Edinburgh, cost 4d each. The next item reads: 'For ii dusan of aris the dusan xxx s; summa iii li' plus 8d for carriage.[15] This galley was seemingly quite small – with only 24 oars.

Archaeological and material evidence

In Britain we lack relevant archaeological evidence. We have the ghost of a Viking boat burial at Scar, Orkney, but no Gokstad, Oseberg or Skuldelev. We have some fragments such as side-rudders and clinch-nails, but few other material remains. We have two undated endposts from the island of Eigg. We have some ironwork on church doors at Stillingfleet, Yorkshire and Staplehurst, Kent.[16] We have some carved stones such as the hogback from Lowther, Cumbria, which shows warriors in a boat with at least one animal-headed endpost and eight round shields along the gunwale. We have some graffiti of boats from Kilchattan, Luing;[17] and on stone and slate plaques from Jarlshof, Shetland, which may have been artists' trial pieces. We also have the seals, the literary evidence and the manuscript illuminations. We have the Highland galley tradition and a continuous line of boat-building craftsmen. We have the mediaeval crosses and grave-slabs of the West Highlands, about 80 of which carry carvings of galleys made in the period c. 1350–1550. By deduction and analogy we must make what we can of it.

Chapter 9

Seals, Heraldic Devices and Manuscript Illustrations

Seals

SOME OF THE EARLIEST PICTORIAL representations of mediaeval boats are on the wax seals appended to official documents. This was not because of the artistic attraction of such vessels; they, and the seals that bore them had an important symbolic function. In the *Chronicles of Man* there is a reference to the fact that in about 1241 the King of Norway made Harald King over the Isles and 'he confirmed them under the protection of his seal to him'. In other words if something was under the king's seal it carried the promise of military assistance should it be needed. What more suitable motif for such a seal than the galley – the principal instrument of such reinforcement within the Kingdom of the Isles.

It is difficult for us, in an age of cars, trains, planes and spaceships, to appreciate the enormous significance of the ship in the Middle Ages. It represented a technological apex; a high point of engineering and craftsmanship. It was to transport as cathedrals were to religious architecture. It was a focal point for innovation and investment; became a metaphor for enterprise, power and wealth. It was part of the mediaeval mindset; the church thought of itself as a mighty ship. No wonder it appeared on coins and seals, used sometimes by religious houses, sometimes by rulers or magnates, perhaps most often by coastal burghs whose wealth depended upon seaborne trade. It represented stateliness, utility, and reach. From the whalers of Spain to the herring boats of Crail and to West Highland galleys, seals were used to carry the images of boats abroad.

In the early mediaeval period the seal of the Isle of Man bore a galley, only later was it replaced by the spiral of three legs. Our first reference is to a seal of Reginald I of Man (1187–1226) which has since been lost. In 1736 it was described as having 'on the reverse the ship under sail'. In 1607 Camden mentions having seen seals of the Kings of Man and the Isles bearing 'a ship with furled sail'. Seventeenth-century facsimiles exist of two seals of Harald, King of

Man. The seals dated from *c.* 1246 but were destroyed in an eighteenth-century fire.[1] They provide some of our earliest visual evidence for vessels that sailed in Hebridean waters. We are not, however, seeing the actual seals, but drawings informed by a seventeenth-century eye. The boats seem shallow and lack the steep stem and stern-posts we might expect. Nevertheless there are striking similarities between these boats and the galleys on late mediaeval West Highland grave-slabs. This suggests a long-lived artistic convention, or a consistency in ship-design, or both.

The seals of the Manx king and Somerled's family were very similar. Somerled had married the King of Man's daughter and his sons would therefore inherit some of her heraldic pretensions. A seal (*c.* 1180) of Reginald, Somerled's son, was described in 1426 as: 'impressed in white wax, in which . . . was engraved a ship full of armed men'.

Our earliest visual impressions of specifically West Highland galleys occur with the seals of Alexander of Lorn, Angus Mor of Islay and his son Alexander, all dated to 1292.[2] The most revealing is the seal of Angus Mor. His boat is double-ended with high stem and stern but no figureheads. It has a single centrally-stepped mast, with yard and furled sail. The tackle consists of forestay, backstay, two braces secured aft and perhaps four shrouds. There are four crew facing out and a stern-rudder. It is difficult to make out but it seems to stretch surprisingly far forward and well below the keel. Every one of these features, including the rudder below the keel-line, is repeated somewhere in the sculptural series. Early craftsmen often derived images and ideas from previous relief models. There is a probable iconographic inheritance from seals to stones. An image library was passed on.

The seal of Angus Mor's son, Alexander, shows a similar but less detailed boat where two crewmen are seen from the side as they attend to the ropes. The seal of Alexander of Lorn is particularly interesting. Unlike the other two his galley appears on a heraldic shield and shows no sail and little rigging. However both endposts carry prominent beast-heads – the ears being a striking feature. This prompts comparison with the Bergen seal of *c.* 1275 – particularly since Alexander's father, Ewen (John), had been King Hakon's 'under-king' in the northern Hebrides. Nevertheless other seals from the thirteenth century, (e.g. Monmouth, Lyme Regis and

Lubeck), as well as Parisian seals in the fourteenth century, all carry beast-heads on the endposts. It was a motif common throughout Northern Europe during this period.

For the later Lords of the Isles some 24 surviving seals have been catalogued – with another six known of.[3] They date to the fifteenth century and in all of them the galley or lymphad appears as part of a heraldic design, as it would on numerous later grave-slabs.

A common thirteenth-century feature is the mike. This was a hook or fork usually attached to the endposts which was used for stowing unwanted gear such as oars. Seals from Calais, Paris and Sandwich all illustrate this. The vessel on the Manx Hedin cross from the Isle of Man has two prongs curving into the boat from stem and stern-post which may represent mikes. No mediaeval graveslabs show Highland galleys with mikes but one at Lochaline has a stem-post ending in three prongs. Was it, like a mike, to support a mast or spar? The Oseberg ship has a simple contraption for stowing oars. Four U-shaped crutches along the gunwale, two on each side, carried this potentially awkward gear in a safe and convenient manner. No doubt the oars could be lashed in during rough weather. The problem of stowing arms is illustrated on one of the Gotland picture stones which shows the spears stacked up in the stern of the boat.

Seals also indicate reef-points on sails. These were places where the sail could be tied up to reduce its surface area. The earliest known representation is on the seal of La Rochelle in the late twelfth century, but we also have examples from Hastings, Rye, Bergen and, most significantly, Dublin in 1297 where the reefing and stitching arrangements give the impression of a sail composed of square sections. There is only one carving of a Highland galley where we find anything comparable but that is the finest, Rodel in Harris, where the reef-points are clearly defined and the sail also seems to be subdivided into squares. At that time it was impossible to manufacture a sail in one piece. It had to be made up by sewing strips of cloth together. These would then be crossed laterally by further bands of material to take the strain of reef-points. The wear and tear of wind and rain, the stretching and pulling of reef and rope would soon weaken the fabric. The reinforcements give the impression of squares in Rodel and Dublin and of diamonds on early carved stones from Scandinavia. The seal of Bergen (c. 1275) is the earliest illustration of reef-points on a Scandinavian vessel and they are shown going right to the top of the sail. More usually, as in La Rochelle and Rodel, they do not extend into the upper portion of sail. Such differences may reflect regional variations.

There is no evidence on Highland boats of a windlass or hoist, which we know from a Winchelsea seal to have been in use from at least the early fourteenth century. Equally there are no suggestions of the masthead fighting-tops, forecastles, sterncastles etc. that according to contemporary seals were appearing on boats elsewhere. Only five years separate the seal of Angus Mor of Islay (1292) and the Dublin seal (1297), but the former shows no sign of the fore and sterncastle of the latter — another indication that Highland galleys were comparatively small and lightweight. It is unlikely that ignorance prevented the adoption of technical advances made elsewhere; rather it was relative economic disadvantage or the unsuitability of such modifications. The first seal of the town of Dunwich (Suffolk), dated c. 1199, shows fore, stern and topcastles a century earlier. With smaller items such as a boathook (Sandwich), which is virtually the same pattern today, we can assume that Highlanders carried something very similar.

On seals the furled sail is usually shown a little below the top of the mast and any topcastle, sometimes one-third of the way down, sometimes as much as half-mast. On several seals (e.g. Hythe, San Sebastian, Sandwich, Faversham, Portsmouth and Yarmouth) men are shown astride the yard-arm, presumably preparing to unfurl the sails before departure. On others they are shown climbing the shrouds (Dover & Damme, Flanders) or stays (Winchelsea, Pevensey) to indicate how they gained access to the yard. This must have been an extremely hazardous practice and it is possible that Highland galleys were generally too small to require much enterprise amongst the rigging. However on one of the English boats in the Bayeux Tapestry a boy at the top of the mast is acting as look-out and we can imagine that similar tasks were expected of the light and agile boys in a galley-crew. Nereabolls (51) shows two crew, the smaller of whom appears to be climbing the aft brace. We also have a carving on a wooden plank from Christ Church Place, Dublin, which shows a man sitting astride the yard at the top of the mast. The sail beneath him is furled so the yard was not necessarily lowered to perform this task.

Seals give us copious information, not directly about galleys, but about developments in boat-building and the types of boats and gear then prevalent. The Highlands were by no means as isolated as we might imagine, or even as they are today.[4]

Heraldic devices

I have largely ignored the numerous representations of galleys that appear as heraldic devices in the later mediaeval period. This is because historical accuracy was sacrificed to heraldic convention. There remain some areas where such research may prove helpful. Galleys appeared very early on heraldic shields – for instance the late fourteenth-century slab to Bricius Mackinnon on Iona or the fifteenth-century effigies at Killean, Kintyre.[5] The transmission of certain devices, such as the three legs of Man to some of the Macleod families, gives us information about their own view of their origins. Some devices give us clues to early naval practice and there is evidence from heraldic boats that galley design changed in the sixteenth century.

Beacons are a good example of a correspondence between heraldic devices and real life. By 1445 the burning mountain or beacon was already part of the heraldic set of the Macleods of Lewis. The traditional origin of this symbol is given by the first Earl of Cromartie (1630–1714). He claimed that Harald, son of Godfrey Dond was obliged 'at a certaine tyme of the yeir to keip tuo fyred beacons, on in Lewes, ane other in the Ille of Sky, for directing the Norvegian shippes in ther navigationes on thes coasts'.

About 1695 Martin Martin says the following of Harris

There are several heaps of stones, commonly called cairns, on the tops of hills and rising grounds on the coast, upon which they used to burn heath, as a signal of an approaching enemy. There was always a sentinel at each cairn to observe the sea-coast; the steward of the isle made frequent rounds, to take notice of the sentinels, and if he found any of them asleep, he stript them of their clothes, and deferred their personal punishments to the proprietor of the place.

He also refers to warning beacons between the coastal forts of Skye, and in Orkney. The elements Ward or Fitty in Orkney hill-names come from the Norse words for beacon and fire.[6] In *Orkneyinga Saga* there is a description of how, after the battle of Tankerness, beacons were built to warn Orcadians of the approach of an enemy fleet:

Late in the spring [1137], *Earl Paul had beacons built on Fair Isle and North Ronaldsay and on most of the other islands, so that each could be seen from the others. There was a man called Dagfinn Hlodvisson, a stouthearted farmer on Fair Isle, charged with the task of guarding the beacon there and setting fire to it if the enemy fleet were to be seen approaching from Shetland.*

Something similar was arranged in the Southern Hebrides when Donald Balloch was sent to ravage Ayrshire in 1455. A set of fire signals was arranged at Kildonan Castle at the south end of Arran

Ane baile [bonfire] *is warning of their cumming, quhat power whatever they bee of; twa bailes togidder at anis they are cumming indeed; four bailes ilk ane beside uther and all at anis as foure candilles, suithefast knawledge that they are of great and meanis far.*

In 1586 an Irish document comments that the inhabitants of the Glens of Antrim can always summon reinforcements from Scotland 'by making of fires upon certain steep rocks hanging over the sea'. We also have a letter from the Earl of Argyle dated 13 October 1615 concerning his suppression of the Islay rebellion

if it had not bene that sum of the tennents were neir to my camp and seing my forces row away in thair boattis – the moone shyning – who presentlie maid on great beakins upone the tope of ane hie hill, The quhilk so sone as Sir James did sie befor my men war at him be sex or seavin myllis of sea, he went to his boat ... utherwayes he could not have escaped.

Fire could serve several different purposes; it could guide, summon or warn.

Manuscript illustrations

Contemporary illustrations provide us with a rich visual library of mediaeval boats. We have all the manuscripts of Europe, all the frescoes, engravings, carvings in wood, stone and ivory – above all the Bayeux Tapestry. It is not just the famous items we should investigate; illustrations of small provincial ferries or fishing boats may be much more revealing of daily life. Among our richest sources are the illustrations of Matthew Paris, monk of St Albans, who died in 1259. It would be easy to assume that a monastic chronicler at an inland English abbey would be ignorant of naval architecture and the West Highlands of Scotland. Nothing could be further from the truth.

Monasteries played a critical role in the economic life of mediaeval Europe. Their enterprise applied to sea as well as land. The first description of a magnetic compass has been attributed to a late twelfth-century Abbot of Cirencester. Equally the thirteenth-century monks of St Albans seem to have compiled tide tables giving high water times at London Bridge. St Albans was also home to Matthew Paris.

Matthew was a polymath who wrote and illustrated his own manuscripts and may well have directed the production of many more. He was also extremely well-connected. After King Hakon of Norway's coronation at Bergen in 1247 Matthew acted as messenger from the French King asking Hakon to join the forthcoming crusade and take charge of the fleet. It was almost certainly whilst he was at Hakon's court that Matthew met or heard of Ewen (John) Macdougall of Lorn. As a result of what he learned he wrote very sympathetically of the plight of Ewen who was caught in a conflict of loyalties between Alexander II of Scotland and Hakon of Norway. In some ways this anecdote is a strange interlude in Matthew's chronicle but he uses it to point a moral in the matter of King Alexander's greed and subsequent death.

Hakon's fleet was among the greatest in Europe and his port of Bergen a marine metropolis. Nonetheless Alexander II could squeeze Ewen at a local level because Ewen held land on the mainland of Scotland. In his *Cronica Majora*, Matthew commented that in 1249 the Count of Dol in France had commissioned a 'splendid' boat from Inverness. He must have known something of Scottish shipping, either from the Hebrides and Ewen or from east coast boats visiting Bergen in 1248. Matthew was a fine artist and responsible for his own illustrations. His pictures of ships were drawn on the basis of first-hand experience and provide particularly valuable evidence. He was possibly even familiar with Ewen of Lorn's own galley which must have been big enough to cross the North Sea. One of Matthew's maps suggests that his geographic knowledge of Scotland was limited, but then the centre usually knows less of the periphery than vice versa.

Boats frequently appear in the marginal illustrations to Matthew's chronicles. Even when they have a Mediterranean context they have a Northern flavour. They are double-ended and clinker-built with a square sail. Some of them have outward-facing animal endposts which feature bird-beaks or prominent ears.[7] Side-rudders appear frequently but he could also draw the rudder on the port side and in a picture of a sea-battle between Pisans and Genoese he shows sharp, triangular rams fixed to the bows of two boats. If he had heard of such devices then so, presumably, had Ewen of Lorn.

There are other contemporary manuscripts which supply invaluable background material. Illustrations from a *Life of St Alban*, probably produced at the monastery of St Albans before 1240, display scenes of embarkation and disembarkation. Gangplanks, down which horses and people walk, lead from the boat to the shore. In the days before harbours and jetties, boats would be beached and gangplanks used for passengers and livestock.

Two very similar pictures from twelfth-century English bestiaries show masts being stepped. In both cases men are standing on top of the stern-post to give them maximum purchase on the ropes in order to raise the heavy mast. As in the Bayeux Tapestry this had been laid towards the bow of the boat. The usual procedure was for some crew to pull on masthead ropes from a point as high as possible in the stern of the boat. A particularly strong man put his shoulder to the mast near its base amidships whilst behind him others pushed the mast upwards from the bow. By means of such pictures we gain insights into the practical boating skills of the mediaeval period.

We have nothing which reflects directly on the West Highland scene but contemporary illustrations from the rest of Europe and Iceland give us a great many clues to the likely scenario in the Hebrides. Matthew saw 200 ships in Bergen Harbour, most of which were probably made in the Viking tradition. There would have been numerous variations between boats from different areas; one of which would have been the Hebrides. What is certain is that Hebridean boat designers would not have been ignorant of developments elsewhere.

Further information as to the actual look of contemporary vessels comes to us from pictures in the *Becket Leaves*, now in the British Library.[8] The *Becket Leaves* have been dated to the period 1220–1240 but they have been assessed as not personally the work of Matthew Paris. Nevertheless they have stylistic links with books which were at St Albans and it may well be that Matthew Paris designed the illustrations and directed the overall work whilst somebody else from a monastic workshop actually executed it.

The stem-post of one of the boats shows an animal-head with eyes, nose, teeth, beard and what appear to be two projecting ears rather than horns. These are so extended that we could be forgiven for thinking that this was artistic licence on the part of the illustrator. However confirmation that this was a current style derives from the graffiti on the 'Bergen Stick', dated between 1183 and 1248, where two of the animal-headed stem-posts have markedly protruding ears. A similar feature occurs in a graffito on the church-wall at Kilchattan, Luing.

Beside the boats a man is being carried ashore to save him getting his feet wet. We know this practice continued in Scottish coastal communities because Burt, one of Wade's staff officers in the eighteenth century, was amazed to see wives carry their husbands ashore from the boats so that they remained dryshod.

What relevance has all this to boat-design and marine practice in the Hebrides? The *Becket Leaves* may not be Matthew Paris's own work, but they bear striking resemblances to it. The boats portrayed may derive directly from his sketches. We cannot assume that galleys in the Western Isles looked exactly like those found in the *Becket Leaves*. We *can* assume that Highland boat-builders would have been well aware of design and practice elsewhere. By analogy we can estimate the appearance of early Hebridean galleys; unfortunately we have no certain knowledge of where lay the similarities, where the differences.[9]

The seals and manuscript illuminations confirm that Highland galleys were within a common North European tradition. There was little, perhaps, distinctive to the Hebrides except the building materials. The tragedy is that whilst the rest of Europe moved on, the Hebrideans did not. The Islay seal suggests they made the same momentous change from quarter to stern rudder in the thirteenth century – so when did they start to lag behind? It is tempting to ascribe it to the ending of Norse control in 1266. This involved a geopolitical realignment that fundamentally affected future Hebridean prosperity. The islands became caught in a technological trap and stood still commercially for centuries. However, it would be irresponsible to imagine that continued Norwegian sovereignty would necessarily have been more propitious. The Norse too went into relative decline during this period – a period that saw the advance of richer states such as England and France. The Highlands still proved capable of some extraordinary early castle-building from the thirteenth century and rich sculpture in the fifteenth century. The reasons for the increasing obsolescence of Highland boats are more complex.

Chapter 10

Carved Stones

THERE ARE OVER EIGHTY REPRESENTATIONS of galleys on mediaeval carved stones in the West Highland series and this does not include the stylised type that later appeared in great numbers on heraldic panels. Most of these galleys are on monumental grave-slabs but they also appear on free-standing crosses, a font, a wall-tomb panel, an altar frontal and even as graffiti.

The West Highland carved stones were analysed at length by Steer and Bannerman who suggested that there were four main schools or production workshops: Iona, Saddell, Oronsay and Loch Awe.[1] Not surprisingly the last-named, (which is inland) shows few galleys on its stones. A glance at the distribution map (Map 2) makes it clear that these stones were concentrated in the area between Kintyre and Mull. Stones in the Northern Hebrides are fewer in number, poorer in quality and later in date. It is an art primarily associated with Argyll and the Southern Hebrides but, ironically, the finest stone comes from St Clement's Church, Rodel, in Harris.

The Rodel galley (*see* Plate 12)

The galley was carved as one of the panels for the magnificent wall-tomb to Alexander Macleod in 1528. Unfortunately it was damaged some years ago but we have some earlier photographs and most of the detail is remarkably well-preserved. This galley has the most oar-ports of any in the West Highland series – seventeen – giving a total of 34 oars. At a crewing factor of three this would give a complement of just over 100.

It has been claimed, not wholly convincingly, that the stem and stern-post are stepped to take the run of the clinker planking, as with the Roskilde boats and the Eigg endposts. The mast shows the hun-bora or pierced wooden hole through which runs the halyard. The sail is square and the yard arm is controlled by two braces which attach to points well in from the ends of the yard. We can even tell the order of ropes at the masthead. They are, reading from top down, forestay, backstay, starboard fore shroud, starboard aft shroud, halyard and parrel. At least four rows of horizontal reefing-bands are visible in the bottom half of the sail. From these depend about six, possibly eight, faint lines which may represent the reef-laces. They could just be stitching seams but the fact that they appear only in the lower half of the sail makes it more likely that they refer to the reefing arrangements. The outer edges of the sail are reinforced by another seam to withstand wear.

There is a horizontal rope or crook just below the hun-bora which represents the parrel. The prow ends in a prong and there is what looks like a line of beading or an extra piece of wood added to the front of the stem-post. This may be a decorative feature but it is unlikely to be a fender since it only appears in the section well above the water-line. The stern-rudder lies at an angle of about eighteen degrees off vertical and widens nearer the base. Metal pins or pintles on the leading edge of the rudder drop into rings or gudgeons on the trailing edge of the stern-post. (MacAulay comments that this technique 'remains virtually unchanged on many island boats today'.)

The planking is shown with great skill. There is a keel, followed by six strakes, then the oarport strake, then the gunwale. The first strake (fliuch-bhord) from the keel is nearly vertical; the second (ruadh-bhord) bellies out, especially in the middle of the boat, but not fore and aft; while strakes five and six are nearly vertical amidships. The stone-carver shows considerable artistry because we are given a remarkably three-dimensional impression of the boat's form. He also indicates the craft of the shipwright because the curvature of the same strake can vary from nearly vertical, fore and aft, to well splayed out amidships where the planks were physically wider. The sense of depth achieved by the Rodel sculptor is unique in the West Highland series. The forestay presses against the sail from behind; the strakes curve out to meet us amidships. By comparison, on the much earlier stone at Texa (62) the clinker planks are indicated by simple incised lines.

Rodel is not alone. We have some fine examples amongst the Oronsay stones, a cross at Pennygown, Mull, and the stones at Kilmory, Knapdale. The remainder, however battered, can sometimes give us clues that are unique. Carvings also varied greatly in quality. Mariota MacDuffie of Colonsay (née MacIan) bought a grave-slab for her brother John at Iona (41) which is considerably better than the one she secured for herself on Oronsay (61).

Galleys were used by sculptors as symbols of power, status and right. Their relevance may have vanished; but they are still evocative and aesthetically pleasing. As sculptural motifs they served an artistic function; they are not a draughtsman's description. However since these 80 or so images are the only concrete evidence we have, their analysis is of the first importance. Such evidence must be used with caution because most stones are weathered and worn. Other observers will confidently state that there is an animal endpost here or a definite number of oarports there whilst I remain dubious. Sometimes appeal can be made to an illustration or description by an earlier witness such as Lhuyd, Pennant, Drummond, Stuart, Graham or White (*see* Bibliography). Their drawings though are of varying quality and they did occasionally make mistakes – even as scrupulous an authority as White. Steer and Bannerman describe Drummond's work as 'little more than a handsome picture-book'. The interests of some of these early authorities were very particular. Graham focused on Islay, White on Kintyre and Knapdale while Lhuyd was primarily concerned with the inscribed stones.

Galley-carvings must be seen in their context. They were not the creative expressions of a solitary artist. They were one of a range of motifs used by sculptors as part of the conventional decorative scheme for a grave-slab, wall-tomb or cross. They had to fit into a confined space and were products of craftsmen working in a particular style and for a particular school. Galleys were shown in specific ways, depending on who carved them and where – Saddell, Oronsay or Iona. This dictated basic design choices such as whether the sail was furled or set, the quantity of rigging, the detail of the rudder etc. It also affected the selection of accompanying motifs. The Kintyre school for instance has characteristic traits which, though not all displayed on every stone, do tend to betray their origins. The sail is typically furled, there are shields and banners at bow and/or stern, miniature trefoils or even a quatrefoil in the spaces between the rigging.

The craftsmen varied in skill and accuracy. For some the galley was just a generalised symbol; for others it was a particular vessel they knew. Sometimes they made straightforward mistakes, either because they didn't fully understand their subject matter or, more likely, were not sufficiently skilled to portray it accurately. For instance we could contrast Texa (62) with Iona (41). In the former stone (late fourteenth-century) the sculptor puts the forestay between the viewer and the sail whereas we feel it should be on the far side. In the latter case (1500–1509) the forestay is hidden by the sail. Best of all is Rodel (63) where the forestay is seen pressing against the sail from behind.

Stem and stern-posts

Elaborate and brightly painted figureheads on the endposts added to the appearance of a warship. Originally their object was semi-magical; to bring fortune, impress, overawe, terrify. In time they became more conventional and lost some of their mystical aura whilst gaining in aesthetic appeal. The early Icelandic *Land-namabok* speaks of the need to remove them on approaching the homeland in case they frightened friendly spirits. *Grettir's Saga* illustrates their magical qualities: 'Later he (Thorir) came out to Iceland and had his ship broken up because he was tired of sea-faring. He set up the figures from her head and stern over his doors, where they long remained foretelling the weather, one howling for a south, the other for a north wind'.

They were detachable and the Bayeux Tapestry indicates socket-holes on a number of endposts. One reason for removing them was the danger of damage in a crowded harbour; their elaborate carving made them expensive to replace. During the storm that so vexed Hakon's fleet in 1263

> *Those who were keeping watch upon the anchor-cables on the king's ship called out, and said that a merchant-ship was drifting from in front into their cables ... The fore-stays of the merchant-ship caught upon the king's ship, in the head; and it took off the nostrils.*

The *Encomium Emmae* describes Svein Forkbeard's fleet prior to embarkation for England

> *On one side lions moulded in gold were seen on the ships, on the other side birds on the mast-tops veered with the direction of the wind, or dragons of various kinds breathed fire through their nostrils. Here were glittering men of solid gold or silver, almost as real as living people; over there were bulls with arching necks and legs outstretched, carved as if they were alive.*

About nine of the West Highland carved galleys bore figureheads – principally Iona (37). These seem to be of animal type but are usually so worn that little can be said about them. They can face the same way (Iona 37) or in opposite directions (Iona 35 & Finlaggan

77). There is notching or beading on the stem-post at Rodel, Harris. This has also been claimed for the graffiti at Kilchattan – where almost anything can be argued – and Lord Archibald Campbell saw a slightly different type of notching on the stern-post of a galley at Kilkerran. Endposts do vary in height, with or without figureheads; some are extraordinarily high, some less so. In some cases, (e.g. Finlaggan 77), the endposts are cut very square. It may be that they were shaped like a hammerhead for ease of securing ropes. MacAulay has remarked on the fact that figureheads do not feature in songs and folklore and certainly the absence of literary mention suggests they were few in number and short in duration.

Most stern-posts have been at least partially straightened to take a stern-rudder but there survives a full range from the double-ended to the vertical. On some galleys – e.g. Kilmichael Glassary (72), where no rudder is shown – the stem is virtually indistinguishable from the stern. At the other extreme the stern-post is shown square to the keel and nearly vertical as in Iona (41) and Oronsay (56). There are many stages in between such as Abbot Mackinnon's cross on Iona (44) which has an uncomfortable dog-leg. The angle of the rudder varied in the carvings, as doubtless it did in practice.[2]

The Eigg endposts

Around 1878 two endposts were discovered in Eigg; one in particular had been stepped so that the ends of the attaching strakes might be fixed inside.[3] These endposts have never been carbon-dated so we cannot tell if they are Viking or mediaeval. They had been buried in the moss, possibly along with a keel, in order to keep them fresh and workable. They were prepared in a slack period for use in a busy one, and by some mishap never reclaimed. One end-post is about 202 centimetres or 6 feet 8 inches long which suggests a boat that was not particularly big.[4]

It is not certain whether the Eigg posts represent stem or stern-posts and whether from one or two different boats. They are gently curved which suggests either they are both stem-posts, since the stern was straightened once a stern-rudder was mounted; or they are early, i.e. pre-thirteenth century, and one is a curved stern-post from the days when boats were steered by quarter-rudder.

Macpherson, writing in 1878, says 'instead of the planks being fixed on the outside of the stem, they seem to have been intended to be fastened inside so as to be protected by it as by a guard'. He adds the footnote 'It is stated that in some Yorkshire villages the stems of the fishing-boats are protected by sheathing on this principle'. Unfortunately no perforations for rivets, treenails or thongs were apparent so we cannot be sure how the strakes were secured. Some manuscripts show the strake-ends riveted or nailed to the endposts from the *outside*.

Sails

Caesar said that the Veneti, a Celtic tribe of NW France, made their sails of hide; the Vikings made theirs of wadmal, (a coarse homespun wool), or flax. Place-names like Lionel and Linshader (Lewis) suggest that the Norse farmed flax in the islands though for what purposes we cannot tell. What about the Highlanders? The evidence suggests wool. Advice contained in the mid-thirteenth century *King's Mirror* is to 'keep on board two or three hundred ells of wadmal of a sort suitable for mending sails'.[5] At their most basic these sails would be monochrome. At the other end of the social and economic scale we know that King Hakon's *Mariasuden* (1256–7) had a sail embroidered with pictures.

The Vikings commonly had white sails but there are also references to blue and red stripes (*Egil's Saga*) and coloured sails. Colours and emblems added to the cost of a sail and so were confined to the boats of the wealthy and powerful. There are pictorial and written references in mediaeval documents to coloured sails and sails embroidered with crosses and coats of arms. They were exceptional in the Hebrides although boats must have used distinguishing flags or pennons. In his account of the Battle of Bloody Bay, Hugh Macdonald describes how the Laird of Ardgour 'displayed his colours' which Angus Og Macdonald mistook for Maclean's. Coloured stripes were probably the cheapest and most effective way of bringing variety to a sail. In Gaelic poetry we find references to 'white sails', 'speckled sails', 'dappled sails' and 'brown sails'.

In his description of a boatyard in Gairloch in the nineteenth century Hugh Miller commented 'Most of the sails themselves were made, not of canvas, but of a woollen stuff, the thread of which, greatly harder and stouter than that of common plaid, had been spun on the distaff and spindle'.[6] One of the problems for early sail-makers was the size of loom available. Usually the sail had to be made in sections that were then joined together. The Bayeux Tapestry shows that Norman sails were composed of several vertical strips which were arranged to make an interesting colour scheme. Our closest evidence for the Irish Sea area is a 1297 seal of Dublin which shows a sail which seems to be divided vertically into seven strips. Superimposed are three rows of reefbands starting about one-third of the way down the sail. This way the reef-points are all in the lower sections of sail and more easily accessible from the deck. The overall impression is of a sail which bulges in individual sections.

Few Highland grave-slabs give us much information. Most are worn and it is doubtful if the original carver was ever concerned with such fine detail. No sail shows vertical strips, many stones have the sail furled and in others the sail gives the impression of having been cut in one piece. This is particularly true of slabs from the Oronsay school where the sail is shown billowing in the wind. On most grave-slabs the sail appears squarish and there is no reason to doubt this visual impression. This contrasts with the Bayeux Tapestry and the Broighter boat which have what is known as a high aspect ratio, i.e. tall rather than wide. It is also at variance with the suspected low aspect ratio of some early Norse boats.[7] Stones vary as to where the yard and sail are set in relation to the height of the mast. Sometimes they are positioned as much as one-third of the way down. Some stones, such as Pennygown (32) and Oronsay (56), show a sail that is slightly narrower at the foot than at the yard.

Sails were regarded as a handsome gift. In *Egil's Saga* Thorolf took a 'good longship's sail' from Skalla-Grim to King Eirik. When Egil wanted a suitable gift for a great friend: 'Egil had had a long-ship sail made and elaborately worked. He gave the sail to Arinbjorn'. In a Highland context they may have been demanded as part of the rent. A rental from Tiree dated 1662 stipulates 60 'elnes' of 'Linning' (linen) and a 'saill and hair taikle to a galey'.[8]

Masts

Most boats had a single centrally-stepped mast.[9] The method of raising the yard was distinctive and derived directly from Norwegian practice. Near the top of the mast was a bulbous expansion with a hole in the middle through which ran the halyard. The hole is known as the 'hun-bora' and a large swelling or bole is left around it to strengthen the mast at that point. This practice first appears on

Gotland stones and was, according to Christensen, still used by nine-teenth-century Norwegian fishermen who tallowed the rope well to reduce friction through the hole. Similarly Sandison comments that the 'halliards of sixareens rove through a hole in the masthead'.

The expansion in the wood also served as a fixing-point for other ropes and stays that had to be attached to the top of the mast. The hun-bora is clearly shown in Rodel, Harris and on several other stones at Pennygown (Mull), Lochaline, Iona and Texa. Economy was important in the construction of Highland galleys and carving the wood in this way dispensed with the need for extra tackle for the halyard. From the numerous illustrations of a furled sail we can assume that the mast was left up more or less permanently and the sail furled. If necessary both yard and sail could then be taken down. Ardchattan (15), Iona (44) and Finlaggan (77) show just the mast and standing rigging.[10]

There are no pennons on the mast-tops as suggested by later heraldic designs; instead there are portable standards within the boat – probably so that they could be taken ashore.[11] Ten boats carry these banners; Nereabolls (51) actually has two. The banners are often toothed and sometimes the pole is set at an angle. Some have claimed a magical significance if there are three pennon-tails. In fact one of the best examples – Iona (44) – has four tails and may also contain a cross on a stepped plinth. That these banners were very much within the Norse tradition is proved by the 'Bergen Stick'. Here a three-tailed banner flies from a standard set in the prow of a boat which also has a weather-vane pointing forwards from the top of the stem-post.

Rigging

Rigging varies in complexity. This was because space dictated the omission of some detail, particularly with regard to the number of stays, braces and shrouds. The minimum arrangements seem to have been forestay (but not necessarily backstay), two shrouds to support the mast and two yard-braces which were almost always tied aft in the boat. All ropes, including shrouds, were secured inside the boat, and not outside.

The maximum arrangement, best shown on the stones at Kilmory, Knapdale, was forestay, backstay or halyard, four shrouds and three braces. (Drummond's drawing of Kilmory (68) shows six shrouds although the stone is now so worn that it is impossible to confirm this. Generally we would expect bigger boats to carry more shrouds.) Two of the three braces lead to the forward end of the yard; one of the braces is secured forward in the boat, two aft. The position of the halyard also shows that masts were raised from the stern and laid towards the bow – as in the Bayeux Tapestry and some mediaeval manuscripts.

On most galleys we cannot tell if the rope from the aft of the boat to mast-head is halyard or backstay. Rodel (63) shows both, but in virtually every other stone it is impossible to say because of the worn nature of the carvings and the sheer number of ropes. In many cases the halyard probably doubled as a backstay if it was secured well aft in the boat and kept taut to apply tension to the mast. At Rodel the back-stay loops over the top of the mast and sits above the expanded hun-bora. The halyard runs through the hun-bora and onto the yard.

The Vikings and Normans used parrel rings or travellers.[12] Their function was simply to keep the yard close to the mast as otherwise they would tend to part company when the sail took the wind. We have surviving examples from Oseberg, an early thirteenth-century level at the Wood Quay site in Dublin and also nineteenth-century Norway. The Wood Quay finds show a wooden crook with rope attachment. The wood went aft of the mast and could have been used with a mast of c. 1.26–1.57 metres in girth, rather bigger than Gokstad. Parrels could also be made of iron or rope with wooden beads. The last offered minimum friction when it came to lowering the yard without the parrel sticking against the mast.

Other ropes included a forestay (mast to stem) and a backstay (mast to stern or frame in aft of boat) and at least two ropes or shrouds to mid-points on either side of the boat. The shrouds always reach within the boat where they were attached to some internal timber. This is unlike the Dover seal of 1305 where the shrouds attach to rings on the outside of the gunwale. On Skuldelev 3 the shrouds also seem to have been fastened to cleats on the outside of the boat.[13] In such a position of course they were very exposed to damage from chafing in port. Galleys employed two ropes as sheets to the clews or lower corners of the sail. The curvature of the sail in stones by the Oronsay school makes this a certainty. There is no evidence for bowlines on Highland galleys – that is a rope from the sail's leading edge forward to the stem.

Cordage

The Norse made rope from the hides of sea-mammals; whale, walrus and seal.[14] Long thin strips could be made by cutting the skins spirally. The Highlanders also did this, particularly with sealskin, but another interesting raw material is revealed in Hugh Miller's account of a visit to a boatyard in Gairloch in the early nineteenth century. Here he noticed a Highlander cutting long thin strips from a piece of moss-fir. This made a rope 'in large use among the fishermen'. It consisted of three strands and was used, amongst other things, for the 'lacing of sails'. Heather was another popular raw material. In 1907 James Macdonald wrote of a typical 'son of Morar' who 'wove his own nets, and made wonderfully tough and flexible ropes of birch and heather'.

Braces

Braces are ropes attached to the ends of a yardarm so that it can be swung to a different angle to take full advantage of the wind. We do not find braces on depictions of Viking boats although there is evidence that they were used from the twelfth century. They are clearly portrayed on a seal of Dunwich dated *c.* 1199.

Very many of the West Highland galleys show braces. These do not attach to the end of the yardarm as we would expect if maximum leverage was the purpose. They are usually set in a little, perhaps to lessen the strain on the yard. One of the braces is often shown running at an angle across the shrouds and mast whilst the other is set vertically. Both tend to be fixed amidships or aft of the mast on some internal timber. The fact that one, or both of the braces often appear vertical led to the suggestion that they were actually made of wood.[15] Braces are portrayed in the same way for at least three centuries. They are clearly shown on a seal of King Harald of Man in 1246 and they appear on the Rodel stone of 1528. They are identifiable by their attachment to the yard rather than the mast and the fact that they are usually set at an angle to other ropes.[16]

The Norse also used a beitiass or tacking-boom. This was a wooden spar for holding the leading edge of the sail forward when sailing close to the wind. Some rather ambiguous wooden sockets just forward of the mast were found on the sides of the Gokstad boat and Skuldelev 1. They are now thought to be seats for a beitiass. It is likely that this was attached to the side or bottom edge of the sail and projected outside the boat. We know of an incident in which a beitiass knocked someone overboard from a passing vessel: 'King Eystein was sitting at the helm as they sailed ... and another ship was sailing at the side of his, when there came the stroke of a wave, by which the beitiass of the other ship struck the king and threw him overboard, which proved his death'.[17] Over time the beitiass was replaced by bowsprit and bowlines. We have no evidence for the use of the beitiass on Highland galleys. The fact that braces appear so often suggests that these were the prime means of altering the angle which the sail presented to the wind.

Oarports

Oars can be secured in a number of ways; by using grommets, thole-pins, rowlocks or oarports. When West Highland galleys show anything they show oarports although it could be argued that the absence of these on many carvings suggests other forms of attachment.[18]

The Gokstad oarports have a diameter of *c.* twelve centimetres which, with the slit for blade, allowed an oar-blade of about sixteen centimetres. Nearly four centuries later, the oarports found at Wood Quay, Dublin, have a diameter of *c.* thirteen centimetres which, with a four centimetres slit, allows a blade of *c.* seventeen centimetres. We can presume something similar for Highland galleys given their close contact with Ireland. Although we have Viking oarports of several different shapes (circular, semi-circular, square, rectangular, trapezoidal), all Highland galleys seem to have round oarports. We know from Scandinavian finds that the optimum distance between rowers was about 91 centimetres. We can estimate the overall length of a boat by multiplying the number of oarports by 91 centimetres and adding an allowance for stem and stern.

Only a few galleys show anything like a full set of oarports but the carving in St Clement's Church, Rodel, even displays the horizontal slit which was cut to facilitate shipping the blade of the oar.[19] Various galleys are shown with 18, 20, 32 or 34 oars whilst others are not complete. If we allocate a crewing factor of three men to an oar the largest boats must have had crews of over 100 which made them impressive instruments of aggression. Thole-pins were preferred to oarports in smaller vessels that had less freeboard. Certainly both were used by Vikings in earlier times and we know thole-pins survived in the Highlands because Alasdair Macdonald refers to them in his 'Birlinn of Clanranald'. Thole-pins would suggest the absence of jetties where they would be easily damaged. The lack of port development along the entire west coast north of Glasgow suggests that landing-arrangements were habitually informal. Boats would be beached and traders would congregate at impromptu beach-markets, as was the case in the Baltic.

Rowing with long heavy oars in an open sea and poor weather would be immensely taxing of a man's stamina. After ten to twenty minutes his efficiency would reduce and it may well be that a high crewing factor was partly to allow regular changes of oarsmen. Oars would not normally be used except for speed, manoeuvring or in calm or adverse winds.

Oars sometimes lay in grommets. In *Egil's Saga* there is a passage describing Egil's skuta lying ready for a quick getaway: 'while the pinnace floated, steering-oar shipped ... with the oars in their loops'. In *Arrow-Odd's Saga* there is a reference to wearing an oar-glove. This may have been no more than a patch of leather but we can imagine it would have been invaluable on long hauls. Alasdair Macdonald's 'Birlinn' is strong on hyperbole but it makes clear that the hands suffered during strenuous rowing.

Rudders and tillers

The single biggest difference between a Viking longship and a West Highland galley is the transition from steering-board to stern-rudder. Viking boats had large steering-boards on the right or starboard side. There were variations in the shape of these steering-boards, as we can see in the Bayeux Tapestry where some have a little curved extension or 'shoe'. Highland grave-slabs show slight variations in rudder shape, the angle at which it is set and its method of attachment. This is as we would expect since there is no ideal shape for a rudder. Its efficiency depends to a certain extent on the speed at which the boat is travelling and in turn this partly derives from its function as trader or longship.

Since the stern-rudder could not be held directly it had to be worked by a tiller. However the tiller and the stern-rudder developed independently. What we know of side-rudders suggests that they must have been worked by a tiller on all except the smaller boats. If boats were below a certain size they didn't require a rudder anyway. With the transfer of the rudder to the stern all that needed to change was the shape of the tiller. Initially this had to curve around the stern-post. Latterly the height of the stern-post was dropped so that the tiller could be straight and horizontal.

Rudder *shape* varies. Some rudders, such as Oronsay (56), have an extremely wide foot while others do not. In most cases the rudder does not extend below the line of the keel, otherwise the crew would have to raise it in shallow waters or when beaching. Nevertheless in boats such as Iona (44) the rudder is definitely shown extending below the keel-line.

Other carvings

We have some graffiti on castle walls, churches and an isolated boulder. Sadly a graffito in Duntulm Castle, Skye, disappeared when a section of walling collapsed a few years ago. A surviving illustration seems to show a three-masted galley with mast-tent but this is now impossible to verify.[20]

More evidence is provided by a set of graffiti on the exterior church wall at Kilchattan, Luing. Here are a number of carvings of Viking-type boats.[21] Some relate them to a Scottish naval expedition in the early thirteenth century but it is just as likely that they were carved at the time of King Hakon's great venture of 1263, in the same way as the runes cut in St Molaise's Cell, Holy Isle, Arran.[22] Unfortunately we cannot distinguish rudders of any particular type which makes dating difficult.

The best-preserved carving shows an animal-headed prow with big ears and what appears to be a mast-tent. There is also a notched endpost(?), a gangplank and what may be a triangular wind-vane similar to that shown on the 'Bergen Stick'. This stick has been dated to between 1183 and 1248 and clearly shows the Norse type of wind-vane – quarter-circle in shape and often of gilded bronze. We have surviving metal examples of these and a description in *Encomium Emmae* suggests they were sometimes in the shape of birds: 'On the other side birds on the mast-tops veered with the direction of the wind'.

A late eleventh or early twelfth-century wooden plank from Winetavern Street, Dublin shows a weather-vane in the shape of an arrow. The yard seems half-lowered (with sail furled) and rests on the stern-post. This implies a long yard and a sail with a low aspect ratio.[23] There also seem to be gaffs for the oars similar to those found in the Oseberg ship. There is a side-rudder and a small towboat astern. If these assumptions are correct then boats in the Irish Sea were very much in the Norwegian tradition; and so probably were boats in the Minches.

Tow-boats

We know of these from Icelandic sources, the Bayeux Tapestry and town seals such as Sandwich. We can assume the Icelandic references apply predominantly to ocean-going knorrs. In *Greenland Saga* we hear: 'they sailed right up to the shore and cast anchor, then lowered a boat and landed'. Three tow-boats were found with the Gokstad ship but I suspect only the largest Highland galleys carried such luxuries. Large vessels may have used gangplanks as illustrated by Matthew Paris.

Anchors

We have no evidence of mediaeval anchors in the Highlands but they quite possibly resembled the Icelandic 'stjori', simply on the grounds of economy. Binns has described this as a pyramidal framework of poles enclosing a heavy stone. It was cheap and expendable but perhaps not very reliable.[24] It was not that Hebrideans were ignorant of better designs. It was just that conventional iron anchors would be expensive and not easily replaced among the islands. The 1297 Dublin seal shows an iron anchor secured outboard against the bow. By contrast in Captain Phillips's seventeenth-century drawings of an Irish currach there is an anchor in the lower sketch which is reminiscent of the Icelandic design described by Binns. A criss-cross of wood with upward-angled ends lies at the base of a conical bag which presumably contained the weight. It looks very home-made, but cheap and functional. In the main drawing it appears again, this time hanging over the side of the currach.

Binns has also argued that beaching was a very important aspect of Viking sea-going and this would be perfectly suited for the Hebridean environment. Jetties, piers and harbours demanded resources the Hebrides did not have and there are innumerable natural coves to offer safety and shelter. In the absence of piers and jetties you beach and carry; therefore your vessels need to be light and manoeuvrable; therefore you build light, shallow boats rather than heavy, deep-draught cargo-ships; therefore you do not require jetties and can make use of any convenient beach. The Scandinavians evolved from this technological trap, not so the Hebrideans. The commercial stimulus was missing.

The *Chronicles of Man* supply an anecdote concerning the beaching of Hebridean galleys. In 1158 Somerled invaded Man with 53 ships where he defeated Godred and ravaged the island. At one stage he was 'at the port called Ramsey'. Gilcolm, one of his chieftains, violated the sanctuary of St Machutus and died a horrible death: 'Somerled and his army were so terror-stricken by his death that, as soon as the tide was in and their ships afloat, they took the fleet out of that port'. It appears that Somerled's 53 boats were beached, even in the port of Ramsey.

Painted, gilded, tarred or tallowed?

How were the boats finished, from a utilitarian or decorative point of view? Were Highland galleys ever painted, gilded, tarred or tallowed? In the context of the Hebrides the last seems the most likely.[25] The Norse regarded winter maintenance as essential to the preservation and long-life of a boat. The thirteenth-century *King's Mirror* contains the advice: 'have it thoroughly coated with tar in the autumn and, if possible, keep it tarred all winter. But if the ship is placed on timbers too late to be coated in the autumn, tar it when spring opens and let it dry thoroughly afterwards'.[26] Tarring even applied to the oars. In *King Harald's Saga* the poet Thjodolf refers to the 'black-tarred oars' of Harald's fleet.

It is possible that painting and gilding were sometimes applied by the story-tellers as a sort of retrospective romantic overlay. The fourteenth-century saga of Arrow-Odd says that Odd 'had the whole of Halfdan's Gift painted and the dragon heads fore and aft gilded, along with the weather vane'. Such a boat would leave a powerful visual impression but it probably only ever applied to the ships of the wealthiest men.

Orkneyinga Saga describes how when Earl Rognvald was planning his trip to the Holy Land his companions agreed that only the Earl's ship would be ornamented. This would reduce unnecessary expense and competition among those going with him. When Rognvald went to Norway to pick up his new boat it is described as 'inlaid with gold upon prow and stern, wind-vanes and so on'. On their voyage back to Orkney the Earl's fleet was overtaken by the ship of Eindridi the Young, a Norwegian chieftain who was accompanying them to the Holy Land. It was 'a superbly built dragonhead, heavily inlaid with gold upon both stern and prow, brightly painted in the bows and all above the water-line'. Rognvald's men complained that Eindridi hadn't kept his word but the Earl merely replied: 'We're not going to plot our course according to his ambitions'.

The visual impression made by gilding is illustrated by a story in *King Harald's Saga* about Harald's return from a raid on Denmark: 'Then a thick sea-fog came down. When the sun rose next morning they saw what seemed to be a host of fires burning on the other side of the sea'. King Harald realised what it was and told them to row away from the nearby Danish fleet: 'The fog must have lifted where they are, and the sun is shining on their gilded dragon-prows'.

Miscellaneous

If they were unable to camp on land the Vikings could make a deck-shelter by dismounting the mast, laying it between vertical trestles at either end of the boat and covering it with the sail. The Gokstad boat gives excellent examples of these T-shaped crutches which support the mast as a tent-ridge. There is a graffito at Kilchattan Church, Luing, which may illustrate this. There is no direct evidence of Highlanders doing likewise but since shelter was essential and since the boats were not decked it remains a possibility. There was probably less need in the Hebrides where land was never far away.

It has been suggested that there may have been weather-vanes on the stem and stern-posts. Such have been found on Viking boats and there may be a graffito of one at Kilchattan, Luing. Some endposts may also have served as mast-supports. At Kilcolmkill, Morvern, there is a stone – Lochaline (21) – showing part of a Highland galley. Here the stem-post is expanded near the top and there appear to be three vertical prongs extending from it with space between them – perhaps for accommodation of the mast or spars.

There are manuscript illustrations which show the stern-post terminating in a U-shaped crutch. We have examples of 'mikes' on mediaeval English seals and possibly on the Manx Hedin stone so they may have been known in Hebridean waters. It has been noticed how often the endposts of galleys finish in a single prong. Since this is always seen from the side it may be that the terminal was in fact a double-prong or mike. We have two surviving mikes from the Wood Quay site in Dublin. These are substantial and could support spars of between 2.5 and 2.7 metres in girth. This would represent a mast twice as big as Gokstad and anything between about 22 metres and 38 metres long. The parrels from the same site would only have fitted masts of 1.26–1.57 metres girth. These mikes may have been substantially bigger than they needed to be so that other items such as the yard and oars could be stacked alongside the mast.

There is no evidence that West Highland galleys ever used topcastles or crow's nests - despite their frequent appearance in heraldry. There is evidence for these in English seals but the situation in the West Highlands was perhaps the same as that shown in one of the Anglo-Saxon boats in the Bayeux Tapestry where somebody just shinned up the mast.[27] It is unlikely they ever fired beacons at the mast-tops.

Baling was a mundane but essential task. In *Grettir's Saga* (early fourteenth-century) we read: 'In those days in sea-going ships there were no scuppers for baling; they only had what is called bucket or pot-baling, a very troublesome and fatiguing process'. In Mac-donald's 'Birlinn' a man is detailed for this task alone – critical in an undecked boat. He had to be strong, tireless and inured to cold:

> *A thick round wooden baling-can*
> *In his swarthy hands,*
> *Throwing out the sea forever.*

(translation by Hugh MacDiarmid)

Functions

What functions did galleys serve? Primarily they were warships and troop-transports, like their Viking ancestors. Several stones carry armed warriors, as on a slab from Lochaline where the bascinet is clearly visible. This display of armour confirms the boat's principal function. Similarly there is a grave-slab at Kilmichael Glassary where a much-worn galley holds six soldiers.

Some of the literary references suggest two types among Highland boats, the lymphad or longship and the birlinn which was somewhat smaller. This literary typology is not reflected in the portrayal of boats on sculptured stones. There are differences, but not obviously between two alternative designs. Galleys on carved stones and seals have a symbolic function. They are symbols of protective power, not commercial enterprise or public service. The clues to the different types of vessel will probably be found in the linguistic and literary sources rather than the sculptural. On seals boats often appear at sea, surrounded by water and, sometimes, fish. In the sculptural series they always appear out of water, in full elevation.

In the case of their Norse predecessors there had been obvious visual distinctions. Longships and knorrs differed in shape. Longships were long and generally thin. Exceptions drew attention to themselves. When King Harald had a new 35-bencher built at Eyrar his saga says 'It was much broader than normal warships'. Where a boat was designed primarily for rowing the sagas say so. In *Orkneyinga Saga* King Ingi gave Earl Rognvald 'a pair of longships, rather small, but very handsome and fast, designed more for rowing'. The same source says of Swein Asleifson on a raiding expedition: 'They had five big ships, all fitted for rowing'. Cargo-ships were shorter and beamier. Longship crews generally unstepped the mast when rowing. Knorrs left their heavy mast in situ. Long-ships had a continuous gunwale, on knorrs these could be stepped.

Were there functional differences between lymphads and birlinns? The sculptural data gives us no hard evidence for such a distinction. We have no stepped gunwales, no strikingly different designs. Although the Gaelic terms *longfada* and *birlinn* suggest separate origins we do not know whether either was designed primarily as a troop-transport or cargo-ship.

Norse byrdingr were apparently smaller than knorrs, with more slender lines, possibly more oarports and a lower freeboard. We know from literary sources that byrdingr could, if necessary, be lengthened into warships. This suggests that the differences between byrdingr and longships were less in design than in size. This argument is supported by the Privy Council minute of 1615 which distinguishes between galleys and birlinns purely in terms of the number of oars. In this case the boats represented on Highland stones could be classed as either lymphad or birlinn depending on the number of oarports alone. Over time, and as boats gradually decreased in size so the general term birlinn came to loosely embrace all Highland galley-types.

There is a fundamental historical contradiction concerning Norse seafaring. Their myth associates Vikings with longships –

which was their weapon of war. In reality their epic voyages of exploration and colonisation were conducted in knorrs – which were trading vessels. The latter drew more water and were better sailers, particularly to windward, since they drifted less. Byrdingr seem to have been something of a design compromise between the two poles – which is why they may be the forerunners of Hebridean galleys. On most galley-carvings the mast is not taken down when the sail is furled. This suggests the mast was heavy and the boat was sailed whenever possible. Equally there was no stepped gunwale so there was a full complement of rowers when required.

Dating

About 30 of the stones bear inscriptions although there are several more that perhaps did so originally. Of these 30 about fourteen are in Lombardic and about fourteen are Black Letter. Since Steer and Bannerman have established that the type of script on graveslabs changed from the former to the latter around 1500 this means that the galley stones are equally distributed on either side of that date. However one early stone from Texa, Islay can be dated to *c.* 1387 and a late stone from Oronsay to *c.*1539 which gives a range of about 150 years for most carvings of galleys.

Inscriptions

What do the inscriptions reveal?

Here lies Lachlan, son of Donald Maclean, Lord of Ardgour. (Lochaline (23))

This is the cross of Colin MacEachern and his wife Katherine. (Kilkerran (5))

Here lies Murchardus MacDuffie of Colonsay who died in the year of our Lord 1539; and Mariota Maclean caused me to be made. (Oronsay (56))

Here lies ... Mariota, daughter of Alexander, son of John MacIan. (Oronsay (61)) – This Mariota also purchased the graveslab of her brother John MacIan of Ardnamurchan (Iona (41)).

(Translations from Steer and Bannerman.)

About sixteen stones have inscriptions that are legible. Of these there are two which commemorate married couples, one was erected by a prior, one is to an abbot and one to a woman. At both Pennygown (Mull), and Ardchattan, galleys are accompanied by representations of the Virgin Mary so they are not emblems we should only associate with warriors. Most of the stones are connected with the great landed families of the day. It was not a democratic art. Galleys were symbolic of power and it is the rich landholders who are remembered. The only exceptions are a few stones to children, craftsmen and possibly merchants.

Accompanying motifs

The evidence from the inscriptions is that it is predominantly the male members of the great families who are commemorated. This is borne out by the accompanying motifs. Much West Highland art was geometric and decorative, but the symbols of power were seldom omitted altogether. Some 28 of the galley-stones also include swords or claymores and a further fourteen have warrior or other effigies. At least eighteen of the stones display stag-hunts and another six carry mounted horsemen. The flavour is unmistakable. These are memorials to an aristocratic warrior caste. The exceptions prove the rule. Only one stone is to a woman, although two more were ordered by women. Only two stones are directly connected to clergymen. One, Iona (44), is to an abbot whilst another, Ardchattan (15), was erected by a prior. Around the galley on Oronsay (57) are a hammer, anvil and tongs which suggest dedication to a smith whilst another slab displays a carpenter's square.

Boat-builders?

We have two slabs which may refer to boat-builders. The most impressive, Inishail (81), is unusually bare of decoration. It has a roll-moulding, a sword, a galley with crew, an axe and a hammer. The prominence given to the galley and the tools, particularly the axe, suggest it commemorates a boat-builder. There are five or six helmeted crew which is a feature only paralleled by the slab at Kilmichael Glassary (72) although the latter bears far more decoration. One of the crew is obviously the helmsman. He is the only one to face forward and wears what looks to be a cowl or hood, peaked at the front with a liripipe at the back. The helmsman was unable to take shelter and had to be well clad. There are plenty of illustrations of this headgear in manuscripts and on seals and this may be another instance of borrowed imagery.

Another stone at Kilmarie, Craignish (74), is also possibly to a boat-builder – judging by the hammer (or adze?) and carpenter's axe shown above a boat hull. In neither the Inishail or Craignish slab is the boat complete which could be a symbolic suggestion that the dead man was a boat-builder. Mast and sail are absent, emphasizing the fact that this particular craftsman was primarily responsible for the hull. Both stones look to be locally produced, both are probably fifteenth-century. From John of Lorn's letters in the early fourteenth century we could expect a boatyard on Loch Etive. The shores of Loch Craignish offer another likely location.

Chapter 11

Surviving Boat-building Traditions

TRADITIONAL SKILLS IN WOOD-WORKING and boat-building have a tendency to last comparatively unchanged for centuries. It is only in recent times with the introduction of new materials such as fibre-glass, new designs and new tools that the building of small boats has been transformed. However changes are now taking place so swiftly that traditional skills and methods will soon be lost or forgotten unless they are recorded. In the nineteenth century Hugh Miller noted the survival of old boat-building methods in the North of Scotland.[1] Although his book *My Schools and Schoolmasters* was published in 1889 he was referring to his youth in the earlier years of the century

> *During the previous winter I had read a little work descriptive of an ancient ship, supposed to be Danish, which had been dug out of the silt of an English river, and which, among other marks of antiquity, exhibited seams caulked with moss[2] ... On visiting, however, a boat-yard at Gairloch, I found the Highland builder engaged in laying a layer of dried moss, steeped in tar, along one of his seams, and learned that such had been the practice of boat-carpenters in that locality from time immemorial.[3] I have said that the ... Highlander ... was engaged in stripping with a pocket-knife long slender filaments from off a piece of moss-fir. He was employed in preparing these ligneous fibres for the manufacture of a primitive kind of cordage, in large use among the fishermen, and which possessed a strength and flexibility that could scarce have been expected from materials of such venerable age and rigidity as the roots and trunks of ancient trees, that had been locked up in the peat-mosses of the district for mayhap a thousand years. Like the ordinary cordage of the rope-maker, it consisted of three strands, and was employed for haulsers, the cork-bauks of herring nets, and the lacing of sails. Most of the sails themselves were made, not of canvas, but of a woollen stuff, the thread of which, greatly harder and stouter than that of common plaid, had been spun on the distaff and spindle. As hemp and flax must have been as rare commodities of old in the Western Highlands, and the Hebrides generally, as they both were thirty years ago in Gairloch, whereas moss-fir must have been abundant, and sheep, however coarse their fleeces, common enough, it seems not improbable that the old Highland fleets that fought in the 'Battle of the Bloody Bay,' ... may have*

been equipped with similar sails and cordage. Scott describes the fleet of the 'Lord of the Isles,' in the days of the Bruce, as consisting of 'proud galleys,' 'streamered with silk and tricked with gold.' I suspect he would have approved himself a truer antiquary, though mayhap worse poet, had he described it as composed of very rude carvels, caulked with moss, furnished with sails of dun-coloured woollen stuff still redolent of the oil, and rigged out with brown cordage formed of the twisted fibres of moss-fir.

Other topographical accounts support Miller's sanguine views. Pennant says that the Loch Broom fishermen made ropes from the inner bark of the Scots fir. Professor Walker travelled in the Highlands and Hebrides between 1760 and 1786 and in his book *Economical History of the Hebrides and Highlands* sheds some light on local boat-building practice. Walker was commenting on the harmful effects of the lack of division of labour

from the want of tradesmen at command, every family is obliged to apply to every thing, and to supply its own necessities. The exercise of so many employments, prevents indeed their excelling in any ... The spades, ploughs, harrows and sledges ... with all their harnessing, are made by the farmer and his servants; as also the boats, with all their tackle. The boat has a Highland plaid for a sail; the running rigging is made of leather thongs and willow twigs; and a large stone and a heather rope serve for anchor and cable.

Traditional boat-building families depended on the patronage of the clan chief. Once this was removed, from 1603 on, there was a decline in support for specialist craftsmen. Boats tended to be smaller, geared to local needs and reflecting local skills. Substitution and restraint kept the manufacture of galleys within the capability of the Highland economy. Boats could be built locally on the basis of traditional skills and knowledge. The raw materials were timber, wool or flax, tallow, and cordage from skin or roots.

Boat-building was a traditional craft, the skills, tools and accumulated technical wisdom being passed from father to son. This was a typical feature of Highland life where particular families monopolised certain crafts or trades. Thus we have the Beatons, who were doctors; the MacCrimmons who were pipers and the O'Brolchans who were sculptors. In 1991 a reconstructed galley called the *Aileach* sailed up the west coast of Scotland. It had been built in Moville, Co. Donegal by a Macdonald family who had emigrated from the Highlands after the 1745 Rising. They settled in Ireland where they have continued the family's boat-building tradition to the present day. Not only did they build the *Aileach* but it has been noticed how similar to Viking longships are some of their wooden boats during the early stages of construction. Some modern fishing-boats with their copper-riveted, clinker-built, larch planks and oak ribs would appear familiar to a Norse shipwright.

The Earls of Argyll employed two such boat-building families, the MacGille Chonnaill on Loch Awe and the MacGille Lucais on Loch Fyne.[4] In 1308 or 1309 John of Lorn claimed in a letter to Edward II that he was building and maintaining galleys on a loch 24 miles long (probably Loch Etive, though some argue for Loch Awe). Perhaps its well-timbered shores made it an ideal boat-building environment. The Revd J MacInnes reported a Dr Ross telling that his mother's ancestors (Macleods) were galley-builders to the Macleods of Harris and Dunvegan and on that account had a croft in Colbost between Glendale and Dunvegan.[5]

The established pattern in Norway was for boats to be built in the sheltered, wooded, inland fjords for fishermen in the exposed outer fjords.[6] Similarly the windswept and sometimes treeless Outer Isles were not ideal for boat-building. The Inner Hebrides such as Skye and Eigg were better; but better still were the well-wooded mainland areas of Argyll and Inverness-shire. Stray references can lead us to boatyards.[7] Matthew Paris indicates that Inverness was a boat-building centre in the thirteenth century. In 1506 we know a certain Donald Gallich was at Kishorn building two galleys because this was where his brothers murdered him

> *Donald Gallich ... walked with his brothers a little below the house to the place where the gallies were building on the stocks. Archibald bowed under the quarter of one of the galleys and said the carpenter had placed a plank there in a very crude manner. Donald Gallich stooping to see the plank was stabbed by Archibald with his long skean or knife.*

What is remarkable about traditional boat-building is that it dispensed completely with the detailed plans held to be so essential for every project today. Proportions were critical, but the eye was the final judge and a story about the making of Olaf Trygvason's *Long Serpent* in Trondheim (*c.* AD 1000) endorses the intuitive skills of a master shipwright. The *Long Serpent* was the biggest ship of her day and naturally a lot of craftsmen were employed in her construction. The shipwright was a man called Thorberg 'Skafhogg' (or 'Trimmer') and after laying the initial lines he had to go home for some time whilst the planks were added. On his return he was not happy with the lines of the vessel despite the fact that the king and all else were. He stole out at night and marked deep notches all the way down one gunwale. The next morning a furious King Olaf demanded to know who had vandalised his boat, threatening the direst punishments. Thorberg admitted responsibility and then proceeded to make good his damage by trimming the length of the gunwale to the depth of his notches. A fresh look convinced the king and all the spectators that this was indeed an improvement and he was ordered to do the same to the other gunwale.

One of the craftsmen in the boat-building scene of the Bayeux Tapestry may actually be a prowright eyeing up the lines of a boat. These skilled craftsmen built intuitively by look. Shape and proportion were judged by eye, not textbook. The breadth of each strake and its angle of join affected the whole shape of the boat. Boat-ells and levels were used to aid accuracy when gauging lines and angles but the design was conceived by the eye rather than the compass and square. Just how intuitive are such craft skills is borne out by recent comments in a book on Ireland's traditional crafts. On a boat being constructed in an Irish boatyard the writer said: 'Construction methods are still very traditional and tools like the adze much in evidence. No elaborate plans are made; the hull is carefully and skilfully built with the use of wooden templates to achieve the correct lines'.[8]

In the early Viking period each frame and strake was shaped by axe and adze, not saw. All wood was split and hewn and particular care would have been taken to select just the right tree for whatever timber was required. This involved an enormous expense of time and energy and was wasteful of timber, although in a primitive northern environment every scrap would find its way onto a fire eventually. Nevertheless the demand for straight-grown forest oaks would put a strain on any mediaeval economy. In the Highlands we would expect to find them using softwoods such as pine, as in northern Norway. Not all of the islands supported trees. In some instances timber may have been exported from the mainland or alternatively the boats built there. In other cases the boats may have been built abroad and imported.

It was an enormously skilled job. Highland galleys did not evolve in the same way as boats elsewhere but local craftsmen still produced beautiful and functional craft that were famously quick at sea. The garboard strakes of an early thirteenth-century wreck from Sjovollen in Norway demonstrate the complexity that clinker-building could involve. (The garboard planks were the ones next to the keel.) Their shape altered along their length from flattish amidships to nearly vertical at either end. Even in the Middle Ages this contortion was often produced by steaming but at Sjovollen the shape required has been cut from the solid wood. It must have taken great skill, patience and persistence. These attributes the Highlanders shared. In the Rodel boat the next strake up from the garboard strake has a curvature similar to that achieved at Sjovollen.

Made in Ireland?

Not all boat-building materials were produced locally and during the sixteenth century timber was exported from Ireland to the Hebrides. Probably one of the first items to be traded was sawn boards. Hewing was so uneconomic of time and timber that there must have been enormous incentive for change in all but the poorest environments. During the thirteenth century this trade was well-established. We have examples of sawn boards in Edward I's galley accounts as well as the evidence from his murage grants to Irish burghs.[9]

Hebridean galleys may sometimes have been constructed in Ireland. The English kings certainly commissioned them, perhaps because of lower timber and labour costs. On 11 February 1235 Henry III asked the justiciary of Ireland 'that he cause to be constructed with the King's money 6 good galleys, 2 of 60 oars and 4 of 40 oars, and that he send them well-equipped to the King in England'. By the next day he had decided he couldn't wait that long for he instructed the same officer to send him 'the galley which Gilbert Marshall ... gave to the king, with 2 more galleys, and all others which the justiciary can acquire for the King's use. At the first fair wind the galleys well equipped shall sail to Portsmouth'.[10]

About August 1241 King Henry III commanded 'his good men of Dublin to cause a new galley to be made, and with the one they already have, to be well-equipped and prepared to go on the King's service'. Similar letters were sent to the men of Waterford for two galleys, and to Drogheda, Cork and Limerick for one galley. Hebrideans maintained relations with Ireland throughout the Middle Ages, perhaps more with the Gaelic chieftains than the merchants of the towns, but it is perfectly possible that some galleys were built in Ireland for customers in Arran, Kintyre and Islay.

Made in Norway?

Writing in 1786 of Captain Alexander Macleod's works at Rodel in Harris, John Knox says: 'He has procured some East Country fishers, with Orkney yawls, to teach the inhabitants'. Knox also commented on the boats from the south end of Skye fishing for herring in Loch Hourn. They were 'not much longer than a London sculler, and many of them, called Norway skiffs, about that size'. Pre-fabricated boats travelled from Norway to Shetland during this period. Did some of them travel still further west to the Hebrides? In Alasdair Macdonald's 'Iorram Cuaim' the author states that a galley he was praising had 'ramh a Lochlainn' (oars from Norway).[11] In 1773 both Johnson and Boswell refer to the Laird of Raasay owning a boat made 'in Norway'. This may not have been unusual in the Western Isles in the eighteenth century and should be taken into account when claiming the survival of local boat-building traditions.

Ratio rules

Traditional skills and stock phrases enshrining the received wisdom of past centuries went hand in hand. Donald Gorm of Sleat was a poet and an expert boat-builder who was visiting MacNeill of Barra to advise him on the construction of a birlinn. He was displeased with his reception and on his departure gave MacNeill's carpenter these cryptic directions

> *On narrow garboard strake engraft*
> *A softly graded rise*
> *Long bevel twist to bilge with craft*
> *And rounded contours fore and aft*
> *Be skilful to devise.*
>
> *And if for keel a yard be spanned*
> *In length, you will discern*
> *A foot for mast-thwart mete; a hand,*
> *Just half as much, for bow beam, and*   .
> *Two thirds for breadth of stern.*

(A. Macleod's translation).[12]

From this Mr Macleod construed the likely proportions of the boat to be

	Keel	Mast-thwart	Bow (beam or depth)	Stern
	3	1	1/2	2/3
e.g.	36 feet	12 feet	6 feet	8 feet

What we have here is not so much an impromptu verse from Donald Gorm as a traditional shipwright's rhyme for the construction of such a vessel, where the crucial factor was proportion rather than any precise measurement. There was an advantage in enshrining such wisdom in verse. It became more memorable and rhyme is more likely to preserve the exact wording. In the same way Andersen quotes a traditional Norwegian rule from Vestland that the mast from heel to halyard hole should equal the girth of the boat at that point. These ratio rules embodied the traditional wisdom of the shipwrights of an area.

Do Viking boat-building traditions survive in areas such as the West Highlands where the old skills can be expected to have lasted longest and changed least? The methods of construction, some of the tools used, the solutions to problems, may reveal patterns that are centuries old.[13]

Nausts/Nousts/Noosts

In the Northern Isles (and other areas) small boats are drawn into 'nousts' or man-made bank-cuttings for shelter. This practice descends directly from Viking times at least.[14] The word can mean either a bank-cutting or a boat-shed. The sagas (e.g. Grettir's) frequently refer to boat-sheds in which vessels were built, repaired and laid up for winter. Where Highland galleys were constructed probably depended on whether the boatyard was incorporated into a castle complex or whether it was situated at the most convenient point for launching. The story of Donald Gallich suggests the latter for Kishorn. If we could find and excavate a boathouse in the Hebrides we could make comparisons with similar sites which have been excavated in Scandinavia.

The launching of boats from a beach would pose a practical problem for Highlanders. In *Grettir's Saga* we read of a 'large sixteen-oared boat' with about 31 crew. Apparently 'she always required 30 men to put her to sea, but the 12 shoved her along the beach at once'. There is an interesting parallel in the launching of the sixteen-oared *Aileach* in 1991. According to Wallace Clark some 30–40 men manhandled her out. They presented their backs to her and grabbed the plank-lands with their finger-tips – almost an intuitive response to the difficulty of obtaining a good hold on a high-sided wooden boat.

The find-site of the Eigg endposts has some intriguing associations. ENE of Laig farmhouse is a flat plain, apparently once a loch, which is separated from the sea by a raised shingle beach. Tradition claims that the Norse used this natural bay as a winter harbour for their galleys.[15] There is a similar site at Rubha an Dunain in Skye. The land was owned for generations by the MacAskill family who had obligations of naval service to the Macleods and who may also have been involved in boat-building. A well-built, stone-lined canal links Loch na h-Airde to the sea. Off the canal appear to be a number of slipways or nausts. Boats could have been dragged up the canal to be overwintered in the loch or one of the bank-cuttings.[16]

In a recent archaeological survey of part of NE Knoydart the surveyors found several nausts and evidence of beach-clearance to secure good landing sites.[17] Some of these nausts were carefully constructed; the sides of one at Inbhir Dhorrcail having been consolidated with masonry whilst another has been cut into the peat. The presence of nausts and beach-clearance is not necessarily a Viking legacy.[18] Great numbers of visiting boats fished for herring in the sea-lochs such as Nevis and Hourn in the eighteenth and nineteenth centuries. We know they used the local timber and the smaller boats may well have lain ashore at certain times. Systematic beach-clearance might have been worthwhile.

What types of wood were used?

Two of the Gaelic boat-names found in poetry are 'darach' (oak) and 'iubhrach' (yew). However there must always have been compromise between what was desirable and what was available. Oak was traditionally required for endposts, keel and ribs, but pine, larch or elm may have been used for the strakes. The survival of Gaelic technical terms – as for the different types of nail used in a boat – may also reveal something of the methods employed.

It has been argued that Viking boat-building was staggeringly wasteful of timber. Oak was best for structural members such as the keel and certainly the oak forests must have suffered drastically. When a reconstruction of the Gokstad boat was built at the end of the nineteenth century they had to obtain the oak for its keel from North America because no tree large enough could be found in Norway. Lots of types of wood were used in boat-building as the Roskilde boats demonstrate. The keel, the most critical timber in the boat, was always of oak; whilst the planks were always of oak, pine or ash.[19] Other woods such as alder, birch, lime, willow and beech were used elsewhere in the vessel.

If the local environment did not offer ideal timber then other types of tree could be and were used. In Northern Norway softer woods like larch or pine were favoured and in the Hebrides boat-builders made use of whatever was locally prolific. Large straight oak would always be scarce on the islands although conditions might have been more favourable in the climatic optimum of the eleventh and twelfth centuries. If suitable timber was not available then it was probably imported from the mainland. A trade in wood between Norway and both Shetland and Iceland was well-established in earlier periods since it was required for all sorts of building and furnishing as well as boats. There was a trade in kit-boats from the Norwegian ports of Os and Stavanger to Shetland between the sixteenth and nineteenth centuries. The chronic shortage of timber in Shetland meant that boats were made-up in Norway, dismantled and then shipped across the North Sea to customers in the Northern Isles.

Chapter 12

Landing-points, Boating-practice and Navigation

Castles, galley-ports, beach-clearance etc.

THE WESTERN SEABOARD HAS MANY fortified sites and RCAHMS surveyors have outlined a number of those which made special provision for boat access.[1] Dun Ara Castle, Mishnish, Mull, was a stronghold of the Mackinnons who had lands in Mull at least as early as 1354. The castle itself is late mediaeval but 'on the SW side ... there is an artificially constructed harbour incorporating a small jetty and a quay and boat-landing, at the upper end of which there are two boat-noosts'. Much of the surviving fabric of the tower of Moy Castle, Mull, can be ascribed to the first half of the fifteenth century. 'On the beach some 36m S of the tower ... there is a boat-landing clearly defined by two rows of large boulders some 4m apart at maximum width. Within the loch an arc of large boulders ... may have served either as a fish-trap or as an anchorage and boat-dock'.

An anonymous report written between 1577–1599 describes Breachacha Castle, Coll, as 'ane great strenth' which

> hes three walls about the rest of the castell, and [ane?] thairof biggit with lyme and stane, ... ane uther wall about that, within the quhilk schippis and boittis are drawin and salvit. And the third and the uttermost wall of tymber and earth, within the quhilk the haill gudes of the cuntrie are keipit in tyme of troubles or weiris.[2]

Ships were more important and better protected than animals. They represented a substantial capital investment.

It is stated of Dunyveg Castle, Islay, that 'at the SW angle of the courtyard there are the remains of a sea-gate which is fronted by a boat-landing formed partly between roughly parallel lines of boulders on the foreshore'. The shoreworks could have been built prior to the present building which is early sixteenth-century – but there was a castle there before that date. An account of the events of spring 1614 demonstrates the continued utility of the sea-gate. Dunyveg had just been seized by Ranald, bastard son to Angus Macdonald of Dunyveg. He in turn was besieged by Angus Oig

Macdonald. Those in the castle resolved to escape and so 'thay in the night eshued at a bak yett in a litle boat with sex oares'.

Certain sites such as Rathlin were favourite galley hideaways. In 1549 Dean Munro says of Rona that it is 'full of wood and heddir, with ane havin for heiland galeys in the middis of it, and the same havein is guyed for fostering of theives, ruggairs, and reivairs, till await, upon the peilling and spulzeing of poure pepill'.

The presence or absence of piers and jetties would always have affected boat-design. The Skuldelev boats show a good deal of wear and tear and certainly continual beaching would require constant maintenance. Running alongside a pier would threaten damage to cleats, thole-pins, shield-rails, oar-gaffs etc. and we can readily see why stepped gunwales would become a favoured feature in cargo-vessels. Side-loading would be more convenient whether on the beach or at a pier.[3]

Boating-practice

One of the most compelling reasons for building reconstructions of ancient boats is that many assumptions can only be put to the test by practical experience under similar conditions at sea. In 1991 Wallace Clark sailed the *Aileach* to the Hebrides and commented that their practice 'of keeping the luff or leading edge of the sail as taut as possible ... was wrong. Square sails pull better to windward with the luff in a harmonic curve and setting it that way reduces very substantially the strain on the mast'. This expresses perfectly the way in which the sail is depicted on the mediaeval grave-slabs of the Oronsay school.

When the *Aileach* reached the Faeroes in 1992 the crew were having rather a struggle against wind and tide in their approach to Torshavn. A Faeroese man, Trondur Paturrson, leapt overboard and 'towed her along the shore helped by islanders who had come to watch. This demonstrated an age-old practice with shallow draft vessels still used in these isles populated by people who revel in open boat pulling and sailing'.

Now this sort of response to a very practical problem may be universal and timeless but it is intriguing to compare it with the account of Sarah Murray who toured the Hebrides in 1796.[4] She desired to view Corryvreckan from the neighbouring island of Scarba. On returning, her boat got into difficulties in the strong current and so: 'When nothing could be done with the oars, the sailors fastened one rope to the head, and another to the stern of the boat, and leaping on the jagged rocks, began to tow it ... Thus we slowly advanced ... till we ... got out of the influence of the tide'. From her description it is clear that the whole procedure was rather perilous. The rope to the stern was to pull the boat off the rocks when she got too close.

Martin Martin noted a curious practice at the end of the seventeenth century. 'The steward of Kilda, who lives in Pabbay, is accustomed in time of storm to tie a bundle of puddings made of the fat of sea fowl to the end of his cable, and lets it fall into the sea behind the rudder; this, he says, hinders the waves from breaking, and calms the sea; but the scent of the grease attracts the whales, which put the vessel in danger'. He was literally putting oil on troubled waters.

It was crucial that galleys offered *two* methods of propulsion.[5] Dangerous tides and currents, volatile wind conditions and a supply of cheap labour meant that the galley-type survived because it was so versatile. Normally it was a matter of choosing between sail and oars but the Scandinavian tale of Bosi and Herraud suggests that if necessary they could use both at once: 'They tried to reach open water as fast as possible by rowing and sailing at the same time'.[6] Having an alternative means of propulsion could be essential. In *Egil's Saga* it says: 'They ... met hard weather, fierce and unfavourable winds, but they pursued their journey doggedly, using the oars'.

West Highland sea-lochs such as Loch Hourn experience notoriously treacherous conditions of wind and tide. Steep-sided glens funnel the wind with dreadful ferocity and in various directions. In squally conditions it is doubly important to complement sail with oar or disaster can overtake very quickly. In 1853 Donald Ross travelled to Knoydart to interview some of the victims of the recent clearance. He took a boat from Kinloch Hourn to Airor

> *The winds and currents, however, are treacherous on all Highland lochs, and this we soon found. We had not proceeded more than 5 miles when both wind and tide appeared against us. A strong current like a powerful river rushed up the loch, boiling and raging, ... We had to change our course, ply our oars, and soon got into smooth water again, and ... reached the pier at Arar ... after a voyage of four hours and a half.*[7]

Since Kinloch Hourn to Airor is nearly seventeen miles he had made good speed but his account shows how essential oars were as a complement to sail.

Folklore

Folklore has a poor reputation with historians but there are tales which may conceal details of former boat-design. One very practical problem facing the *Aileach* – which is an undecked boat – is how to keep her from filling up with water if she lies ashore untended for any length of time. The answer has been to drill a plug-hole in her. Now Hugh Macdonald, the seventeenth-century Sleat historian, gives an account of how Somerled won Ragnhildis, daughter of King Olaf of Man. Maurice MacNeill, a friend of Somerled's and foster-brother of Olaf, drilled holes in Olaf's boat and filled them with tallow and butter. When the holes opened and Olaf was near to sinking Somerled came to the rescue, on condition of gaining Ragnhildis!

Another tale comes from the collection of JF Campbell of Islay.[8] The subject is the competition between native and Norwegian carpenters. The local champion is MacPheigh from near Loch Gilp

> *It was thought in those times that the carpenters of Lochlann were far more skilled than either the Irish, Scottish or English carpenters. When the Lochlann carpenters heard it reported how expert and skilful the Carpenter MacPheigh was, a company of their best carpenters arranged together that they would go to Scotland to ... compete against him ...* [In the ensuing contest MacPheigh worsted the Norwegians, partly by deviousness. Then] *while the others were in the hostel, the Carpenter MacPheigh went to inspect the wooden horses belonging to the Lochlann carpenters, and find out how they were made. He examined them very thoroughly, and upon finding out how they were made, took a tiny wooden peg out of each one of them, and went away and left them.* [The Norwegian carpenters then departed but] *when they were well out to sea, the wooden horses became unserviceable for lack of the pegs that the Carpenter MacPheigh had taken out of them, and when the wind arose, the rolling of the waves drove the horses to pieces, and the Lochlann carpenters were drowned. And never again did any one come from Lochlann to trouble the Carpenter MacPheigh.*

It is a good story, or myth, and conjures some intriguing possibilities. Were Norwegian carpenters once pre-eminent and did their longships have wooden plugs? Did the Gaels borrow the metaphor of wooden horses (ships) from the Norse and copy Scandinavian vessels? Was there ever a ship-building yard at Loch Gilp?

Maintenance

The Norse were very careful about maintaining their boats. The *King's Mirror*, which was written in the 1240s, sets out some good advice

> *Always buy shares in good vessels or in none at all. Keep your ship attractive, for then capable men will join you and it will be well manned. ... Keep reliable tackle on shipboard at all times, and never remain out at sea in late autumn.*
>
> *Whenever you travel at sea, keep on board two or three hundred ells of wadmal of a sort suitable for mending sails, if that should be necessary, a large number of needles, and a supply of thread and cord ... You will always need to carry a supply of nails, both spikes and rivets, of such sizes as your ship demands: also good boat hooks and broad-axes, gouges and augers, and all such other tools as ship carpenters make use of.*[9]

Over time Viking boats acquired benches. We cannot be certain of this in the Hebrides and in 1773 Dr Johnson remarked on the lack of seats in island boats: 'I never saw a boat furnished with benches, or made commodious by any addition to the first fabrick'. Again, when leaving Mull by boat he commented that 'the seat provided for our accommodation was a heap of rough brushwood'.[10] Since he was rowed on several occasions it makes us wonder whether the oarsmen sat or stood? If they sat, what did they sit on?

Dr Johnson's remarks may have a bearing on the layout of mediaeval boats. Galleys were often used for cattle-raiding, and cattle, whether live or carcass, would prove a bulky, awkward cargo. It might not have been very convenient if the interior space was taken up by rowing-benches. It would have been important to have some transverse thwarts but heavy freight would need to be stowed as low as possible.

Early topographical accounts such as Martin Martin's voyage to St Kilda can also be revealing. Of their units of measurement he writes 'The *cubit*, or in their language, *lave keile*, i.e., an hand of wood, is the distance from the elbow to the finger's ends; this they only use in measuring their boats'. If we take the cubit to be 18 inches then the single boat belonging to the St Kildans in 1697 was 24 feet long.[11] The whole population was employed in hauling the boat from the sea and when it lay ashore – presumably face down – it was covered with turf to protect it from the sun. Martin Martin commented favourably on the stamina of the St Kildans, and also the

Lewismen who 'will tug at the oar all day long upon bread and water, and a snush of tobacco'. Poles were important to keep the boat from being broken against the rocks when landing – a theme which also occurs in mediaeval manuscripts but which we now tend to overlook. Virtually anything associated with maritime practice could help inform us what the Hebrideans owed to their Norse ancestors, what to their Irish. Fishing methods, fishing implements, even fishing taxes, may prove relevant.

Navigation

There is little we can say on the subject of navigation that derives directly from West Highland sources. However we can say something by way of analogy. Hebrideans had frequent contact with boats and mariners from other nations and would not have been ignorant of developments elsewhere. We have a graffito from Kilchattan, Luing, which seems to show two triangular weather-vanes on the endposts of one of the vessels. We know of these from Viking sources and, whilst we have no direct evidence, it is quite possible they were carried by Highland galleys. The graffiti at Kilchattan could represent Norse, Hebridean or Scottish boats, the first being the most likely.[12] We also have a remarkable rutter, or book of sailing directions, by Alexander Lindsay, which dates to the first half of the sixteenth century. It could well have been prepared especially for James V's naval expedition to the Western Isles in 1540 but drew on many years experience and observation.[13]

The word rutter derives from the French word 'routier' and refers to a set of sailing directions for use by pilots in coastal waters. Written sailing directions have a long history and in the Mediterranean world we have evidence for Italian 'portulans' from the thirteenth century onwards. In the more exposed waters of the North we would expect something similar and there is evidence from Adam of Bremen that such existed from the eleventh century. Of course the Vikings embarked on their epic voyages long before this and must have accrued a wealth of navigational data in the course of their travels. Much of this would have been transmitted orally but it is probable that there were written directions which have simply not survived. Our earliest clues (such as snippets in the Icelandic *Landnamabok*) date from the thirteenth and fourteenth centuries.

The navigational skills of the Vikings have long mystified later seafarers. Just how did they travel such great distances so accurately and so regularly without the aid of compass or chronometer? They undoubtedly used the relative position of the midday sun and evening pole star to reckon their latitude (which they were much better at reckoning than longitude). They amassed practical knowledge of prevailing winds and currents, local weather conditions and the presence or frequency of sea-birds and ice-floes. Over time they may have learned to use some artificial aids such as lodestones and floating sundials, wind-vanes and sounding-lines. As they explored so their knowledge base expanded and no doubt most of it was transmitted orally and never committed to paper. Some of this knowledge may well have been far older than the Vikings. Advice written in the 1240s in the *King's Mirror* condenses their practical common sense

> *Observe carefully how the sky is lighted, the course of the heavenly bodies, the grouping of the hours, and the points of the horizon. Learn also how to mark the movements of the ocean and to discern how its turmoil ebbs and swells; for that is knowledge which all must possess who wish to trade abroad.*

Coastal pilots set courses from one headland or point to the next. Time, distance, tide, direction and depth could all be measured and logged, as were harbours, havens and hazards. Nothing of this sort has survived from the Gaelic world but we can be sure that such knowledge existed and was passed down the generations. Martin Martin's comments at the end of the seventeenth century make it clear that there was a comprehensive marine knowledge-base about tides on the west coast of Scotland and local variations such as Kyleakin.

A pilot's equipment included a sounding-line for reckoning depth, a sand-glass for measuring time, and a traverse board which was a board for marking the amount of time run upon a certain course and so estimating the distance travelled. It is reckoned to have been most useful when travelling great distances in poor visibility, or out of sight of land. A fine example of such a board dating from *c.* 1600 was found in Barra in 1844. Given the piratical habits of Clanranald and others around Barra in the early years of the seventeenth century it is not difficult to imagine how it may have been acquired. By then the Dutch were established as traders in Stornoway, so Highlanders may have been aware of the navigational aids used by these experienced seamen.

No doubt the Norse transmitted their navigational skills to their

Hebridean descendants but the latter did not often require the ocean-going expertise of their ancestors. There are few places in the Hebrides where, on a good day, you cannot see the mainland or a number of other islands. Navigational skills probably required less in the way of long-distance dead-reckoning and a lot more knowledge of wind, tide, currents and local weather conditions. Finding land was less of a problem than coming safely to it.

Lindsay's modern editors have assessed his rutter to be both accurate and useful. It covers the coastline of Scotland from east to west and whilst the north-west coast from Cape Wrath to the Crowlin Islands is regarded as least satisfactory they conclude that there is no part of the coast for which he was badly short of information. Typical entries read

> From Kylra [Kylerhea] to Ardemurthen [Ardnamurchan], by the isles called Egg, Rum, Muck and Canna, the tide runs E. and W. ....
> From Kylra to Ardemurthen thirty-three miles, course S-SW.
> The Tarbat of Dura [Jura] is a good anchorage for ships, as also the Road of Ila, except that the tide runs with a strong current.[14]

Danger-points such as Corryvreckan[15] deserve special attention

> Betuixt Scarba and Dura is the most dangerous stream knowing in all Europe, for manie of the seas which flowethe betuixt the Mulle of Cantyr and Yla passeth throwe this narrow channell and in the passyng they fall with such a great violence upon the coast of Scarba that they retourne to the cost of Dura with a great noys, making in thair returning a depe horlepoole quhairin if schippis do enter thair is no refuge but death onlie. Notwithstanding the best tyme that may be had of it is the tyme of full sea and low watter. This passage is called Corriebreykin.

This was precisely the sort of information a seafarer wanted. Other early writers like John Major and Dean Munro paid close attention to safe havens and sure anchorages. Barbour commented on the strong currents to be met as Bruce travelled to Rathlin. He was probably referring, in part, to the seas off the Mull of Kintyre. Prevailing winds, currents and tides all helped to determine a boat's position. Shetland fishermen were supposed to be able to navigate in a mist using the underlying swell patterns.

Martin Martin describes how St Kildans forecast the weather by watching sea and sky, told the time on dull days by the state of ebb or flow, and watched the moon in order to reckon the tides. 'When they fail they use no compass, but take their measures from the sun, moon, or stars; and they rely much on the course of the various flocks of sea fowl; and this last is their surest directory'. They predicted approaching winds by the behaviour of birds such as the fulmar.

Fire was used as a navigational aid in the Hebrides from Norse times (*see* Chapter 9). We can assume from Martin Martin that this persisted into the seventeenth century at least. According to Barbour, when Bruce was rowing from Arran to Carrick he followed the light of a signal fire 'for yai na nedill had na stone'. Barbour was writing *c.* 1375–77 of February 1307 so we can infer that by his time the lodestone was in general use, but not 70 years previously on a Highland galley.

Chapter 13

The Evidence from Language

Etymological evidence

THE ETYMOLOGY OF A BOAT-WORD may have historical implications. In *Norse influence on Celtic Scotland* Henderson details all Gaelic nautical terms which he claims derive from the Norse. However it is not simply a matter of tracing a lineal descent from Norse to Gaelic or English. The three languages have interacted for centuries and it is perfectly feasible for words like 'scutt' or 'reef' to have been mediated through Dutch – the language of some of the greatest of mediaeval seafarers. Here follows a list of some of Henderson's suggested loan-words. I have omitted those, including 'sgoth', which are disputed by Oftedal.[1]

acairseid	anchorage
bac	rowlock
carbh (Islay)	
or carbhair	
(Lewis)	from N. karfi, a fast boat for the fjords
cnarra	a Norse trading boat (knorr)
creigeir	a grapple
falm	helm
falm-adar	tiller
lonn	roller put under boat for launching, mid-part of oar
put	a large buoy usually of inflated sheep-skin
rac	parrel or traveller, a ring that secures yard to mast
scalpa	a kind of boat
	(so Scalpaidh – Lochalsh, Scolpaig – Griminish, N Uist, Scalpay – Harris, Scalpay – Skye)
sgiobair	a skipper
sgod	sheet of sail, sheet-rope
sgud	ship, from Old Norse 'skuta' – a small boat for use on rivers or coasts
sparr	beam, joist, spar

Local knowledge of Gaelic terminology is invaluable with regard to the borrowing of specific shipbuilding terms. These can vary from one part of the Highlands to another.[2] Words may be borrowed, mediated through another tongue, or translated literally into the receiving language. Direct borrowing is more likely when there is no functional equivalent. Early Irish currachs had masts and yards, so Gaelic had no requirement to borrow these terms from the Norse; but it may have borrowed mast-step (stalla(G), stallr(N)), and traveller or parrel (rak(G), rakke(N)).[3]

Norse place-names are widespread throughout the Hebrides and the mainland west coast. They are heaviest in the Northern Hebrides and dilute towards the Southern. Norse impact on the Gaelic language seems to be limited to at most some 300 loan-words. Many of these are confined to the relatively peripheral areas of boats, fishing, navigation and toponymy. Few Norse words seems to have found their way into the heart or structure of the Gaelic language. Norse influence may also have imposed itself on the intonational patterns of some dialects of Scottish Gaelic.[4]

Nautical terms

The words most commonly used for West Highland sailing-vessels were galley, birlinn, longfada and naibheag. The first of these is not Gaelic and is a widely used descriptive term for a boat that can be rowed. Such boats were used in Classical times and throughout the Middle Ages. They were common even in the sixteenth century and there is a manuscript drawing showing a French galley landing troops before the battle of Pinkie in 1547. Similar contemporary terms were galleon and galliass.

Birlinn is a word used in Gaelic though it probably derives from the Norse 'byrdingr' or ship of burthen (i.e. cargo-ship). Two other Gaelic terms are longfada and naibheag, i.e. long ship and little ship.[5] (Longfada is usually anglicised as lymphad. In Ireland a naevog is now a type of currach.) It has been claimed that naibheags, being more manoeuvrable, were better suited for Hebridean waters and represent the triumph of Gael over Gall. It is more likely that the distinct terms simply denote a difference in size. Both types continued in use in the Highlands throughout the Middle Ages; the construction of one rather than the other being largely a matter of wealth.[6]

Place-names and topography

The place-name evidence is crucial in mapping the nature and intensity of Norse settlement in the Hebrides. It is also of interest what the Norse named. Norse influence on Gaelic is patchy, but perhaps strongest in things to do with the sea and toponymy. This is what we would expect of colonists who came by boat.

There are many place-names of general significance such as the fjords (Moidart, Sunart & Knoydart); the islands (Grimsay, Eriskay, Pabbay); the points (Ness, Skipness) and the hills (Askival, Hallival, Ainshval etc.) all of which indicate the Norse mariner's interest in landmarks. The Vikings would have found much of the west coast reminiscent of Norway and significant features would soon have earned themselves Norse names, whatever their Gaelic or Pictish ones. Rum, for instance, was of very little interest in agricultural terms but its hills are visible from many miles away. Nearly every peak on Rum has a Norse name.

In a few locations the mediaeval boat-name has survived directly. There are two examples of Port na Birlinne (SE Jura and by Pennycross, Mull), and an Innis na Birlinn (Lochaber). MacAulay has drawn attention to Laimhbhrig na Birlinn (Berneray), Leac na Birlinn (Harris) and Loch na Birlinn (by Scadabay, Harris). The Gaelic word 'long' (ship) appears frequently in coastal place-names and there are odd references to precise boat-types or boat-accessories.

Portage

Features such as anchorages or portage points had practical meaning for sailors. Where two stretches of water are separated by a narrow piece of land it is often more convenient to haul the boat – or carry its cargo – across the isthmus. This system of portage was frequently practised in early times when journeys might otherwise be delayed or extended by contrary winds.

The Norse word 'Eid' and the Gaelic 'Tarbert' indicate portage points and we have examples of both in modern Highland topography. Aoidh (Eid or Eye) appears by Stornoway and possibly Loch Eye (Black Isle). Aith (Shetland) is still pronounced locally as 'Aid'. A list of Tarberts would include Jura, Gigha, Harris, Canna, Uist and Eilean Shona among islands; Loch Fyne, Loch Lomond, Loch Nevis, Loch Sunart to Loch Linnhe, Loch Sunart to Loch Shiel,

Loch Shiel to Loch Eil, and from near Handa Island to Loch Laxford on the mainland. Some of these portage points, such as Tarbert, Canna; Tarbet, Loch Nevis, or Tarbert, Gigha, are of purely local significance. Others, like Tarbert, Loch Fyne, were of major strategic importance. Moreover the last-named had value long before the Vikings arrived which suggests that portage was already a well-established feature of Hebridean life.[7]

According to the Irish records Tarbert, Loch Fyne, was burned in 712 and again in 731 in the wars between the Dalriadic tribes of Cenel Loairn and Cenel Gabrain. It was one of the two principal strongholds of the Cenel Gabrain, the other being Dunaverty at the south end of Kintyre. The entry in the *Annals of Ulster* for 712 shows that the Cenel Loairn destroyed Tarbert and besieged Dunaverty in that year, evidently making a clean sweep of it as far as Kintyre and the Cenel Gabrain were concerned. Tarbert was obviously regarded as a centre of some strategic importance and therefore worthy of attack.

In 1098 Magnus Bareleg, in order to claim Kintyre as well as the west coast islands, had his boat hauled across the narrow isthmus at Tarbert at the north end of the peninsula. As his saga puts it

> *when King Magnus came north to Kintyre, he caused [his men] to draw a skiff across the isthmus of Kintyre, and to set the rudder in place: the king himself sat in the after-deck, and held the helm. And thus he took possession of the land that then lay to the larboard. Kintyre is a great land, and better than the best island in the Hebrides, excepting Man. A narrow isthmus is between it and the mainland of Scotland; there long-ships are often drawn across.*

The phrasing is very similar in *Orkneyinga Saga*: 'the isthmus connecting it to the mainland is so narrow that ships are regularly hauled across'.

During Hakon's expedition in 1263 a Norse raiding party was hauled between Loch Long and Loch Lomond from whence they plundered the Lennox. (In practice it seems to have been largely composed of the smaller boats of Hakon's Hebridean supporters.) The smaller Irish curraghs could possibly have been carried or pulled on sleds at these portage points; the heavier wooden boats of the Norse would have to be hauled on rollers.[8] Whale-ribs were apparently ideal for this task as they took on a polish with usage. In Shetland such whale-ribs are known as 'linns' which is reminiscent of the Gaelic 'lonn' or roller – both terms deriving from the Norse. Sandison, writing of the Shetland sixareens, says

> *As in the days of which the Sagas tell, whale ribs were much valued as 'linns' to slide the boats up and down the beaches. They are remarkably slippery when wet and have the further advantage over wood that they are just heavy enough to sink in water, and so to stay put while the boat is got in position ... some of these will still be seen in the noosts around the shores.*[9]

Only relatively small boats could be easily portaged. Magnus Bareleg's boat in 1098 may have been a skiff of sixteen oars or so but it cannot have been too small or it would not be described as having a helm or rudder. Lightness for easy portaging may well have been part of the design brief for certain classes of boat. Luggage and movable fittings would be taken out of the vessel before haulage.[10]

Certainly at popular crossings such as Tarbert an infrastructure may have been built which allowed the carriage of bigger vessels. We can imagine a trackway, a convenient supply of rollers, oxen for haulage etc. Even here there must have been a cut-off point as far as size of vessel went. Above a certain weight or length and the expenditure of effort would just not be worth it. The higher the freeboard the more difficult it would be to pull or support the vessel. Photographs of the crew beside the *Aileach* in their attempt to portage it at Tarbert are instructive – a tractor had to be called in! A passage in *King Harald's Saga* recounts a raid in Denmark

> *One summer King Harald put to sea with a small number of light skiffs and a small force of men. He sailed ... into Limfjord. This fjord has a very narrow channel at its mouth, but farther inside it seems as wide as the open sea ... King Harald now heard from his spies that King Svein had arrived at the mouth of the fjord with a large fleet; but it was taking them a long time to enter the fjord, because only one ship could pass through the channel at a time.*
>
> *King Harald sailed his ships farther up the fjord to its widest point, to a place called Livobredning; at the far end of the creek there, only a narrow neck of land separates the fjord from the North Sea. Harald and his men rowed there that evening; and during the night, under cover of darkness, they unloaded their ships and dragged them across the isthmus. Then they loaded the ships again, and were all ready to sail before dawn ... King Harald said that next time he came to Denmark he was going to have a larger force and bigger ships.*

In the course of his dispute with Earl Hakon (*c.* 1064) Harald mounted a punitive expedition. 'King Harald sailed south to

Konungahella, and ... assembled all the light skiffs he could get and travelled up the Gota river. The boats had to be hauled overland at every waterfall they came to, and by this means they brought the boats to Lake Vaner'.

Some of the Tarberts in Scotland are so long that it has been argued that boats were never pulled across these or indeed any other portages. Such for instance are the crossings between Loch Sunart and Loch Linnhe (c. 7 miles) and between the head of Loch Shiel and Loch Eil (c. 4 miles). These east-west portages lie parallel to each other, the latter about twelve miles north of the former. In both cases they represent shortcuts to and from the west coast and were probably for commercial rather than military traffic. In a commercial context it was only possible to portage small, light boats while on a military expedition several crews could be utilised in hauling each boat in turn. Most boat-portages probably took place for military purposes. For trade it would not be cost-effective – the goods would move on rather than the boat.[11]

Loch Ness

Captain Richard Franck, a Cromwellian soldier who toured the North in 1656 or 1657, describes a portage between the sea and Loch Ness in his *Northern Memoirs*. The exchange is between Arnoldus (Franck) and Theophilus (a friend)

Arn. *The famous Lough-Ness ... and here it is, in these slippery streams, that an English ship, by curious invention, was haled over the mountains to this solitary Lough; brought hither on purpose to reclaim the Highlander.*

Theoph. *Do you romance ... ?*

Arn. *If eye-sight be good evidence, there's enough to convince you; behold the ship.*

Theoph. *How came she here? Was she not built in some creek hereabouts?*

Arn. *No*

Theoph. *By what means then was she moved into this small Mediterrane? ...*

Arn. *Why thus it was: In the time of war betwixt the King and Parliament, this navigate invention was consulted by Maj. General Dean; who to compleat a conquest over the Highlanders, ... he accomplished this new navigation of sailing by land ...*

Theoph. *But how? ...*

Arn. ... *which to accomplish, the sailers and the souldiers equally contributed. For a regiment (or it may be two) about that time quartered in Inverness; who, by artifice, had fastned thick cables to her fore-castle, and then they got levers and rollers of timber, which they spread at a distance, one before another; whilst some are of opinion these robust engineers framed a more artificial and politick contrivance: but thus it was, and no other wise, I'le assure you; save only they fastned some cheeks and planks to the solid sides and ribs of the ship, the better to secure her from crushing upon transportation.*

Theoph. *And did she pass in this manner as you tell me, to this famous Ness?*

Arn. *Yes, she relinquished the brinish ocean, to float in the slippery arms of Ness. But to keep her steddy in her passage, and preserve her from rocking and rolling by the way; they consulted no other project than what I tell you: save only some additional supplies from Inverness, that with ropes and tackle haled her along to this very place where you now observe her.*

Franck's testimony is borne out by James Fraser, author of the *Wardlaw MS.* Writing between 1666 and 1699 he describes the building of the citadel in Inverness by the thousand-strong Cromwellian regiment stationed there. Of the period 1655–7 he says

They fixt a garrison at Inverlochy, and carried a bark driven uppon rollers of wood to the Lochend of Ness, and there enlarged it into a statly friggot, to sail with provision from the one end of the loch to the other; one Mr Church governour [helmsman?], *and Lieutenant Orton captain of this friggot, and 60 men aboord of her to land uppon expeditions where they pleased. I happened myselfe ... to be invited aboord by Orton, where we were gently treated.*

With a thousand soldiers at their disposal such a large-scale portage becomes understandable. It also sheds some retrospective light on what could have been achieved by Magnus Bareleg or Robert Bruce.

Bruce and Tarbert, Loch Fyne

In the early fourteenth century Bruce paid particular attention to Tarbert, Loch Fyne. Magnus Bareleg's symbolic annexation of Kintyre had great mythic significance in the West Highlands. Why else would Robert I go to such trouble to exorcise this ghost over two centuries later? Basically Robert repeated Magnus's act, but in reverse. According to Barbour he reclaimed Kintyre and the Isles for Scotland in late 1315 or 1316. Technically the Hebrides had been ceded by Norway in 1266 but popular imagination is slow to eschew its old affinities and no doubt Robert was aware of the enormous propaganda value of his performance. Barbour's *Bruce*, composed *c.* 1375-7, makes this quite clear

> *Till the Tarbard thai held thar way*
> *In galayis ordanit for thair fair.*
> *Bot thame worthit draw thar schippes thar:*
> *And a myle wes betuix the seis,*
> *Bot that wes lownyt all with treis.*
> *The King his schippis thar gert draw,*
> *And for the wynd can stoutly blaw*
> *Apon thair bak, as thai wald ga,*
> *He gert men rapis and mastis ta,*
> *And set thame in the schippis hye,*
> *And salys to the toppis te,*
> *And gert men gang thar-by drawand.*
> *The wynd thame helpit, that wes blawand;*
> *Swa that, in-till a litill spas,*
> *Thar flot all weill our-drawyn was.*
>
> *And quhen thai that in the Ilis war,*
> *Herd tell how the gud Kyng had thar*
> *Gert schippis with the salys ga*
> *Out-our betuix the Tarbartis twa,*
> *Thai war abasit all utrely.*
> *For thai wist throu ald prophesy*
> *That he that suld ger schippis swa*
> *Betuix the seis with salis ga,*
> *Suld wyn the Ilis swa till hand,*
> *That nane with strynth suld him withstand.*[12]

This has a mythic quality, as does the contrary local legend that at Lag na Luinge, (Hollow of the Ship), Robert's boat made an unscheduled departure from its route. Both Magnus and Robert had been involved in a symbolic 'beating of the bounds'. Hakon omitted to use Tarbert in 1263, not because of a threat from Tarbert Castle, but simply because all his Norwegian boats were far too big. Equally most of Bruce's boats were probably too big in 1315. It was a purely symbolic manoeuvre.

The beginning of *Orkneyinga Saga* recounts a similar incident as part of the earliest history of Norway. In the days of inexact geography we can imagine a situation where groups of islands were defined, not by listing names (and countless unnamed islets and tidal islands) but by giving a catch-all definition such as: 'Nor was to have all the mainland and Gor the islands, wherever a ship with a fixed rudder could be sailed between them and the mainland'. Notionally it was a sensible way of settling territorial disputes but greed must have prompted a more devious manoeuvre - whether first in fact or story. 'He had one of his ships hauled over ... with Gor sitting aft, his hand on the tiller. So he laid claim to all the land lying to port, a sizeable area with many settlements'. Its appeal lies in its mixture of chicanery and humour. In Kintyre we see one of the last and perhaps one of the most flamboyant expressions of an ancient ploy.

Bruce also spent a good deal of time and money fortifying the area. The earliest surviving Scottish Exchequer Rolls from 1326 show a number of payments made for building works in Tarbert. These included the walls of Tarbert Castle, a new fort in West Loch Tarbert and some sort of road or trackway between the two Tarberts: 'pro itinere faciendo ab uno Tarbart usque ad alium' (for making a road from one Tarbert to the other). It was likely built with an eye to the requirements for hauling boats. In this context Barbour's couplet 'And a myle wes betuix the seis, / Bot that wes *lownyt all with treis*' may refer to a wooden trackway or road.[13]

This western encroachment of the Scottish kings was too erratic and fitful to guarantee success. The burgh established in Tarbert did not develop into a major commercial centre and the increasing size of merchant ships meant that portage was no longer a realistic option for bulk cargoes.[14] In 1656 Thomas Tucker reported that the inhabitants of Glasgow trade

> with theyr neighbours the Highlanders, who come hither from the isles and westerne parts; in summer by the Mul of Cantyre, and in winter by the Torban to the head of the Loquh Fyn, (which is a small neck of sandy land, over which they usually drawe theyr small boates into the Firth of Dunbarton), and soe passe up in the Cluyde with pladding, dry hides, goate, kid, and deere skyns, which they sell.[15]

Pennant's description of Tralaig, Islay, in 1775 displays his scepticism of the size of Hebridean war-fleets

> Ride along the head of the bay; at Tralaig, on a healthy eminence that faces the sands, are three deep hollows; their insides once lined with stone: these had been the watch-towers of the natives, to attend the motions of any invaders from the sea. Observe near them a great column of rude stone. Pass by two

channels, at present dry; these had been the harbour of the great Macdonald; had once piers with doors to secure his shipping, a great iron hook, one of the hinges, having lately been found there.

The vessels then in use were called Birlings, probably corrupted from Byrdinga, a species of ship among the Norwegians: but by the size of the harbours, it is plain that the navy of this potentate was not very considerable.

Documentary sources

The numerous official references to galleys are mainly written from a Lowland Scottish standpoint. From at least the thirteenth century the Scottish kings regarded the western islands and their semi-independent chieftains with great suspicion. They, and their allegiance to the foreign power of Norway, posed a direct and powerful threat to the ambitions of the Scottish kings. In some respects the history of the West Highlands from the thirteenth to the eighteenth centuries can be seen in terms of a struggle between these two conflicting cultures. From the late fifteenth century the independence of the islands was a lost cause but in the earlier period it seemed much less so; which explains the remorseless hostility of the Scottish state.[16]

Until 1266 the Hebridean lords had military obligations to the Norse kings for their islands, to the Scottish for their mainland estates. This situation meant divided loyalties once their masters came into conflict, as they did increasingly in the first half of the thirteenth century. Scottish expansion under Alexander II and III was designed to bring matters to a head and the issue was resolved by the cession of the Hebrides in the Treaty of Perth in 1266. There then followed the chaos of the Wars of Independence when the Hebridean chiefs vied for regional supremacy, enjoying the privilege of playing one master off against another, the Scottish against the English kings. The Macdonalds of Islay emerged triumphant over the Macdougalls of Lorn, only to succumb in later centuries to the Campbells.

Bruce re-established the bonds of military obligation in the west, but this time to the Scottish kingdom.[17] A whole series of land-grants stipulated ship-service of such-and-such a boat for so many days. Unable or unwilling to crush them he was making a conscious effort to regulate and make subservient the miniature navies of the west.

In 1314 he gave James Macdonleavie lands in Kintyre for 'unius navis viginti et sex remorum cum hominibus et victualibus' (a ship of 26 oars with men and provisions).

An ounceland of 20 pennylands to Gillespic, son of Walter ... for 'servitium unius navis viginti sex remorum cum victualibus quindecem dierum' (for the service of a ship of 26 oars with provisions for 15 days).

The Isle of Man to the Count of Moray, one of Robert's supporters, c. 1310 for 'sex naves ... viginti sex remorum cum hominibus et victualibus sex septimanarum'; (i.e. for 6 ships of 26 oars with men and provisions for 6 weeks).[18]

Privy Council Minute 1615

One of the most revealing of official documents is the minute of the meeting of the Privy Council held in Edinburgh on 25 June 1615. The members were taking measures against Sir James Macdonald and Coll McGillespic by establishing a naval force and 500 troops to be commanded by the Earl of Argyll's brother the Earl of Lundie. Argyll was expected to provide half the soldiers whilst other prominent Highland chiefs such as Maclean, Macleod of Harris, Clanranald etc. were providing smaller contingents. Towards the end of the minute is a note concerning what information the Privy Council had about the availability of naval forces in the Isles, (given here as a table)

	Galleys	**Birlinns**	**8-oared boats**
McLeod of Harris	1		Some
Donald Gorm		1	Some
Clanranald		1	
Clanranald's brother	1		
McKinnon			1
McLean	2	8	
Laird of Coll	1	2	
Laird of Ardgour		1	
McPhie		1	
Earl of Argyll	1		
Total	6	14	Several

The minute adds that a galley is a vessel of 18–24 oars, a birlinn is a vessel of 12–18 oars. The complement of a galley or birlinn and the number of men of war they are able to carry is estimated according to the number of oars, counting three men to every oar. The number of galleys and birlinns required of each chief is set out according to their ability to supply.

The Earl of Argyll had soldiers, but apparently very few boats. (In fact the only Highland chief who had a substantial naval force was Maclean. Did he need it to hold his own against the encroachment of rival clans or was he something of a commercial shipping magnate?) There are three references to boats 'of aucht airis'. This has the ring of a stock phrase and they appear as a separate but smaller class of boat. We are informed that the distinction between a galley and birlinn is based on the number of oars. Crews, according to the contemporary reckoning could be anything between 36 for the smallest birlinn and 72 for the largest galley. A glance at the sixteen-oared reconstruction, the *Aileach*, suggests that it is unlikely she could carry 48 men and their weapons. The crewing-factor is probably an over-estimate. It may have been possible on the largest galleys; on the smaller birlinns it was very ambitious.[19]

Chapter 14

The Literary Evidence

ONE OF THE MOST IMPORTANT written sources is poetry. There are dangers in relying on such evidence – principally because of poetic licence. When poets use metaphor they are interested in effect rather than fact. A good example is a poem by Murchadh Mor mac mhic Mhurchaidh (d. *c*.1689) in which he compares the virtues of a past and possible future wife. He assesses them by typifying each as a boat. In 33 lines of verse he uses at least eight different words for boat – none of them 'birlinn'. They include 'curach' (currach), 'ochdramhach' (eight-oared boat), and 'sguda' (from skuta?) – all of which have distinct origins as particular boat-types. Such 'evidence' has to be handled warily![1]

It has been claimed that poetry contained within the Norse sagas is often considerably older than the surrounding prose which makes it even more valuable as historical evidence. Numerous stanzas by Earl Rognvald are quoted in *Orkneyinga Saga* and some of these contain clues about sailing habits. He refers to the 'leathery anchor-line' holding his boat in a storm off Spain. As they are tacking up to the straits of Gibraltar the Earl says 'now let's adjust sails, lower and lash them to mid-mast'.

There are many references in verse to galleys and their accoutrements. One of the earliest is a poem about an expedition against Castle Sween, Knapdale about 1310

Tall men are arraying the fleet
which takes its course on the swift sea-surface;
every hand holds a trim warspear
in the battle of targes, polished and comely.

The prows of the ships are arrayed
with quilted hauberks as with jewels,
with warriors wearing brown belts;
Norsemen - nobles at that.

The prows of the brown-sailed ships
are decked with swords which have gold and ivory settings;
[the second ?] rank is composed of bright pointed spears;
shields hang from the long sides of the ships.

188

Behind the shields on the dappled ships
is a gleaming pile of stones of gold;
[a festooning] of fair hats and collars
beside the yards which are so sharp and strong.

(Above translation by Derick Thomson)[2]

A strong wild wind blows on the shoulders of the swift barks
while they are being loaded by the shore;
a stout rank [   ] of blades,
a set of shields lean by the barks' planks.

... a loop of purple satin adorns each mast-top.

... the lofty, peaked, smooth ships.

They have a straight stern-wind behind them,

...

their dappled sails are bulging,
foam rises to vessels' sides.

(Above lines translated by WJ Watson)[3]

What is particularly telling in this poem, as Thomson has pointed out, is the complimentary reference to the Norse element of the expedition. The tall warriors, an aristocracy of well-equipped fighting men, are referred to as 'Lochlannaigh' or Norwegians. The author wrote within 50 years of the last Norse expedition in 1263 and his overt recognition of Scandinavian influence has to be weighed against other evidence suggesting its relative dilution. His reference to shields, however, is pure Norse. Poole has translated part of Thjodolf Arnorsson's poem on the Battle of Nissa as follows: 'I saw the leader's comrades place their shields to overlap above the rowlocks ... so that each shield touched the next'.[4]

Barbour's *Bruce*, probably composed *c.* 1375–77, is, in its own way, like a saga for Robert the Bruce. Quite apart from the Tarbert crossing there are plenty of other references to Robert's travels by sea. This is particularly true for the first desperate year or two after Comyn's murder when he was so dependent on the galleys of Angus Og of Islay. In one incident the Earl of Lennox is being chased by boat and only escapes after lightening his own ship by throwing out all the surplus luggage. This is reminiscent of a scene in *King Harald's Saga* when Harald escapes King Svein of Denmark by throwing his booty and prisoners overboard. Authors are as capable of borrowing motifs from each other as visual artists are.

Certain clans, particularly the Macleods, clung to the idea of their Norse heritage long after it had ceased to have anything but sentimental meaning. In a Macleod lullaby taken down by Alexander Carmichael in the nineteenth century we find these lines which contrast the Macleods with other Highland clans

> Thou art not of the Clan Kenneth,
>> Ho bhirinn ho bho
> Thou art not of the Clan Donald,
>> Ho bhirinn ho bho ...

> But of a clan dearer to us :
>> Ho bhirinn ho bho
> Clan Leod of the galleys,
>> Ho bhirinn ho bho
> Clan Leod of the hauberks,
>> Ho bhirinn ho bho
> Norway was thy native country,[5]

This theme of a Norwegian heritage for the Macleods is reiterated and gives a sense of how the idea of a distinct racial origin endured for centuries.

Sea-metaphors which were part of Scandinavian vocabulary and syntax may have been conceptually transferred from Norse to Gaelic. This way ideas and images would survive even when the language didn't. The sea was an integral part of the Scandinavian linguistic and cultural set. It became part of the Hebridean consciousness. Sea-metaphors underwrite much poetry and thought. Boats were visualised as horses or birds.[6] Can we draw a precise line of descent for such images or are they universal? The line, the grace, the speed of their boats were as rooted in the psyche of mediaeval Hebrideans as they were in their Viking forebears. Such vessels enabled them to maintain a culture in a hostile environment, in a miserable climate, against richer and more powerful neighbours – so that the idea and image of it survived into our own times.

There are two extraordinary satires in the *Book of the Dean of Lismore* which demonstrate such concepts.[7] The author is described as 'The Bard Macintyre' and he plainly suffered from a strong misogynist streak. His editor, WJ Watson, knew of no parallels in Gaelic and it is difficult to guess at the object of his vitriol. However in both poems he uses the comparison of a rotten ship to lambast whatever or whoever he had in his sights. The concept of sea-worthiness was so deep-rooted in the Gaelic consciousness that it would have been a telling metaphor. Neither poem is later than about 1520

> *An old ship without anchors, without oak timber;*
> *we have not known its like;*
> *she is all one ship of leather:*
> *she is not a ship complete for sea-going.*
>
> *Boards of the wings of black beetles*
> *from her stem downwards in her sides;*
> *nails without grip joining her together,*
> *on the high chill ocean.*
>
> *What is yon crew in the black ship,*
> *pulling her among the waves?*
> *A crew without fellowship, without sense,*
> *a woman-band of mind disordered. ...*
>
> *Let us leave on the stormy stream*
> *the evil leaky ship,*
> *and its load of noxious women, in the brine,*
> *without psalm or sea-creed.*

The religious theme expresses how vulnerable a ship would be without the protection wrought by singing the appropriate psalm or sea-chant. The verses combine the author's dislikes – a poor ship and women. The reference to leather sounds like a slight on currachs.

There is Norse precedent for this in the story of Bosi and Herraud. Busla's prayer (or curse) displays an acute awareness of the qualities of a good boat

> *When you set sail*
> *May your rigging fail,*
> *Your rudder-hooks snap*
> * in heavy seas:*
> *The sheets will rip*
> *On your sinking ship...*
>
> (Palsson & Edwards – *Seven Viking Romances*)

The metaphor of sea-worthiness recurs in other Gaelic poems where problems at sea are used as images for political disorder. Iain Lom

described the position of the young Charles II, crowned but power-
less in 1651, 'like a ship on the sea without rudder, oar, or harbour
to make for' – i.e. without means of steering, means of propulsion,
or a safe destination.[8] Similarly in the last verse of his poem on the
Massacre of Glencoe an otherwise unknown Muck poet claims that
'the rudder has leapt from its socket'.[9]

Mary Macleod, in a lament for Sir Norman Macleod, compares
her predicament to that of a storm-ravaged boat with torn sails and
broken rudder. The images of skilled seamanship were commonly
used in eulogies; mishap or disaster in laments. Whilst there is an
element of convention involved, the metaphoric code would have
immediate meaning for an island audience.

Magic, superstition and taboo

Sailors and fishermen have always been superstitious; some of them
remain so today.[10] The Norse ascribed magic potency to figureheads, runes and iron

> *He is named Helgi: you never can*
> *Hope to do him harm.*
> *His ships are surrounded by shields of iron:*
> *No wishes can work against us.*
>
> (from 'The Lay of Helgi' – translated by Auden and Taylor).

> *Sea-runes you should know to save from wreck*
> *Sail-steeds on the sea:*
> *Carve them on the bow and the blade of the rudder,*
> *Etch them with fire on the oars;*
> *Though high the breakers and blue the waves.*
> *You shall sail safe into harbour.*
>
> (from 'The Lay of Sigrdrifa' – translated by Auden and Taylor).

The Norse in the Hebrides seem to have converted to Christianity
relatively early so runes were probably replaced by Christian
symbols. Less Christian though is the practice noted by Martin
Martin in the late seventeenth century: 'It was an ancient custom
among the islanders to hang a he-goat to the boat's mast, hoping
thereby to procure a favourable wind'.

Martin Martin also reported that Lewismen visiting the Flannan
Isles had a strong superstition against calling either them or St Kilda
by their proper names. Several other words such as 'water', 'rock'

and 'shore' were regarded as taboo and euphemisms substituted. Similarly the natives of Canna called their island 'Tarsin' (i.e. Tarsainn, 'across') when at sea, whilst those of Eigg had to refer to their home as 'island Nim-Ban-More, i.e., the isle of big women' (Eilean nam Ban Mor). Some, such as the tenant of Fladda, off Skye, 'are very careful when they set out to sea that the boat be first rowed about sunways; and, if this be neglected, they are afraid their voyage may prove unfortunate'. To set against these pagan throwbacks there was the belief that a particular stone on Iona was propitious for helmsmen.

The Birlinn of Clanranald

The most famous Gaelic sea-poem is the 'Birlinn Chlann Raghnaill', written by Alasdair Macdonald in the middle of the eighteenth century. By this time galleys and birlinns were almost a memory. Clanranald, as a prominent chief, was probably among the last to possess one. The poem describes a sea-passage from Uist to Carrickfergus in Ireland in the midst of a raging tempest. As well as long descriptive passages of the storm it includes a catalogue of the crew members, their skills and numerous details about the tackle.[11]

The poem begins with a ship-blessing followed by a blessing of the arms. Then there comes an 'Incitement for Rowing to the Sailing Point' and a iorram or rowing-song. There follow descriptions of the crew and their ideal characteristics as they are appointed to their various tasks: the helmsman; a man for the shrouds; a man for the sheet; a man for tacking; a pilot; a halyard-man; someone to watch the seas at the stern; a baler; two more men to control the sail-ropes and six men to stand by in case of necessity. The poem then goes on to describe a stormy and stressful voyage which finally ends in safety

> *They hoisted the sails – speckled,*
> *towering, close-woven;*
> *they stretched the ropes – stiff,*
> *tough and taut, to the long, tall masts,*
> *red-resined, pointed.*
>
> *They were tied in trusty knots,*
> *efficiently,*
> *through the eyes of iron hooks*
> *and round ring-bolts.*

Macdonald reinforces the concept of order on a boat when discussing the role of the man appointed to watch the seas at the stern

> *Let there be no teller of high seas*
> *except that one :*
> *flurry, chatter and babble*
> *make for confusion.*

(translations by Derick Thomson)[12]

And from the iorram

> *Cheeks be lit all blazing red,*
> *Palms of skin all casing shed,*
> *While sweat off every face and head*
> *Thumping pours. ...*
>
> *Row as one, cleanly, clearly;*
> *Through flesh-thick waves cut sheerly;*
> *A job that's not done wearily*
> *Nor snail-wise.*

(translation by Hugh MacDiarmid)[13]

Both Norse and Hebrideans viewed rowing and sailing styles with a degree of machismo.

Singing songs to keep time to the oars is a very old custom. From the Anglo-Saxon period we have a description by Eddius Stephanus of Bishop Wilfrid returning from France: 'While they were crossing the British sea ... the priests were praising God with psalms and hymns, giving the time to the oarsmen'.[14] Thus are interwoven the two strands of rowing and religiosity. Seamen, because they experienced constant danger, were often of a superstitious or mystical turn of mind. It was natural for oarsmen to sing religious songs, as Pennant was to find in the Hebrides. It is quite possible that the tradition of boat-songs is very ancient among the islands. Anderson drew attention to the phrase 'Scotland of melodious boats' in *Berchan's Prophecy*, (twelfth to fourteenth century), and wondered if this referred to oar-songs.

Iorram[15]

Hebrideans, like many other peoples, sang songs to accompany tedious, repetitive tasks. These helped to overcome the pain and discomfort as well as relieve the monotony. They created a sense of community and restated a purpose. Such are the waulking-songs which groups of women sang as they fulled the home-made cloth. Another class of songs are the 'irrims' which were chanted by the crew as they rowed the galleys – here described by Thomas Pennant in 1775

> *Our boat's crew were islanders (Skyemen) who gave us a species of marine music called in Erse (Iorrams). These songs when well composed are intended to regulate the stroke of the oars, and recalled to mind the custom of classical days. But in modern times, they are generally sung in couplets, the whole crew joining in the chorus at certain intervals, the notes are commonly long, the airs solemn and slow, rarely cheerful, it being impossible for the oars to keep quick time. The words generally have a religious turn, consonant to that of the people.*

It is clear from Macdonald's 'Birlinn' that the man on the bow-oar led the rowing-chant and so regulated the rate of rowing. Effectively he acted as 'stroke', which, by a curious reversal, is now done by the oarsman nearest the stern.[16] Macleod, in his notes on the 'Birlinn' comments that Pennant didn't fully appreciate the connection between the rowing-chant and the purpose of many early sea-passages.[17] Iorram also means dirge or lament and throughout the Middle Ages the burial of important men required a stately sea-passage to Iona, their favoured resting-place. Galleys would have borne much funeral traffic and there was a close connection between the tempo of the rowing-song and the purpose of the voyage.

From 'An Iorram Dharaich': Rowing Song of the Oaken Galley

> My treasure and my ransom and my hoard
> Are the men of the black and brown locks
> Who would pound the ocean,
> Who would souse her oaken timbers,
> Who would drink red wine in waves
> And who would carry off a spoil . . .

> 'S na hada hia hi 's na hi ho hua

> My treasure and my ransom and my dower,
> When thou wouldst go to sea
> Truly thy hand was not found feeble
> Though thou wast but a child;
> Wooden pins would be twisted from her oaken planks,
> She would shed the rove from every rivet's head;

Thy craft was not decayed,
And thy sailing was not inshore.

'S na hada hia hi 's na hi ho hua[18]

These verses capture the longing, the yearning, of the woman left behind; but whose imagination travels with her lover, or son. The images of stress in the wooden craft are similar to those employed by Alasdair Macdonald. The daring of the hero is implied by the fact that he does not sail close to shore.

Galleys, like Viking longships, were built for rowing. That was an essential design feature. Skill in rowing was celebrated in both Norse and Gaelic literature. In *King Harald's Saga*, Thjodolf the poet admires rowing style and invests it with an element of machismo

As one, King Harald's warriors
Lift long oars from the ocean;
The womenfolk stand watching,
Wondering at their sea-skill.

(Magnusson & Palsson)

Certain members of the *Aileach's* crew found that they broke oars with alarming regularity. The idea of oars being strong enough to withstand hard rowing occurs in both Norse poetry and Alasdair Macdonald's 'Birlinn'.

Apart from relieving monotony the whole point of a rowing song was that its rhythm helped establish fluency and consistency in the communal task. Rowing had to be smooth, confident, even, clean, and this involved sympathy between the oarsmen. Alasdair Macdonald was aware of the critical importance of a smooth and measured rowing action and this theme surfaces both in the 'Birlinn' and elsewhere in his poetry

Like one oar 'tween the tholepins sounding
There are mighty strokes abounding.

Men torture oars, their strength they try
In iron grip, seas running high.

Smooth-bladed oars, the very best
And stout men put them to the test.

With handles smooth, fists clenched they sit;
Saliva on their palms they spit.[19]

(translation by A & A Macdonald)

At its best a good rowing-song proved to be both an antidote to pain and an incitement to action. In 1796 Sarah Murray toured the Hebrides and she describes her journey from Ardtornish (Morvern) to Aros (Mull) in a four-oared boat on a hot, calm, summer's day

> *I requested the seamen to sing Gaelic songs, which they did the greatest part of the voyage. It is astonishing how much their songs animated them, particularly a chorus, that made them pull away with such velocity, that it was like flying more than rowing on the surface of the water.*

An important function of these rowing-songs was to distract from the pain and tedium of the task. The last word goes to a description by Mr John Knox who toured the Highlands in 1786. He was travelling along the coast of Sleat

> *In this day's voyage, we observed a number of Highland boats, with four oars, and containing, generally, six or seven men. – They were returning from the fishery in Loch Urn [Hourn] to the south coast of Sky. The wind being contrary, these poor people were forced to labour at the oars from ten to twenty, or twenty-five miles, before they could reach their respective huts. They take the oars alternately, and refresh themselves now and then with water, though generally in a full sweat. They sing in chorus, observing a kind of time, with the movement of the oars. Though they kept close upon the shore, and at a considerable distance from our vessel, we heard the sound from almost every boat. Those who have the bagpipe, use that instrument, which has a pleasing effect upon the water, and makes these poor people forget their toils.*

Ship-blessings

Being a religious, as well as a superstitious people the procedure for blessing a ship commanded the full attention of Highland mariners. It was a profound and solemn occasion, bearing in mind the risks run in Hebridean seas.

> *The manner of blessing a ship going to sea. Let one of the crew say thus:-*
> The Steersman *Bless our ship*
> The rest respond *May God the Father bless her*
> The Steersman *Bless our ship*
> Response *May Jesus Christ bless her*
> The Steersman *Bless our ship*
> Response *May the Holy Spirit bless her*
> The Steersman *What do you fear and that God the Father is with you?*
> Response *We fear nothing*

The Steersman *What do you fear and that God the Son is with you?*
Response *We fear nothing*
The Steersman *What do you fear and that God the Holy Ghost is with you?*
Response *We fear nothing*
The Steersman *May the Almighty God, for the sake of his son, Jesus Christ, through the comfort of the Holy Ghost, the one God who brought the children of Israel through the Red Sea miraculously, and brought Jonah to land out of the whale's belly, and brought the Apostle Paul and his ship, with the crew, out of the great tempest, and out of the fierce storm, save us, and sanctify us, and bless us, and carry us on with quiet and favouring winds, and comfort, over the sea, and into the harbour, according to his good will. Which thing we desire from him, saying our Father which art in heaven, etc. Let all the rest say So be it.*[20]

The blessing reveals much of contemporary fears of the sea as well as the commanding position of the Steersman within the boat's hierarchy.

This invoking of divine protection for a vessel has a long history. The Norwegian kings who built the 30-room 'great ships' of the twelfth and thirteenth centuries often gave them overtly religious names: *Mariasuden, Kristsuden, Kross-suden* (Mary's-ship, Christ's-ship, Cross-ship). When King Sverre launched the *Mariasuden* in 1183 or 1184 he made a speech invoking the Virgin Mary's aid: 'I give it into the protection of the blessed Mary, naming it *Mariasuden*, and I pray the blessed Virgin to keep watch and ward over this ship'. King Sverre then gave vestments to the church and had sacred relics inserted into the crossbeams at the endposts.[21]

Sea-travel frequently involved danger and it wasn't just at launching that divine aid was called upon. Prayers from *Carmina Gadelica* capture the hope, and fatalism, of a religious but vulnerable people – and provide a fitting epilogue.

From 'The Ocean Blessing'

> Bless our boatmen and our boat,
> Bless our anchors and our oars,
> Each stay and halyard and traveller,
> Our mainsails to our tall masts
> Keep, O King of the elements, in their place
> That we may return home in peace;

From a 'Sea Prayer'

HELMSMAN	What can befall you And God the Father with you?
CREW	No harm can befall us.
HELMSMAN	What can befall you And God the Son with you?
CREW	No harm can befall us.
HELMSMAN	What can befall you And God the Spirit with you?
CREW	No harm can befall us.
ALL	God the Father, God the Son, God the Spirit, With us eternally.
HELMSMAN	What can cause you anxiety And the God of the elements over you?
CREW	No anxiety can be ours.
HELMSMAN	What can cause you anxiety And the King of the elements over you?
CREW	No anxiety can be ours.
HELMSMAN	What can cause you anxiety And the Spirit of the elements over you?
CREW	No anxiety can be ours.
ALL	The God of the elements, The King of the elements, The Spirit of the elements, Close over us, Ever eternally.[22]

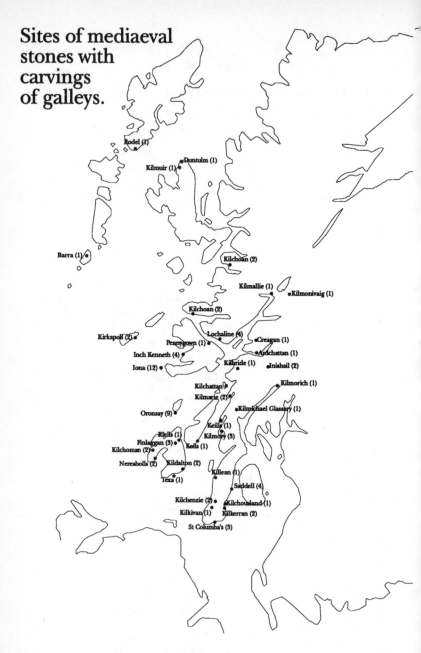

Sites of mediaeval
stones with
carvings
of galleys.

Rodel (1)

Duntulm (1)

Kilmuir (1)

Barra (1)

Kilchoan (2)

Kilmallie (1)

Kilmonivaig (1)

Kilchoan (2)

Kirkapoll (2)

Lochaline (4)

Creagan (1)

Pennygown (1)

Ardchattan (1)

Inch Kenneth (4)

Kilbride (1)

Inishail (2)

Iona (12)

Kilmorich (1)

Kilchattan (1)

Kilmarie (2)

Oronsay (9)

Kilmichael Glassary (1)

Keills (1)

Kiells (1)

Kilmory (3)

Finlaggan (3)

Keils (1)

Kilchoman (2)

Nereabolls (2)

Kildalton (2)

Killean (1)

Texa (1)

Saddell (4)

Kilchenzie (2)

Kilchousland (1)

Kilkivan (1)

Kilkerran (2)

St Columba's (3)

Map 2

Appendix

Catalogue of Mediaeval Carved Stones with Galleys

(References are primarily to the RCAHMS Inventories – where applicable)

No	Location	Reference
1	Kilchenzie, Kintyre	Argyll Vol 1, 280, 5
2	Kilchenzie, Kintyre	Argyll Vol 1, 280, 8
3	Kilchousland, Kintyre	Argyll Vol 1, 281, 1
4	Kilkerran, Kintyre	Argyll Vol 1, 285, 2
5	Kilkerran, Kintyre	Argyll Vol 1, 285, 3
6	Kilkivan, Kintyre	Argyll Vol 1, 286, 7
7	Killean, Kintyre	Argyll Vol 1, 287, 4
8	Saddell, Kintyre	Argyll Vol 1, 296, 2
9	Saddell, Kintyre	Argyll Vol 1, 296, 6
10	Saddell, Kintyre	Argyll Vol 1, 296, 10
11	Saddell, Kintyre	Kintyre Magazine No. 24
12	Southend, Kintyre	Argyll Vol 1, 300, 2
13	Southend, Kintyre	Argyll Vol 1, 300, 3
14	Southend, Kintyre	Argyll Vol 1, 300, 5
15	Ardchattan	Argyll Vol 2, 217,10
16	Inishail	Argyll Vol 2, 247,13
17	Lerags Cross, Kilbride	Argyll Vol 2, 253
18	Kilchattan, Luing	Argyll Vol 2, 256
19	Creagan	Argyll Vol 2, 373
20	Lochaline, Morvern	Argyll Vol 3, 267, 13
21	Lochaline, Morvern	Argyll Vol 3, 267, 14
22	Lochaline, Morvern	Argyll Vol 3, 267, 16
23	Lochaline, Morvern	Argyll Vol 3, 267, 17
24	Inch Kenneth, Mull	Argyll Vol 3, 288, 1
25	Inch Kenneth, Mull	Argyll Vol 3, 288, 3
26	Inch Kenneth, Mull	Argyll Vol 3, 288, 4
27	Inch Kenneth, Mull	Argyll Vol 3, 288, 5
28	Kilchoan, Ardnamurchan	Argyll Vol 3, 293, 1
29	Kilchoan, Ardnamurchan	Argyll Vol 3, 293, 2
30	Kirkapoll, Tiree	Argyll Vol 3, 310, 4
31	Kirkapoll, Tiree	Argyll Vol 3, 310, 7
32	Pennygown, Mull	Argyll Vol 3, 320, 1
33	Iona	Argyll Vol 4, 6, 127
34	Iona	Argyll Vol 4, 6, 150
35	Iona	Argyll Vol 4, 6, 151
36	Iona	Argyll Vol 4, 6, 152
37	Iona	Argyll Vol 4, 6, 153
38	Iona	Argyll Vol 4, 6, 154
39	Iona	Argyll Vol 4, 6, 155
40	Iona	Argyll Vol 4, 6, 156
41	Iona	Argyll Vol 4, 6, 183

42	Iona	Argyll Vol 4, 6, 207
43	Iona	Argyll Vol 4, 6, 208
44	Iona	Argyll Vol 4, 6, 214
45	Kiells, Islay	Argyll Vol 5, 327, 1
46	Keils, Jura	Argyll Vol 5, 331, 2
47	Kilchoman, Islay	Argyll Vol 5, 366, 15
48	Kilchoman, Islay	Argyll Vol 5, 366, 16
49	Kildalton, Islay	Argyll Vol 5, 367, 15
50	Kildalton, Islay	Argyll Vol 5, 367, 21
51	Nereabolls, Islay	Argyll Vol 5, 384, 8
52	Nereabolls, Islay	Argyll Vol 5, 384, 10
53	Oronsay	Argyll Vol 5, 386, 14
54	Oronsay	Argyll Vol 5, 386, 15
55	Oronsay	Argyll Vol 5, 386, 16
56	Oronsay	Argyll Vol 5, 386, 17
57	Oronsay	Argyll Vol 5, 386, 20
58	Oronsay	Argyll Vol 5, 386, 26
59	Oronsay	Argyll Vol 5, 386, 28
60	Oronsay	Argyll Vol 5, 386, 29
61	Oronsay	Argyll Vol 5, 386, 30
62	Texa	Argyll Vol 5, 391, 1
63	Rodel, Harris	Outer Hebrides etc. No. 111
64	Barra	Outer Hebrides etc. No. 436
65	Kilmuir, Skye	Outer Hebrides etc. No. 537
66	Kilmory, Knapdale	Argyll Vol 7, 76, 17
67	Kilmory, Knapdale	Argyll Vol 7, 76, 18
68	Kilmory, Knapdale	Argyll Vol 7, 76, 25
69	Kilchoan, Knoydart	PSAS Vol 45 pp363-4
70	Kilchoan, Knoydart	PSAS Vol 45 pp364-6
71	Keills, Knapdale	Argyll Vol 7, 45, 22
72	Kilmichael Glassary	Argyll Vol 7, 69, 3
73	Kilmorich, Loch Fyne	Argyll Vol 7, 74
74	Kilmarie, Craignish	Argyll Vol 7, 67, 22
75	Finlaggan, Islay	Argyll Vol 5, 404, 4
76	Finlaggan, Islay	Argyll Vol 5, 404, 5
77	Finlaggan, Islay	Argyll Vol 5, 404, 11
78	Kilmonivaig, Lochaber	
79	Kilmallie, Lochaber	
80	Kilmarie, Craignish	Argyll Vol 7, 67, 26
81	Inishail, Lorn	Discovery and Excavation in Scotland, 1991, p53

Glossary of Relevant Boating Terms

Many of these terms have a long history and their meanings have changed over space and time. I have given those definitions I think most suitable in a mediaeval West Highland context.

adze – axe-like tool for shaping wood, especially in shipbuilding

backstay – rope from stern to masthead to help secure mast

bail/bale – to empty water out of a boat by hand, usually by means of some sort of scoop or bucket

bark/barque – general term for a sailing-ship

birlinn – (Gaelic) a general term for a West Highland galley. It derives from byrdingr (Norse) which was a small cargo-ship built with the lines of a longship rather than a knorr.

boat-ell – a measuring-stick used in boat-building (an ell is a measure of length)

bonnets – additional pieces attached to the foot of the sail

braces – ropes attached to yard in order to change its angle

brails – ropes to edges of a sail for taking it in

carvel – a method of building ships by constructing a frame or skeleton first and then adding a skin of planking. Each strake lies flush with the next, not overlapping as with clinker. It is more usually associated with Mediterranean than with Northern ships.

caulk – to insert a fibrous material into the seams between planks to make them watertight

clench/clinch-nail – the nail holding two overlapping planks together, hence the word 'clinker'. The nail is driven through the wood and a metal rove hammered over it from the inside. The point of the nail is then bent over to clench nail, wood and rove together.

clinker – a system of building the skin of a boat by a series of overlapping planks – each of which is 'clinched' to its neighbour. The keel and skin are constructed first, the internal framework fitted subsequently.

cog – a boat-type distinguished from the Viking type by its flat bottom and sharp angles between the keel and endposts.

coracle – small skin and wicker boat, now mainly associated with Wales – for inland use

creach – (Gaelic) plunder or pillage, often in the context of a cattle-raid

crear/crayer – small trading vessel (term used from about fourteenth century)

crompstre/crompster – a small ship, a kind of galley

currach/curragh – skin (now canvas) and wicker boat, usually larger than a coracle and certainly sea-going *double-ended* – a boat with symmetrical ends, i.e. the stem is the same shape as the stern

forecastle – fortified structure at the stem of the boat. In the sagas the forecastle-men were amongst a boat's foremost warriors.

forestay – rope from stem to masthead to help secure mast

freeboard – the height from the lowest point of the gunwale amidships to the water-line

furl, furled – the process by which a sail is rolled up and hung in bunches from the yard

galley – a general term for a boat that can be rowed as well as sailed

garboard – the line of planking next to the keel

grommet – a loop of skin or fibre to attach the oar to thole-pin or gunwale

gudgeon – ring into which the rudder pin or pintle slotted. The gudgeon was fixed to the stern-post whereas the pintle was part of the rudder

gunwale – timber fixed along the sides of a boat above the top line of planking

halyard / halliard – rope to haul up the yard and sail

hulc / hulk – a boat-type with a distinctive curved or banana-shaped hull

hun-bora – pierced wooden bole at the top of the mast on a Viking ship. The halyard ran through this and the bulbous expansion also served as a fixing-point for other ropes.

keel – main structural timber running lengthways along the bottom of the boat or a general term to describe clinker boats built within the Viking tradition

keel-scarf – the scarf or join in a keel which was made from more than one piece of wood.

knorr / knarr – substantial Norse cargo-ship

land / plank-land – where two clinker strakes overlap

larboard / ladeboard – left-hand side of boat when looking from stern to stem. Since the early nineteenth century this term has been replaced by 'port' to avoid confusion with the word 'starboard'.

lee – the side away from the wind

leech – the side or vertical edge of a square sail

limmar / lymmer – rogue

liripipe – the long hanging tail of a hood or cowl – (as worn by helmsmen in mediaeval illustrations)

lymphad – anglicised version of Gaelic 'longfada' or longship where 'long' = ship and 'fada' = long

mast – vertical timber to carry yard and sail

mike – wooden crutch or support which helped to stow mast, spars or oars out of the way on board ship – (*mitch* in Caithness)

naibheag / nyvaig – (Gaelic), literally little-ship

naust / noust – a boat-house, ship-building yard, or bank-cutting for the winter-shelter of a boat.

oakum – fibre used in caulking, usually obtained by unpicking old rope *oarports* – holes below the gunwale through which the oars could be passed for rowing

parrel (or *traveller*) – ring of wood and rope which kept yard attached to the mast

paying – treat planks with pitch or tar etc. to protect against effects of water

pennon – flag, often with trailing triangular tails

pintle – downward-pointing pin on rudder which slotted into the gudgeon on the sternpost

plank – wooden board, one or several of which made up a strake along the side of a boat

port – left-hand side of boat when looking from stern to stem

portage – the carriage of boats or freight across a piece of land separating two stretches of water

quarter-rudder – another term for side-rudder

reef – the business of shortening or reducing a sail by tying up reef-points or reef-laces with reef-knots. Reef-bands are reinforcements in the sail material to help it take the extra stresses.

robands – small pieces of rope through eyelets in the top of the sail which were used to tie it to the yard

rocker – the amount of spring or upwards curvature in the shape of a boat

roves – little washers or plates of metal impaled on the point of a clinch-nail which was then bent over. In this way they helped 'clench' the nail and the planks in position.

rowlocks – either a U-shaped space cut into the gunwale or (now) a metal crutch fitted to top of gunwale to act as fulcrum for an oar

rudder – board or oar for steering, placed either at the side or at the stern of the boat

scarf – a joint between two pieces of timber

sheer – the upward curve at each end of the boat

sheet – line to lower (lee) corner of sail

shrouds – ropes to support the mast (across the boat) – in Highland galleys usually secured inside the boat amidships

side-rudder – rudder fixed forward of the stern, usually on the right or starboard side of the boat

sorning – exacting free quarters and maintenance at expense of others

square sail – sail set at right-angles to the centreline of the vessel

starboard – literally 'steering-board' side, or right-hand side of boat when looking from stern to stem

stem – bow or front of boat

stempost – the endpost at the bow of the boat

step – to put the mast up and into its base fittings

stern – aft or rear of boat

sterncastle – fortified structure at the stern of a boat

sternpost – the endpost at the stern of the boat

stern-rudder – rudder fixed at stern of boat

strake – line of planking forming part of side of boat

sweep – long oar used in some boats for steering

tack – line to lower (weather) corner of sail, also procedure by which sailing ship makes to windward

tallow – animal fat

thole-pin – pin acting as pivot for oar, to which it can be secured by an oar-loop (grommet) or via a pierced block of wood on the oar (bull)

thwarts – cross-timbers which can also be used for seating

tiller – a wooden arm for holding and steering the rudder

topcastle – fortified structure at the top of the mast

trenails/treenails – wooden pegs or dowels used to fix timbers together in boat-building

unstep – to take a mast down

wadmal – a coarse, homespun wool used by the Vikings for sails

windlass – machine for hauling or hoisting rope etc.

yard – wooden spar from which was suspended the sail. It was spread horizontally in Highland galleys.

Footnotes

Abbreviations

CDI	*Calendar of Documents Relating to Ireland*
CDS	*Calendar of Documents Relating to Scotland*
COM	*Chronicles of Man*
CRA	*Collectanea Rebus Albanicis*
CSP	*Calendar of State Papers*
ER	*Exchequer Rolls*
ES	*Early Sources (AO Anderson)*
HP	*Highland Papers*
KIST	Magazine of the Natural History & Antiquarian Society of Mid Argyll
MM	*Mariners Mirror*
NMM	National Maritime Museum
OSA	*Old Statistical Account*
POAS	*Proceedings of the Orkney Antiquarian Society*
PSAS	*Proceedings of the Society of Antiquaries of Scotland*
RCAHMS	Royal Commission on the Ancient and Historical Monuments of Scotland
RMS	*Register of the Great Seal (Registrum Magni Sigilli)*
RPC	*Register of the Privy Council*
SHR	*Scottish Historical Review*
SHS	Scottish History Society
TGSI	*Transactions of the Gaelic Society of Inverness*

Chapter 1 – Historical Antecedents (pages 3–12)

1 Hornell in S McGrail – *Ancient Boats in NW Europe* p. 184

2 Joass – *PSAS* XV p. 179

3 Skene attributes this account to the grandson of the man who supposedly built the dugout. Skene – *Blackwood's Magazine* Vol. 114 1873 pp. 408-9

4 There is a single surviving example in Elgin and Fenton has surveyed the evidence of their use in fishing and logging, principally on the Spey. Fenton – 'The Currach in Scotland', *Scottish Studies* Vol. 16

5 Fenton – op. cit. p. 67

6 In 1945 a well-tarred 'coracle' was used on Loch Dubh behind Samalaman in Moidart and in the 1950s one was stored on Inverailort Estate. Isobel Grant reported that the 'old people of Skye can still remember hearing of the use of curraghs'. IF Grant – *Highland Folk Ways* p. 252. The term currach features in Gaelic poetry as late as the seventeenth century – see M Bateman & C Ó Baoil – *Gàir nan Clàrsach* p. 52 & p. 154

7 Winterbottom (ed.) – *Gildas* pp. 22-3

8 *King Harald's Saga* – p. 67

Chapter 2 – The Early Mediaeval Period (pages 13–33)

1 Stevenson – *Documents illustrative of Scottish History 1286-1306* Vol. II pp. 187-8

2 'et naves in servitio domini regis existentes infra communitates ecclesiarum comburi faciebant'

3 *Accounts of the Lord High Treasurer of Scotland* Vol. I p. 248

4 Stevenson – op. cit. pp. 189-191. The first letter uses forms of 'navis' (ship) three times and 'galea' (galley) not at all. The second letter uses 'naves' once and forms of 'galea' eight times. This suggests that the two letters had different scribes, if not different authors. Similarly the first letter uses the name 'Rolandus' which, according to Steer & Bannerman (p. 138), was the Latin equivalent of the Gaelic name Lachlann; whereas the second letter uses the name 'Lochlanus' or 'Lachlan' – spelled in several different ways.

5 Both Lochlan and Alexander were married to daughters of Alexander Macdougall of Argyll. (See Figure 1)

6 'duae magnae galeae fuerant, quibus in insulis non fuerant majores' ('were two great galleys, than which there were none bigger in the islands').

7 Local timber was used for building ships in Lochaber before *c.* 1630. Macfarlane – *Geographical Collections* Vol. II pp. 158 ff.

8 *CSP (Ireland)* 1293-1301 No. 555 & ff.

9 'Flanders Galleys' – *MM* Vol. 12 pp. 145 ff.

10 *CDS* Vol. II pp. 434-5 The phrase 'foreign isles' suggests a literal translation of the Gaelic term for the Hebrides, 'Innsegall' or Foreigners' Isles – in this case Norse. The name 'Inchegall' occurs several times in English documents and can only have come from Irish or local informants. William's reference to doing 'justice' in the isles was presumably in connection with his office of Sheriff of Skye, part of the institution of three West Coast Sheriffdoms by Balliol's first parliament.

11 Barrow – *Bruce* p. 177

12 *ES* Vol. II p. 649

13 Munro – *Acts of the Lords of the Isles* pp. 4 ff. The Latin says 'componere seu fabricare' which I read as 'collect together or build'. I am unsure whether 'componere' is used in the sense of 'bringing together' individual ships which might belong to others; or in the sense of 'construct'.

14 *Court of Chancery Calendar of Close Rolls* preserved in the PRO (Edward I) Vol. V p. 482

15 Barrow's translation, op. cit. p. 179. (See also *CDS* Vol. III p. 16). Barrow reckons March 1308 as the date. Arguments have been advanced for both Loch Awe and Loch Etive as the loch referred to.

16 *CDS* Vol. III pp. 26 ff.

17 *CDS* Vol. V pp. 229-31

18 John's grandfather, Ewen, had invaded Man in 1250 but his claim to be 'King of the Isles' was received with some hostility by the Manxmen. In 1266 Man was ceded to Scotland by Norway but in 1275 there was an attempt by Godfrey, illegitimate son of the last King of Man, to regain the island. The Scots king, Alexander III, assembled a fleet of more than 90 ships to crush this rebellion. One of his commanders was Alexander of Lorn, (John's father), and very probably a large proportion of the fleet consisted of West Highland galleys. In John's

case it was only 50 years since the Kings of Scotland had annexed Man and perhaps he nurtured some dynastic ambition. The seannachies or genealogists played an important role within the leading Highland families and in Somerled's house the tradition of a claim to Man still had life at the end of the sixteenth century.

19 *CDS* Vol. III p. 80 (Perhaps the men were from Carrick.)

20 *Court of Chancery, Calendar of Close Rolls* in the PRO Edward II Vol. II p. 218

21 *CDS* Vol. III p. 84

22 *Court of Chancery, Calendar of the Patent Rolls* in the PRO (1313-1317) p. 696

23 Another candidate is the 'Gotherum' who is described as brother to Donald of Islay in March 1315 when Edward empowered John of Argyll to receive both these magnates into his peace, presumably in an attempt to reduce the number of his Highland opponents.

24 *Exchequer Rolls* Vol. I pp. 52 ff. & *KIST* 34 pp. 1-7.

25 *KIST* 34 pp. 9-10. Large timbers which may mark the old roadway were unearthed recently near Tarbert. The site of the fort at West Tarbert has probably been discovered on ground close to the loch and in view of the castle at Tarbert itself.

26 AAM Duncan – *Acts of Robert I* p. 622. Perhaps it was this very 'birling' that the six men took to Arran. They may represent the minimum crew for such a boat when proceeding under sail alone.

27 RG Nicholson – *Irish Historical Studies* XIII

28 Gregory – *History of the Western Highlands & Isles* p. 175 where he quotes the opinion of the Irish Privy Council concerning the Irish expedition to Scotland in November 1545 – that this was the largest force to leave Ireland for 200 years.

29 There are striking parallels in political structure between the Kingdom of the Isles under Man and the later Lordship. It continued to work as a federation, rather than a tyranny.

30 Aristocracies sometimes have an anti-commercial mentality. The dominance of such a set may have disadvantaged the Hebrides at a time of growing merchant classes in England, Scotland and Ireland.

31 *CDS* Vol. II pp. 12 ff. The crew included Master Alan, the 'gubernator' (helmsman and skipper?), and Gilfolan Kerd, whose name may be the Gaelic word 'ceard' for a smith or metal-worker.

32 Presumably 'Coupeland' refers to Copeland Island off Belfast and the term 'goods' implies that John's men were trading with Ireland. Copeland could also be written 'Copman', probably from the Norse 'kaupman' or merchant.

33 In the murage charter of Dublin in 1297 there occurs a levy on 'each ship laden with the weight of 40 hogsheads of wine for sale anywhere, 16d'. In 1991 the *Aileach* took on some empty whisky barrels off Islay and found that ten hogsheads would fit easily in a boat of 40' overall length. Merchant vessels of the late thirteenth century must have been substantially larger.

34 *KIST* 48 p. 16

35 In 1714 there is a payment in the MacLeod accounts of £66-13s-4d to John Campbell 'as the freight of the Loadning of his Birline of Lyme shells brought from Barra for the use of Dunvegan House'. (*TGSI* 1966 p. 335).

Chapter 3 – The Later Middle Ages (pages 34–52)

1 *CSP Ireland 1592-6* p. 412

2 Sandison gives some examples of speed for Shetland sixareens (six-oared boats). One boat rowed for nine hours to get to her station just before the great gale of 1881. There were seven men aboard and they averaged 3.8 knots in a smooth sea. Under sail they came back in four hours – averaging perhaps nine knots. (C Sandison – *The Sixareen* pp.17ff). In 1992 the *Aileach*, a sixteen-oar galley reconstruction, achieved a mean of 7.5 knots in a force 7 wind with three reefs in. Her maximum speed was over 12 knots and on long passages she could average 2.8 knots – all under sail. Under oars she could make a top speed of some 4 knots but her sustained speed was about 3 knots. It seems fair to assume that mediaeval Hebrideans, who inherited centuries of practical experience, could achieve at least equal results. Crumlin-Pedersen reports an average 4.5 knots with 24 rowers on the 57' reconstruction of Skuldelev 5 (a warship). There was only a slight reduction in speed when 12 men rowed so perhaps oarsmen on Viking longships worked in shifts. (Crumlin-Pedersen – *The Earliest Ships* p. 119). There have been several attempts to estimate the speed of Viking boats on the basis of crossing-times given in the sagas. When Hakon's *Kristsuden* of 74 oars crossed from Bergen to Shetland in 1263 it averaged about 3.7 knots. Bergen to Man is about 765 miles so assuming the same speed the journey would take about 8.5 days.

3 D Waters – *The Art of Navigation in England* NMM p. 576

4 *CSP Ireland 1601-3* p. 317. Howth is just North of Dublin and the distance to Strangford is about 72 miles.

5 This raid is reported elsewhere as 600 men in only seven galleys.

6 Carew MSS – *James I* p. 149

7 *RPC (1630)* pp. 428 ff.

8 Further when writing of the Glens of Antrim he remarks that the area 'is backed ... on the other part with the sea, on which side there are very small creeks between rocks and thickets, where the Scottish galley[s] do commonly land ... The force of this country is uncertain, for they are supplied as need requireth from Scotland with what numbers they list to call, by making of fires upon certain steep rocks hanging over the sea'. His remarks are confirmed by an anonymous map (No 25, probably *c.* 1602) in the Dartmouth Collection, National Maritime Museum, Greenwich. In the north-eastern corner of Antrim, beside the shortest crossing from Kintyre, there is a sketch of a bonfire on a hill and the note 'Here the Scotts make their warninge fyres'. These Scottish 'warninge fyres' appear in other contemporary maps of Ulster e.g. Trinity College Dublin 1209/16 and 1209/17 – both by Jobson.

9 Carew MSS – *Elizabeth* p. 375

10 Hayes McCoy has pointed to the Scandinavian element in the mercenary system. (Hayes McCoy, *Scots Mercenary Forces in Ireland*)

11 One of the best known took place in 1460 but is merely one in a sequence. *Odyssey II* (ed. W Kay) p. 79 & Macinnes, *West Highland Sea Power TGSI* 1974 p. 537.

12 Facsimiles of National MSS of Scotland Vol. III 29: 'we have come therefore, most potent prince, to your Majesty's country of Ireland, attended by four

thousand soldiers; in that place (and also wherever your highness shall wish) according to the wish and desire of ... [the Earl of Lennox], to offer most diligent service'.

13 We can question if Grany really had 20 boats at her behest because in 1593 there is a reference to her predicament as a result of 'her galleys by a tempest being broken'.

14 The O'Malleys liked this size of boat because one of Donald's brothers lost his 30-oared galley to the English ship *Tramontana* in 1601.

15 The *Moon* was the name of the vessel used by Ochiltree in his Hebridean expedition of 1608. The Highland chiefs were invited aboard to hear a sermon by the Bishop of the Isles before imprisonment and conveyance to Edinburgh. Ochiltree had a nice sense of the appropriate forms of spiritual and temporal retribution.

16 *Scots Mercenary Forces in Ireland* pp. 250-1

17 W Clark – *Lord of the Isles Voyage* p. 81

Chapter 4 – Ship-Service (pages 53–63)

1 See section on land-assessment in the Bibliography

2 This term is not found in Ireland, whence it must have originated, but seems to have been introduced to Pictland by the Dalriadic Scots. There it embedded itself into the system of land-organisation from Caithness to Galloway.

3 Bannerman, *Studies in the History of Dalriada* p. 49. Lamont (*Scottish Studies* 25 p. 68) has argued for a different interpretation of the Senchus, viz. one boat with forty-two crew for each group of twenty houses. Given that these were currachs I favour two boats with sixteen crew apiece. A seven-thwart boat is small, perhaps only 25-30 feet long. The practice of building in skin would have restricted boat size and there were probably large numbers of small boats.

4 H Marwick – *Leidang in the West* p. 21

5 Thomson in Macgregor & Crawford (eds) – *Ouncelands & Pennylands* p. 34

6 Crumlin-Pedersen and Olsen have reckoned a levy for Denmark of up to 1100 ships but such a figure looks rather high – even though Denmark formerly included South Sweden. (Crumlin-Pedersen – *Five Viking Ships* p. 111) In 1295 Eric of Norway agreed to help Philip of France against the King of England with a fleet of 200 galleys, 100 large ships and 50,000 soldiers – W Laird Clowes, *The Royal Navy* Vol. 1 p. 209.

7 Skene – *Celtic Scotland* Vol. III Appendix pp. 428 ff. This description of the Isles written *c.* 1577-1595 claims that the Hebrides could raise 6,000 men; 2,000 of whom should be clad in aketons (quilted protective garments), haubergeons (mail-shirts) and 'knapshal bannetts' (metal headpieces), – 'as thair lawis beir'. Galley-crews in the Viking and Hebridean tradition were not slaves or low-born men.

8 Marwick *POAS* Vol. 13 p. 24 & Clouston – *POAS* Vol. 6 p. 23. Within each shiprede in Norway there were smaller units known as manngerds or lides which were responsible for providing one man with food and equipment. Marwick believed that the Orkney skatland or quarterland (4.5 pennyland) was the same as the manngerd or lide. Given the number of tax-paying eyrislands

in Orkney (*c.* 175) he reckoned the total number of men who could be called upon for ship-service was about 700. Assuming that a standard Orkney warship was 40 oars he calculated Orkney's naval strength at about 17.5 ships. If, alternatively, we reckon on the basis of one man per pennyland then Orkney could have supported nearly 80 boats of 40 oars apiece which seems much too high in the light of the other historical evidence. Clouston came to a similar conclusion to Marwick and reckoned the Orkney total was 16 ships.

The memory of Orkney boat-service was still alive at the end of the seventeenth century when Martin Martin wrote: 'The isles of Orkney were formerly liable to frequent incursions by the Norwegians, and those inhabiting the western isles of Scotland. To prevent which, each village was obliged to furnish a large boat well manned to oppose the enemy'.

9 Orkney and Man had a roughly equal number of ouncelands (Orkney eyrisland = Manx treen or tirung), so we might expect an equal number of boats.

10 This might suggest that boats were supplied on a sheading basis rather than by treen or quarterland. (A sheading is an administrative division in Man and derives from the Norse word 'settungr' or sixth part). On the other hand it could reflect a declining number of galleys between 1264 and 1310.

11 A McKerral – *PSAS* 1950-1 p. 62

12 On the basis of the *Senchus Fer n'Alban* it was almost two men per house and it may be that a house was the functional equivalent of a pennyland. Some historians have argued on the evidence of shore-based military service for a rate of one man per pennyland. However in all the references to naval levies I can only find two cases with a ratio as high as this (and one is a political threat rather than charter evidence). Neither do we find support for Marwick's ratio of one man per quarterland although this does seem closer to the mark. There are only limited references to precise numbers of oarsmen and not all of these specify the exact amount of land involved.

13 G Barrow – *Robert Bruce* p. 289

14 Figure 2 confirms this but I have only referred to those charters where naval service is precisely stated. It is also mentioned elsewhere in general terms, as service 'by sea and by land'. For the Sheriffdom of Perth in 1304-5 we have an entry which allows us to compare a monetary and a naval service: 'From said sheriff by the hands of Sir Alexander of Argyll, for the farms of the land of Loghaua [Lochawe] and Arscodenche [Ardskeodnish/Ardscotnish] ... £26-13s-4d [i.e. 40 marks]'. (*CDS* Vol. II p. 439). This is land that Robert I gave to Colin Campbell in 1315 for service of a boat of 40 oars with men for 40 days. In Bruce's charter the land is specified as 'Louchau et Ardscodinche'. The galley is the largest to be mentioned in any mediaeval charter and this presumably reflects the land's value. On this basis one mark of rental equated with one oarsman's service for 40 days.

Chapter 5 – Numbers and Sizes of Boats (pages 64–78)

1 *Reliquiae Celticae* Vol. II p. 159

2 The Bayeux Tapestry and a coin from Hedeby imply that the shields were hung *inside* the gunwale. On the other hand the Lowther hogback stone suggests they could have been hung *outside*. (Bailey – *Viking Age Sculpture* p. 27 & plate 35).

3 Brogger – *The Viking Ships* p. 174. It was possible to manage with only one man per oar, even in a sizeable boat. We know that Earl Thorfinn went to Norway *c.* 1047 with two 40-oared boats, each of which seems to have had a crew of only 50 or 60. By contrast Earl Erling's 32-bench boat (995-1000) had a crew of over 200. On King Sverre's 30/32-room boat *Mariasuden* the ratio was as high as 5 men per half-room giving a total crew of about 320. On King Hakon's *Kristsuden*, (27 or 37 rooms), built especially as the flagship for his 1263 expedition to Scotland, we even know the names of some of the rooms and the men who occupied them. 'These were in the middle room (i.e. amidships where the room was the broadest and most spacious of the whole vessel) ... Thorleif ...; Askatin ...; four priests, and the chaplains of the king; ... and many more ...' (i.e. at least 15, possibly 20 to a room, 8-10 to the half-room). Likewise for the narrow room before the poop (stern) we have another nine names – including Eric Macruari! 'Most usually there were four men in [each] half-room'. Assuming 37 rooms with at least eight men per room we arrive at a crew of about 300.

4 *RPC* Vol. X pp. 346 ff.

5 M Bateman (trs) *Gàir nan Clàrsach* – p. 49. (See also IF Grant – *The Macleods* pp. 189-90 where the lines are translated with a different sense.)

6 For a horse stepping over the side at Pevensey, see Bayeux Tapestry. For gangplanks see *Life of St Alban* by Matthew Paris, Trinity College, Dublin, (MS 177).

7 Donaldson – *Northern Commonwealth* p. 143

8 The oars are found in the proportions of eight before and sixteen aft of the mast which is set slightly forward in the boat. This contrast between oars fore and aft is also found in those Bayeux Tapestry boats which have stepped gunwales – but not in Highland galleys.

9 The lookouts may have positioned themselves with one at the prow and the other beside the helmsman as described in 'The Birlinn of Clanranald'. The former had a particularly important job. Nicolson (p. 318) gives the proverb: *'Is olc don luing an uair a dh'eigheas an stiuireadair* – It's ill for the ship when the steersman sings out'; (i.e. this is the duty of the bow lookout, if the helmsman has to do it then the boat is in trouble).

10 In a letter of 25 April 1763 Captain Fraser of Beaufort writes that he 'has been looking out for Boats, but cannot get them for the sum allowed. They demand there £18-15s-0d for a small boat 25 feet in the keel with six oars, including sails, nets, hooks, fishing lines etc., and more than twice that sum for a large boat fit for cod and herring fishing, 28 feet in the keel, with eight oars'. (Millar – *Forfeited Estate Papers* p. 81.) For comparison a Shetland sixareen (six oars) called the Spinnoway, built in 1889, had a keel length of 19 feet 6 inches and an overall length of 30 feet. See also a contract from 1662 to build a 6-oared boat with a 30 feet keel in A Allen 'Orkney's Maritime Heritage' (p. 20).

Chapter 6 – Naval Battles (pages 79–89)

1 *Orkneyinga Saga* (trs Hjaltalin & Goudie, ed. J Anderson) p. 75. The Highlanders were also very keen on archery and abandoned the bow much later than their contemporaries. Their skill drew wry compliments from their English opponents in sixteenth century Ireland. In November 1617 Kenneth McAlayne of

Glenelg stole goods from Alexander Johnsone, burgess of Inverness, including 'aucht dussine arrow-hades' and 'thrie dussine bow stringis'. (*Book of Dunvegan* Vol. I pp. 116 ff.)

2 The early shields of the Vikings, as on the Gokstad ship, were round although they later became elongated (see the kite-shaped shields on the Bayeux tapestry or those of the Lewis chessmen). Highlanders may have derived some of their distinctive military attributes, such as round shields, bows and axes, from Scandinavian practice.

3 However we only have four instances in the whole of the West Highland series where archery is portrayed on grave-slabs; and in three of these the context is a deer-hunt. One is at Rodel, Harris where a quiver is shown. Two more are in Arisaig and there is a fourth at Kilchoan, Knoydart, just a few miles north of Arisaig. We can regard these last three as a group since two of them seem to derive from the third and principal stone at Kilmory, Arisaig.

4 Earl Hakon of Orkney's mistress was Helga, daughter of Moddan, a rich farmer in Caithness. Ingibjorg, a daughter of Helga and Hakon, was the second wife of Olaf the Red, King of Man and the Hebrides. Another of Moddan's daughters was Frakokk who brought up a grandson called Olvir Brawl on her estates in Sutherland. Frakokk's brother Ottar was Earl of Thurso. Moddan's family therefore was powerful in Caithness and Sutherland and well-connected in the Hebrides. *POAS* Vol. 6 pp. 21-25.

5 It is interesting to contrast the paltry forces which Olvir collected from the Hebrides in 1136 and the much more substantial numbers Somerled led against Man only 20 years later. It may be that Olvir's recruiting only took place in the Northern Hebrides – perhaps recruitment in the Southern Hebrides was not open to him.

6 *ES* Vol. II pp. 331-341

7 Since King Sverre had been collecting support in the North of Norway this may imply that the average size of boats in North Norway was smaller than those built in the South. Perhaps we should expect this in terms of the underlying economic strength of the areas and the habit of building in pine rather than oak in the North.

8 For account written by Hugh Macdonald about 1628 see *CRA* pp. 316-7

9 Lethbridge in *PSAS* LIX pp. 105 ff. Friel (p. 63) and others have drawn attention to the large numbers of clinch-nails required to build a clinker boat.

Chapter 7 – Decline and Demise (pages 90–112)

1 We have a series of entries in the Privy Council Registers from the end of the sixteenth and beginning of the seventeenth centuries. These give proof of the government's antipathy to Highland boats – but less compelling evidence of their destruction. (WC Mackenzie *History of the Outer Hebrides* Chapters VII-IX.)

2 *RPC* Vol. V p. 468

3 He claimed he used no weapon himself, being busy steering the galley. A supporter, William McAllan, owned one of the birlinns; the other was probably owned by Murdoch's brother, William. *RPC* Vol. XIV Appendix to Introduction.

4 *RPC* Vol. VII pp. 84-5

5 In case it is thought that the names 'lymphad', 'galley', 'boat' and 'birlinn' distinguished four different boat-types it should be noted that the Council minutes, like all legal documents, relished the roll of redundant terms.

6 *HP* Vol. III pp. 111 ff.

7 A Privy Council minute of June 1615 shows that Maclean still had two galleys and eight birlinns which makes it even more doubtful that Ochiltree destroyed any boats at all in Mull.

8 *RPC* Vol. IX p. 13

9 *RPC* Vol. X p. 720

10 *HP* Vol. III pp. 177 ff.

11 In a letter from the Earl of Tullibardine to Lord Binning the boats are described as 'tua crearis, with sum wthir boittis that Sir James him self gat in Ardmurche, and supprysit in wthir pairtis'. *HP* Vol. III p. 254

12 *RPC* Vol. X pp. 346 ff.

13 *HP* Vol. III p. 292

14 *HP* Vol. III p. 179

15 *Book of Dunvegan* Vol. I pp. 52-4

16 *RPC* Vol. X pp. 772 ff.

17 *RPC* Vol. X pp. 634 ff.

18 NMM – *Dartmouth Collection* p. 49 Map 25. One piece of evidence which may eventually help identify the author is the use of the Spanish word 'parada' when describing the annual expeditions of Highland galleys. From a dictionary we might expect it to have the sense of 'display' or 'show of force' but in this context it could almost mean rendezvous or assembly-point. Research into other early Irish maps may turn up further clues. Francis Jobson's maps (e.g. Trinity College Dublin MS 1209 Nos 15 & 17) also show galleys of the new design – in particular the changed ends and the cabin at the stern. One example (TCD MS 1209, 15) has a transom at the stern and two masts. MacAulay (p. 32) defines a *fleogach* as having two masts.

19 A good example is the Campbell blazon of the 'Erll of Ergyle' illustrated facing p. 13 of Lord Archibald Campbell's *Argyllshire Galleys*. It is now in Inveraray Castle.

20 From the seventeenth century onwards we have more prices for boat-building items as they appear in compensation claims or the account books of great families. In November 1617 one Kenneth McAlayne of Glenelg was reported to have stolen a series of items from Alexander Johnsone, Burgess of Inverness. They included 'twa stone wecht hemp pryse thairof ten pund XIIIs & 4d'. (*Book of Dunvegan* Vol. I p. 118 – *cf.* also *Accounts of the Lord High Treasurer* Vol. IV p. 465 where hemp cost four shillings per stone in January 1513.)

We have accounts for what is probably the repair rather than the construction of a Macleod birlinn in 1706 and 1713. In both years the word 'beating' is used, which has the sense of mend or repair. In 1706 the various items under wages, white plaiding for a sail, oak, oakum and nails totalled £117-7s-0d. In 1713 'Saill, Oak, Ropes for rigging and the wages of three Wrights for beating MacLeods Birline' come to £117-10s-4d – almost exactly the same sum. (*TGSI* Vol. XLIV 1966 p. 318 & p. 334.) The price of MacLeod's sail at 24 merks

(£16) in 1706 compares very favourably with the value of sail and tackle (£40) in a Tiree rental of 1662. In 1705 Macleod bought a boat for the man who ran the ferry between Skye and Harris at a cost of £53-6s-8d. In 1712 he paid for a boat for the people of St Kilda at the cost of £97-13s-4d. This was worth more than a year's rent from the island.

From a map of Kentra, Ardnamurchan, dated 1734 we have sketches which indicate that the galley-type still survived on Loch Shiel. The double-ended craft has a single mast, squarish sail, two crew, flag, two lines to the bottom corners of the sail and what looks to be a row of oarports below the gunwale. (B Megaw – *Scottish Studies* Vol. V pp. 96-99.) The contemporary Gaelic poet, Alasdair Macdonald, refers to thole-pins in his 'Birlinn of Clanranald'. Since he knew Loch Shiel intimately we must conclude that both forms survived and coexisted in the Moidart area. We might expect oarports in boats with plenty of freeboard, thole-pins in smaller boats with less.

There are early nineteenth-century paintings by William Daniell (e.g. of Loch Duich and of Loch Coruisk), which show small, single-masted, square-sailed boats in West Highland sea-lochs. From their size relative to other vessels, number of crew etc., we can estimate them to be between 20-30 feet in length. They appear alongside other types of sailing-boat and may indicate either the survival of local models or, conceivably, Scandinavian imports.

21 In the *Forfeited Estates Papers* there is correspondence showing that in 1752 the factor of Lovat Estate was ordered by the Exchequer to supply 'as much timber out of Lord Lovat's wood as would repair the King's Gally upon Loch Ness'. Such a galley was essential for speedy communications between the forts of the Great Glen but it would have been quite different to the traditional Highland type.

22 One of the mysteries of Highland history is the slow growth of the fishing industry on the west coast. The adaptation of West Highland designs to fishing is a story in itself and attention should focus on traditional boat-types like the Ness 'sgoth' – a name which may itself derive from the Norse.

23 In 1568 James VI made a grant of Free-Forestry in Glenfalloch, Perthshire, to Campbell of Strachur. This allowed him 'to mak plant big and repair ane fre forrest ... to mak and big dykis about it and to ... set growing trees therintill'. The fact that he was also allowed to regulate the hunting of deer and the grazing of animals suggests an awareness of conservation issues. – *HP* IV pp. 36-7

24 H Cheape – *Woodlands on the Clanranald Estates*

25 J Macdonald – *Tales of the Highlands* p. 17

26 This problem is being experienced today at Rahoy, Morvern, partly because of the choking effects of bracken.

27 *CRA* p. 309

28 Small has suggested that in parts of Lochaber the rights of landowners to use of the foreshore derive from Norse udal custom. (Small in *Dark Ages in the Highlands* p. 83)

29 B Crawford – *Earl and Mormaer*

30 Norse names, including several dale-names, are scattered throughout the Rough Bounds (Moidart to Knoydart).

31 J Fraser – *Chronicles of the Frasers* (W Mackay ed.) p. 297. Fraser also described the building of the soldiers 'citadel' in Inverness which began in 1652. 'All their oake planks and beames was carried out of England in ships to Cessock rode; all their firr, logg, spar rofe beames, sold ther out of Hugh Fraser of Struyes woods. I saw that gentleman receave 30 thousand marks at once for timber ...' (p. 414)

32 Carew MSS – *James I* pp. 150-3

33 *CSP Ireland 1565-1625* pp. 666-7

34 *CRA* p. 153

35 *CRA* p. 34 The lack of a current dictated against rafts and we can assume that the boats must have been of reasonable size. On rivers such as the Tay the wood was simply floated downstream as early as the beginning of the sixteenth century.

36 Cheape has commented on how late the adze was used in a Highland wood-working context – for instance in shaping floor-boards. This may have been the case with ship-boards also.

37 The OSA return for Arisaig and South Morar in 1795 showed there were 2 small vessels, with an average crew of 3, and 65 small boats. This represents a complete upheaval in naval affairs. Instead of relatively few large boats in the hands of aristocrats and clan chiefs, we have lots of small ones in the hands of tenants who used them for small-scale fishing.

Chapter 8 – The Shared Tradition (pages 115–126)

1 There are two words in Gaelic which may be cognate. A 'sgoth' is a type of clinker-built boat associated latterly with the men of Ness in Lewis. Both Macbain and Maclennan define it in their dictionaries as a 'Norway skiff'. Dwelly gives it as a large winter fishing-boat or boat with vertical stem and stern. 'Sgud' appears in Dwelly as a ship or ketch, is absent from MacBain but is given in Maclennan as a 'style of boat, slow and clumsy but capacious; often a term of contempt for a boat'. Maclennan derives 'sgud' from Old Norse 'skuta'. The problem is compounded by the fact that in mediaeval Scottish documents we often find the word 'scutt' used to describe small boats and in English one sense of the word 'scout' means a small fast boat used for spying out the enemy. It seems reasonable to suppose that all these words: 'sgoth', 'sgud', 'scutt' and 'scout' are cognate with Norse 'skuta'; whether they passed directly into Gaelic and English or whether they were mediated through Dutch. (Middle Dutch 'schute', Modern Dutch 'schuit' – pronounced remarkably like the English word 'scout'. The Dutch had a close connection with the British Isles throughout the mediaeval period and were heavily involved in the herring fishery off Scotland). GVC Young (*The Hebridean Birlinn, Nyvaig and Lymphad*, p. 20) has pointed out a Manx boat-type called the 'scoute' which was *c*. 26 feet long, with a square sail and eight oars.

2 This last refers to the habit of letting precious objects into the actual wood of the stem-post. (See also Chapter 14 note 10.)

3 Our earliest evidence for stern-rudders comes from the Tournai fonts at Winchester and Zedelghem which are dated to the late twelfth century. It is

probable that both the Winchester and Zedelghem vessels represent hulcs. The town seal of Ipswich in 1200 is the first seal which clearly shows a stern-rudder. It is thought that this fundamental change in boat-design took place in the second half of the twelfth century. An illustration in an early fourteenth century English manuscript (The Holkham Bible) shows a tiller composed of two curved pieces of wood held fast by a ring. This device gave purchase on the rudder *around* the stern-post. Perhaps Highland galleys had something similar.

4 The graffiti may be associated with one of the big naval expeditions between 1221 and 1263 but we can give no firm date and cannot distinguish the steering arrangements. Some have claimed to see a side-rudder but given the state of the carvings I am sceptical of firm conclusions. Angus Mor's seal shows a stern-rudder.

5 Anderson *MM* 14 & Tinniswood *MM* 35

6 Some of the English accounts use terms such as 'brandr' and 'rack' which come straight from the Norse – the latter word also finding its way into Gaelic as 'rac' or parrel.

7 Further confusion stems from the fact that the Latin word 'clavus' is sometimes translated 'bolt', sometimes 'nail'. An alternative explanation is that the bolts may have been required in the fixing of stem and stern-pieces to the keel. The implication seems to be that by this means Godred restricted the size of any potential competitor's fleet.

8 Exactly the same problem recurs with the *Paul* in 1373 where we know the keel measured 80 feet and the oarsmen also numbered 80.

9 W Clark – *The Lord of the Isles Voyage* p. 156

10 By 1336 the sail of *La Phelipe* was made of canvas, not wool, at a cost of 3d per ell. We have some surviving accounts of Robert the Bruce for Tarbert, Loch Fyne, and in 1326 there is a payment of 7s 2d for '28 ells of canvas bought for sacks for lime'. This works out at just over 3d per ell. Accounts for one of the London galleys built under Edward 1 show that the cloth cost 2.25d per ell. Canvas can mean either hemp or flax; if hemp then it may have been imported; if flax then it might have been made locally. Writing of Lewis at the end of the seventeenth century Martin Martin says 'they have also flax and hemp' (p. 86). See also Chapter 7, note 20.

11 The stern-rudder sometimes hung lower than the keel, as on the cross-shaft of John, Abbot of Iona (44), and was presumably fixed *after* launching.

12 This ancient boat-launching scheme persisted in Britain into the nineteenth century and is portrayed in John Constable's *Boat-building near Flatford Mill.*

13 A Gunn – Dissertation 1986 p. 14

14 Knees are internal timbers for supporting thwarts etc. Thwarts are cross-timbers providing seats for rowers.

15 i.e. 'two dozen oars, 30 shillings a dozen, total £3'.

16 Stillingfleet – *Saga Book of the Viking Club* Vol. V pp. 247-250; Staplehurst – *Archaeologia Cantiana* Vol. 9 p. 189 ff.

17 M Campbell – *KIST* 22 & FS Mackenna – *KIST* 26

Chapter 9 – Seals, Heraldic Devices, etc (page 127–136)

1 See B Megaw 'Ship Seals of the Kings of Man', *Journal of the Manx Museum* Vol. 6 Plate 241. Of the two seals one is less detailed and shows a clinker hull with mast, forestay, backstay and probably 6 shrouds. No steering gear, sail or yard is visible and the mast is stepped slightly fore of centre. The other seal is more informative. The sail is furled near the top of the mast, there are two forestays, two backstays, four shrouds and three braces – making a total of eleven ropes. The braces appear to be secured one fore, two aft – which is how they appear in those mediaeval Highland carvings which show three braces rather than two. There are signs of four crew members. The seal is damaged at the stern so we cannot distinguish the steering arrangements.

2 Seals of Angus Mor and Alexander of Islay – PRO ref E39/95/14 & 15; Alexander of Lorn's seal – PRO ref E39/96/12. Alexander of Islay's seal is illustrated in A & A Macdonald, *Clan Donald* Vol. 1 (plate facing p. 88). See also *PSAS* 126 pp. 582–4.

3 J & R Munro – *Acts of the Lords of the Isles*, Appendix E

4 West Highland heraldic or sculptural designs owe much to the earlier image library of the seal-engravers. A good example is the stone at Nereabolls where the crewman climbing the rigging is reminiscent of English seals such as Dover (1305) and Sandwich (thirteenth-century).

5 There is a galley on a shield on the seal of Evir Campbell of Strachur dated *c.* 1499. (*Highland Papers* IV p. 22). The Campbells of Strachur had used galleys on their heraldic shields from at least as early as 1355. (*Argyllshire Galleys* p. 15.) We have a record of 1478 which refers to their service with a 'cymbe' ('cumba' is Latin for small boat). – *HP* Vol. IV pp. 19-20 & *ER* Vol. IX p. 679. Matthew Paris has left us with a drawing of the shield of Hakon of Norway (mid thirteenth-century) which consisted of 3 gold longships on a red background.

6 A Allen – *Orkney's Maritime Heritage* p. 17.

7 Another common endpost design is like a half-hammerhead set at an upward incline, but there is also one with a trefoil. Matthew's sterncastles suggest that at this stage (*c.* 1240s) they were very rudimentary affairs. We have no evidence for fore, stern or top-castles in any Hebridean galleys despite the presence of the first two on the Dublin seal of 1297. The most we have is an ambiguous reference in the *Chronicles of Man* for 1238 which talks of a shipwrecked boat having upper and lower decks. (Broderick – *COM* f45v. With a crew of nearly 80 this must have been a large vessel.)

8 Backhouse & de Hamel (eds) – *Becket Leaves*

9 Some argue that in both seals and in mediaeval sculpture boats are given an unduly high stem and stern as they are compressed to fit into the space available. However the boat pictures of Matthew Paris show that even when there was room available vessels were still drawn with the same extremely high stem and stern.

Chapter 10 – Carved Stones (pages 137–157)

1 Steer & Bannerman – *Late Mediaeval Monumental Sculpture in the W Highlands*. There are stylistic differences between the schools which must be taken into account in any

analysis. Saddell tends to show galleys with their sails furled; Oronsay masons show them with their sails set and billowing. There is also a carving of a galley on a rock outcrop above Loch Creran, Argyll – RCAHMS Argyll Vol. 2 No. 373.

2 There was generally no fore and aft rocker or spring in Highland boats. The keel is straight – except in a carving on a font from Kilmorich, Loch Fyne.

3 *PSAS* XII pp. 577 ff.

4 In S Greig's *Viking Antiquities in Scotland* (p. 179) there is a report that a boat-find similar to Eigg was made in a peat-moss near Tormore in Arran.

5 Larson – *Portable Mediaeval Reader* (eds Ross & McLaughlin) p. 147

6 H Miller – *My Schools & Schoolmasters* pp. 284-5

7 In 1706 Macleod needed 30 yards of white plaiding for the sail of a birlinn he was repairing. (*TGSI* XLIV p. 318) If we presume 30 yards for length and a standard width of 1 yard then we can guess that the sail was made of 6x5-yard strips giving proportions of about 18 feet by 15 feet and a total sail area of only 270 square feet. This looks small by comparison with the *Aileach's* 360 square feet which itself was substantially less than she might have carried. See also GVC Young (*The Hebridean Birlinn, Nyvaig and Lymphad*, pp. 23-4).

8 *SHR* 1911-12 p. 344 The linen was worth £20, the sail and tackle £40. By contrast a cow and calf at Whitsunday were worth £10.

9 It has been claimed for single-masted ships that masts are optimally stepped 8-10 per cent of the keel's length forward of its mid-point. There is some support for this among West Highland carvings of galleys although the majority appear central. Since it is aesthetically more satisfying to have the mast follow the centre-line of the stone it may be that most sculptors fudged realism in order to maintain symmetry within the grave-slab. Nevertheless the mast is shown forward of centre on Iona (34) and Iona (35).

10 Early Vikings lowered the mast completely when sails were not in use but in later times the mast was often left up. The yard could remain aloft or partially lowered and the sail furled. Sometimes the yard was detached completely. As boat-size increased so raising or lowering the mast became increasingly arduous but leaving it in position brought problems of increased windage. At the end of September 1263 Hakon's ships were caught in a great equinoctial storm off the west coast of Scotland. Some ships drifted, some were driven ashore and even the King's ship drifted up the sound despite having seven anchors out. Hakon's saga comments: 'On the Monday, the storm became so violent that some hewed down their masts'. Virtually all Highland carvings show the mast up, even when there is no sail present.

11 In the poems of Mary MacLeod (c. 1615-1707) we find references to satin pennons on the mast. Either they inclined towards this over time or they carried both.

12 The Gaelic word 'rac' (parrel-ring) derives from the Norse word 'rakki'.

13 We have no surviving rope fittings but we can get a good idea of the type used from Viking relics and detail on the Rodel tomb. In one of the panels a huntsman holds two dogs by means of a lead connected to a swivel hanging from his wrist. No doubt similar devices were common on galleys.

14 Martin Martin says (c. 1695) of the seals off Uist 'The skin is by the natives cut in long pieces, and then made use of instead of ropes to fix the plough to their

horses'. Both he and Dean Munro (1549) drew attention to the great slaughter of seals on certain islands. In St Kilda he found there were three ropes, each 24 fathoms long. 'The chief thing upon which the strength of these ropes depends, is cows hides salted, and cut out in one long piece, this they twist round the ordinary rope of hemp, which secures it from being cut by the rocks'. By contrast the fowlers of Barra used a rope of horse-hair.

15 Lord Archibald Campbell thought that these were two vertical wooden spars to *support* the yard-arm (Lord A Campbell, *Argyllshire Galleys* p. 17). It could be argued that yard-arms on Highland galleys would have benefited from some sort of structural support. Unfortunately all ropes on grave-slabs are shown as straight lines of equal thickness and it is impossible to distinguish between a rope and a wooden spar. However the fact that at least one of the braces is always shown at an angle suggests that they were actually ropes. Unless set vertically it is difficult to imagine how a wooden spar could be effective as a support. On the Rodel stone it is almost as if one of these braces is marked with cross-lines to show the fibres of the rope. The seals of Dunwich (*c.* 1199) and Dover (1305) show the ropes to the end of the yard as curved and slack.

16 There is a problem explaining why some boats (such as King Harald of Man's or those at Kilmory, Knapdale) show three braces whilst most Highland galleys only feature two. It may be that the third brace was a function of size; or perhaps sculptors left it out when they felt the extra detail would clutter an image. The Rodel sculptor omitted two, possibly four, shrouds and a third brace, presumably for the sake of clarity.

17 Atkinson, *Viking Ships* p. 35

18 Friel has argued, on the basis of thirteenth-century customs dues in London, that oarports were characteristic of larger boats. (Friel p. 111)

19 At Rodel this slit is horizontal whereas on the ninth century Gokstad ship from Norway it was cut at an upward angle to prevent damage from a chafing oar during rowing. In both cases the cuts are aft of the hole.

20 R Miket & D Roberts – *The Mediaeval Castles of Skye & Lochalsh* p. 63. Further Irish evidence may come to light. We know of a galley on the wall of the gatehouse at Dunluce, a carving on the door of a round tower at Roscrea, Tipperary, and graffiti from the chapel of Barrymore Castle, near Cork.

21 In the RCAHMS inventory it is suggested that they may be the work of children since they are low on the wall. Against this it is probable that the original ground level was lower. RCAHMS *Argyll* Vol. II pp. 144-5.

22 Some of these runes refer to a 'Vigleikr Stallari' (Vigleikr the Marshall or Chancellor) who was in Hakon's expedition and is mentioned as one of the leaders of the forays to Kintyre and Loch Lomond. *KIST* 22 & 26

23 The use of an endpost to provide support may have a parallel in Lochaline (21) – although in the latter case it is the stem-post which has prongs.

24 A Binns – *The Navigation of Viking Ships* p. 114. MacAulay has commented on the longevity of the 'cruaidh' or simple stone anchor in the Hebrides – particularly for rocky coasts where a fluked anchor is more likely to be lost. Stones can be carved or 'waisted' to hold a rope better and were also used as weights for fishing.

25 In the Lord High Treasurer's accounts there was a payment in January 1513

for 4 'scheip skynnys to mak moppatis for the tallowyng of the James'. Although this context may be Lowland we can assume something similar in the Highlands. Friel (p. 76) says that tallowing was designed to help the vessel move through the water faster. Nicolson (p. 404) gives the proverb '*Tha taobh dubh 's taobh geal air, mar bha air bata Mhic Iain Ghearr* – He has a white side and a black side, like the boat of Short John's son'. Apparently this Archibald MacDonell was a noted pirate and had his boat and sails coloured differently on each side.

26 Larson – op. cit. p. 147
27 In Nereabolls (51) one of the crew appears to be climbing the aft brace.

Chapter 11 – Surviving Boat-building Traditions (pages 158–166)

1 H Miller – op. cit. p. 284
2 He was possibly referring to the discovery of a mediaeval boat in the River Rother in 1822.
3 'Three stones Ocum' were used on Macleod's birlinn in 1706.
4 Macleod states that the latter were employed down to 1780. A Macleod – *Sar Orain* p. 126
5 J MacInnes – *West Highland Sea Power TGSI* 1974 p. 527
6 AE Christensen – 'Boats & Boatbuilding in Western Norway' in Fenton & Palsson (eds) *The Northern & Western Isles in the Viking World* p. 86
7 Cheape comments that 'There is a vague tradition that the chieftains of Clanranald had their galleys built at Gasgan on Lochshielside'. Only half the work was done there, leaving the problem of what type of work this constituted and where it was completed. Any such division of the task may have reflected the local availability of different types of timber for certain parts of the boat. Cheape gives details about the types of wood used: 'It is said that oak was used for the stem and stern-posts, keel, ribs and gunwale. Elm was preferred for the strakes'.
8 D Shaw-Smith – *Ireland's Traditional Crafts* p. 94
9 A murage grant allowed a community to raise customs duties for a fixed number of years in order to build town walls. The items on which customs could be levied provide a good idea of what was being traded at the time. We have several of these documents from places like Dublin, Drogheda, Clonmel and Tipperary for the period 1295-1300. One in particular, that for Drogheda (Meath), reads as if it had been 'customised' for the particular needs of that community. If the following were typical imports then Drogheda was probably a ship-building centre in 1296:

Item	Levy
100 lbs of pitch and rosin	1/2 d
100 large boards for ships	1/4 d
Each mast of a ship	1/4 d
2 ropes for rigging of ships	1/4 d
Each hundred of canvas for ships	1/2 d

There were also items such as iron and nails which would have been used in ship-building. A letter dated 26 April 1298 concerns William le Ware, a burgess of Cork. William had applied to Edward for permission to 'cut through the wall of the city of Cork in order to convey to the water through such opening a ship which he had lately caused to be constructed within the circuit of the said wall, provided that he repair the wall at his own expense'. William felt that his investment was only secure if construction took place *inside* the walls of the city (*CDI* 1293–1301 p. 237).

10 In 1235 the King of England operated on a similar naval scale to the King of Norway. Sixty-oar boats were amongst the largest currently being built and Hakon's flagship in 1263 was not greatly larger at 37 rooms (74 oars). In 1248 Matthew Paris claimed that his ship was the largest of more than 200 in Bergen harbour. (*Illustrated Chronicles* pp. 75–6.) Edward I's building program suggests that galley size grew out of all proportion in the second half of the thirteenth century.

11 J MacInnes – op. cit. p. 528

12 A Macleod – op. cit. pp. 126–9

13 Investigative work such as Sandison's on the Shetland sixareen might cast some retrospective light on the evolution of boat-building techniques. However we cannot just assume that West Highland boats were the same as those in Shetland. They may have had much in common, but Hebridean boats were more likely to have been influenced by Irish practice.

14 Naust appears as a place-name element in the sagas – e.g. Naustdal and Naustanes in *Egil's Saga*. We know of an Eilif from Naustdalr (Naustdale) who took part in the Battle of Largs on the Norwegian side and 'acted very boldly'. It may lie behind Scottish place-names such as Nostaig, (Islay), Nostie (Loch Alsh), Noster (Loch Seaforth), Glen Noustapal (S.Uist) and Naast (Loch Ewe) – as well as several more in Orkney and Shetland.

15 A nearby rock is called Sron Laimhrige or the landing-point, although it is now well inland. The channel, by which boats were supposedly led to and from their winter harbour, is presumably at NM 472882.

16 Report from Roger Miket, Skye. Miket also believes there is a good chance some boat-timbers may be preserved in the silt.

17 RCAHMS – Knoydart: *An Archaeological Survey* 1991

18 In his study of Irish curraghs Hornell noticed that in some areas, such as Achil Island and Iniskea, they were housed bottom-up in low stone-walled pens when not at sea. Curraghs need to be protected from the wind but perhaps the different types of boat-shelter had a common origin.

19 Vikings in England, there principally the Danes, were long known as 'aescmen' or ash-men.

Chapter 12 – Landing-points, Boating-practice, etc (pages 167–175)

1 In a report compiled in 1915 for the Royal Commission Inventory for the Outer Hebrides, Skye and the Small Isles there is the following comment in connection with the 'dun' on the island of Geirum More off Mingulay: 'it is said ... that there is a boat-slip above high-water mark on the eastern end'. The latest Argyll inventory (Volume 7) shows an increased awareness of boat-landings at early island sites. People have always taken advantage of natural coves but occasionally these have been 'improved'. At Eilean na Circe (Caol Scotnish, Loch

Sween) there are some rock-cut steps above the boat-landing. Below Dun Mhuirich (on Linne Mhuirich off Loch Sween) there is 'a rudimentary wharf, from which three roughly built jetties project; at its S end there is a small boulder-faced recess resembling a boat-noost'. These are probably later than the original construction of the dun but no date has been assigned. In 1881 Nicolson (*Gaelic Proverbs* p. 94) referred to a MacLeod who kept his galley at Duntulm in Skye 'where the groove is still shown, worn in the rock of the beach up and down which she was launched or drawn up'.

2 Skene – *Celtic Scotland* Vol. III p. 437

3 Yet not a single one of the boats in the West Highland series of grave-slabs displays a stepped gunwale. The only two examples with a Hebridean context are the Hedin slab on the Isle of Man and the Sigurd stone at Iona – both much earlier.

4 S Murray – *The Beauties of Scotland* p. 172

5 Mather quotes the claim that Shetland sixareens were always rowed unless the wind was fair and 'that tacking was unknown as a technique or at least not practised'. Mather – *Boats & Boatmen of Orkney & Shetland* p. 24.

6 *Seven Viking Romances* (trs) Palsson & Edwards p. 222. MacAulay – Birlinn p. 32 – refers to the 'long-luirist', a type of boat associated with the Monach Isles, which could be rowed whilst under sail.

7 D Ross – *The Glengarry Evictions* p. 5. The tricky section of his voyage probably refers to the passage through the narrows at Caolas Mor.

8 A Campbell – *The Carpenter MacPheigh* in *KIST* 51

9 Larson op. cit. pp. 147-8. Nicolson (p. 17) quotes the Gaelic proverb *'Am fear a ruitheas an eathar shalach, thèid e air sgeir-mhara uair-eigin'* – He that sails a foul-bottomed boat will some day run on a rock.

10 One of the lines of Iain Lom's poem 'Iorram do Bhata Mhic Dhomhnaill' (*c.* 1664) mentions the word 'faradh', which means the litter used in a boat which carried horses or cattle. (AM Mackenzie – *Orain Iain Luim* pp. 102-3). Perhaps this was what Dr Johnson sat on.

11 If, by analogy with their number of agricultural divisions, we assume that the boat was subdivided the same way we arrive at a ten-oared boat with five oars per side. This seems about right in relation to its length.

12 *KIST* 22, *KIST* 26

13 A Lindsay – *A Rutter of the Scottish Seas* NMM.

14 Tarbert in Jura seems to have been something of a congregating-point for Highland galleys on their way south to Ireland.

15 At the end of the twelfth century Gerald of Wales wrote 'Not far to the north ... is a certain wonderful whirlpool in the sea. All the waves of the sea from all parts, even those remote, flow and strike together here as if by agreement. .... If a ship happens to touch it, it is caught and pulled with such violence of the waves that the force of the pull downwards immediately swallows it up for ever'. Gerald is writing in a rather vague geographical context. His previous sections had been about the Scottish Isles and Iceland. It may be, as his translator John O'Meara suggests, that he was writing about the maelstrom on the west coast of Norway. He could just as easily be talking about Corryvreckan – which was a lot closer to Ireland. Gerald of Wales – *The History & Topography of Ireland* p. 67 & note 28.

Chapter 13 – The Evidence from Language (pages 176–187)

1 Henderson – *Norse influence on Celtic Scotland* pp. 136 ff. Oftedal – *On the frequency of Norse Loanwords in Scottish Gaelic*, Scottish Gaelic Studies pp. 116 ff. Henderson claims that the 'Birlinn of Clanranald' contains about 33 words from Norse.

2 The six pages of nautical definitions given by Dwelly under 'bata' reveal how much can still be done through linguistic analysis. He notes under 'sgoth' that 'the mast is lowered a-stem, not a-stern as in other boats'. This alone may indicate different historical antecedents.

3 The story of Carpenter MacPheigh suggests a Norse origin for plug-holes. MacAulay derives the relevant term, osar(G), from osekar(N). He also draws cipean(G), a type of fulcrum for the oar, from keipe(N) – MacAulay, Birlinn, pp. 112-118. In both Gaelic and Norse the term for sewing or stitching is applied to wooden clinker boats. The earliest wooden boats in Norway did use some withy ties rather than nails but it is difficult to know if the association derives from this or the fact that even earlier hide boats were used by both cultures.

4 This essentially impressionistic conclusion should eventually be capable of objective verification. It has also been argued that the Norse origin of Hebridean place-names becomes obvious when the words are pronounced by a local speaker.

5 It has been suggested that 'naibheag' gives the name Dunyveg (literally Dun-of-the-little-ships) and that another Islay place-name, Nereabolls, derives from 'knorr', a merchant-ship, when it is more likely to come from 'nidri' meaning lower or nether.

6 Given the Privy Council distinction on oar-numbers we could surmise that longfada denotes a galley, naibheag a birlinn.

7 Tarbert means literally a 'bearing' or 'carrying over' – a portage point. The Norse name for the Tarbert crossing was Satiris-Eid which has not survived. However on the Cowal shore, just opposite Tarbert to the East, there is an Eilean Aoidhe which is joined to the mainland by a tiny isthmus. This seems to be the Gaelic version of 'eid' as with Aoidhe for Eye by Stornoway. It is interesting to see the Norse name survive so near to Tarbert and so far south in the Hebridean world. As if to confirm that Eilean Aoidhe is a true 'eid' and not just an aberration we find another site about 4.5 km NNW of this called Dun Caisteal Aoidhe. Other 'tarberts' may yet come to light. In a manuscript map by Timothy Pont, whose fieldwork dates to the period 1583-96, there is a 'Terbard' marked on the north side of Kinlochleven. This is probably the Tarbert near Lundavra marked by Morison on his survey of 1772.

8 It is just possible that the 'Sigurd' stone on Iona, which dates to the Viking period, shows two rollers acting like chocks – one at either end of the boat. RCAHMS *Argyll* Vol. IV p. 212

9 Binns has commented that Yorkshire fishermen used the term 'footing-trees' for the oars of a coble. This is a type of boat whose oars are used as rollers to move it over a beach. In practice the rollers don't actually rotate or roll. What happens is that boats slide over the top of them, possibly with the aid of grease or seaweed. Moving boats over rollers or whale-ribs works on the principles that the area of contact is reduced and the process aided by something slippery.

Nicolson (p. 251) quotes the Gaelic proverb *Is corrach culaidh air aon lunn* – A boat is unsteady on one roller.

10 Sandison reckoned that the weight of the bare hull of a 30 feet sixareen would be about 16 cwt – making it perfectly feasible to haul.

11 Maclean describes a story from Mull of a feud between Allan Macdonald of Clanranald and Maclean of Duart. In order to escape the latter, Clanranald's men dismantled their birlinn at Salen by 'withdrawing the wooden pins', then carried the planks to Shielfoot before launching it again. The Highlanders may have had some boats that could be dismantled and then reassembled. JP MacLean – *History of the Clan MacLean* p. 337

12 W Mackenzie (ed.) – *The Bruce* by John Barbour pp. 269-70

13 Some large timbers were turned up during the construction of Tarbert Heritage Centre. More were exposed by deep-ploughing in a field nearer to West Loch Tarbert. These were long and straight-grained and evidently from forest oaks – the longest being nearly 5m in length. Attempts to date them dendrochrono-logically have so far been unsuccessful. One lay about 55 cm below the present surface so, if they have anything to do with a mediaeval trackway, then more evidence may be discovered. *KIST* 49.

14 The practice of portage at Tarbert may have continued on a small scale through-out the mediaeval period. H Cheape – 'A critical View of Mediaeval Reportage in Fenton & Palsson' (eds) *The Northern & Western Isles in the Viking World* p. 212.

15 Over the centuries Tarbert, Loch Fyne, and Crinan have been rivals for a short cut to the West Coast. Negotiating the Mull of Kintyre was a lengthy and tricky voyage and travellers have long considered alternatives. In the days of portage Tarbert seems to have been pre-eminent. We know of its importance in Dalriadic times, we know of Magnus Bareleg's and Bruce's crossings and we know of Bruce's trackway between West and East Loch Tarbert. Crinan though was always a contender. Marion Campbell quotes a local tradition that a Viking boat was brought up the Add and hauled overland to Lochgilp (M Campbell – *Mid Argyll: A Handbook of History* p. 16).

16 On several occasions between the thirteenth and the sixteenth centuries the Highland chiefs were in league with the Kings of England against the Scottish crown. In 1328 the Treaty of Northampton expressly forbade such contacts to the Highlanders. In 1461 the Treaty of Westminster-Ardtornish was signed between the Macdonald chiefs and the King of England. In 1545 Donald Dubh's emissaries sought and gained help from King Henry VIII in their planned rebellion against the Scottish king. In all of these negotiations the power, or supposed power of the Highland naval forces was a factor.

17 G Barrow – op. cit. pp. 289-291

18 *RMS* I, App. I, 105; *RMS* I App. I, 107; *RMS* I, App. I, 32

19 Theoretically this naval force offered more than enough carrying capacity. At 3 men per oar, and assuming the smallest boat in each class, the 6 galleys could carry at least 324 men and the 14 birlinns at least 504 men – making a total of 828. If we add in the capacity of several 8-oared boats this represents very ample provision for a force supposed to total 500 men.

Chapter 14 – The Literary Evidence (pages 188–199)

1 M Bateman & C Ó Baoill – *Gàir nan Clàrsach* pp. 154-7

2 D Thomson – *An Introduction to Gaelic Poetry* p. 28

3 WJ Watson – *Scottish Verse from the Book of the Dean of Lismore* pp. 7-13

4 RG Poole – *Viking Poems on War & Peace* p. 62

5 *Carmina Gadelica* Vol. V pp. 209 ff., Scottish Academic Press

6 The Norse often described their boats as steeds. The Gaelic poet Murchadh Mor mac mhic Mhurchaidh (d. *c.* 1689) wrote a poem comparing a boat to a mare – to the disadvantage of the latter. See M Bateman & C Ó Baoill – *Gàir nan Clàrsach* pp. 148-153

7 WJ Watson – op. cit. pp. 219-233

8 AM Mackenzie – *Orain Iain Luim* pp. 56-7.

9 M Bateman & C Ó Baoill – *Gàir nan Clàrsach* pp. 190-199. Nicolson (p. 56) gives a Gaelic proverb with a similar theme: *Bean ga threigsinn, is stiuir ga dhiultadh* – Wife forsaking him, and helm disobeying.

10 MacAulay comments that 'it is still common practice to place coins in the joint between keel and stem on new boats, for good fortune'. Ian MacDonald reports that 'it was common for fishermen or sailors to place a hand on iron after someone had inadvertently broken a taboo'.

11 A Macleod – *Sar Orain* pp. 21-129; D Thomson – *An Introduction to Gaelic Poetry* pp. 172-80, Alasdair Mac Mhaighstir Alasdair, *Selected Poems* pp. 132-165; H MacDiarmid – *Golden Treasury of Scottish Poetry* pp. 65-85; A Nicolson – *An Gaidheal* (1877) Vol. VI pp. 55-61.

12 D Thomson – *An Introduction to Gaelic Poetry* pp. 176-7

13 H MacDiarmid – *The Golden Treasury of Scottish Poetry* p. 71

14 B Colgrave – *The Life of Bishop Wilfrid* p. 27

15 We can distinguish between *iorram* as the name for a particular style of poetry and *iorram* as the name for an oar-song. I use it in the latter, restricted sense here. (For an analysis of this difficulty see 'Eachann Bacach & other Maclean poets' ed. C Ó Baoill 1979 pp. 279-81).

16 A Nicolson (*Gaelic Proverbs* p. 134) states that the song was generally raised by the man at the helm. He gives the proverb *Chan urrainn domh h-èigheach agus a h-iomradh* – 'I cannot raise the boat-song and row her'.

17 A Macleod – op. cit. pp. 75-6

18 *Carmina Gadelica* Vol. V pp. 17 ff., Scottish Academic Press

19 A & A Macdonald – *The Poems of Alexander Macdonald* p. 365

20 Sixteenth-century ship-blessing preserved in the Inveraray Archives. JB Craven – *Records of Argyll & The Isles* pp. 11 ff.

21 In *Grettir's Saga* 'It is related that Thorir asked the bishop to consecrate a large sea-going ship he had built in the forest, and the bishop did so'. Boats in the Middle Ages often bore religious names. Sadly we know none of the names of Highland galleys but two boats which King Ingi of Norway gave to Earl Rognvald of Orkney about 1150 were called *Bog Cotton* and *Help*. Iain Lom (*c.* 1624 – *c.* 1710) refers to a boat called the *Black One of Knoydart* in one of his poems. See AM Mackenzie, *Orain Iain Luim* pp. 104-5, and p. 278 for *An Dubh-Ghleannach* which was MacDonald of Glenaladale's boat. (For the latter see also B Megaw – *Scottish Studies* Vol. 5 pp. 98-9). Murchadh Mor mac mhic

Mhurchaidh (d. *c.* 1689), in a poem about a storm-struck fleet on its way to Lewis, describes a conversation between himself and *Anna*, his boat. – *TGSI* XX.

22 *Carmina Gadelica* Vol. I p. 325 & pp. 333-335, Scottish Academic Press. Martin Martin wrote of the St Kildans (p. 442) 'They use a set form of prayer at the hoisting of their sails'.

Select Bibliography

Source Material

Accounts of the Lord High Treasurer of Scotland, 1473-1566, Dickson T., & Balfour Paul, Sir J., (eds), (1877-1916) – Vol. IV

Anderson, A.O., *Early Sources of Scottish History*, Vols.1-2, Stamford (1990)

Bannerman, J., *Studies in the History of Dalriada*, Edinburgh (1974)

Broderick, G., (trs) *Cronica Regum Mannie & Insularum*, Isle of Man (1979)

Calendar of Documents relating to Ireland (1252-84 etc.), Sweetman (ed.), London (1877->)

Calendar of Documents relating to Scotland, Bain et al. (eds), Edinburgh (1881->)

Calendar of State Papers - Carew, Brewer & Bullen (eds), London (1867)

Calendar of State Papers Ireland, Hamilton et al. (eds), London (1877)

Calendar of State Papers relating to Scotland, Boyd et al. (eds), Edinburgh (1898->)

Cameron, A., *Reliquiae Celticae*, Vols. 1-2, Inverness (1892-4)

Collectanea de Rebus Albanicis, Edinburgh (1847)

Duncan, A.A.M., (ed.), *The Acts of Robert I*, Edinburgh (1988)

Exchequer Rolls of Scotland, Stuart, J., et al. (eds), Edinburgh (1878-1908)

Facsimiles of the National MSS of Scotland, London (1867-71)

Highland Papers, Vols. I-IV, SHS (1914-34)

Macfarlane, W., *Geographical Collections relating to Scotland*, SHS (1906-8)

Nicolson, A., *Gaelic Proverbs*, Edinburgh (1996)

Register of the Privy Council of Scotland, Hill Burton, J., & Masson, D., (eds), Edinburgh (1877 ->)

Registrum Magni Sigilli Regum Scottorum, Thomson, J.M., (ed.), Edinburgh (1984)

Rotuli Scotiae, MacPherson, D. et al. (ed.), London (1814-19)

Stevenson, J., (ed.), *Documents Illustrative of Scottish History 1286-1306*, Edinburgh (1870)

The Vikings

Crawford, B., *Earl & Mormaer, Norse-Pictish relationships in Northern Scotland*, Groam House Museum (1995)

Crawford, B., *Scandinavian Scotland*, Leicester (1987)

Donaldson, G., *Northern Commonwealth*, Edinburgh (1990)

Fenton & Palsson (eds), *The Northern and Western Isles in the Viking World*, Edinburgh (1984)

Grieg, S., *Viking Antiquities In Great Britain & Ireland (Part II – Viking Antiquities in Scotland)*, Oslo (1940)

Henderson, G., *The Norse Influence on Celtic Scotland*, Glasgow (1910)

Megaw, B., 'Norseman & Native in the Kingdom of the Isles' in Davey, P. (ed.), *Man and Environment in the Isle of Man*, BAR, Vol. 54 (1978)

Oftedal, M., 'On the frequency of Norse Loanwords in Scottish Gaelic', *Scottish Gaelic Studies* IX (1962)

Small, A., 'The Viking Highlands – A Geographical View' in *The Dark Ages in the Highlands*, Inverness Field Club (1971)

Boats

Allen, A., *Orkney's Maritime Heritage*, NMM

Anderson, R.C., 'English Galleys in 1295', *MM* 14

Atkinson, I., *The Viking Ships*, Cambridge (1980)

Auden, G.A., 'A Viking ship on a church door (Stillingfleet)' in *Saga Book of the Viking Club*, Vol. V, London

Backhouse, J., & de Hamel, C., *The Becket Leaves*, British Library (1988)

Brogger, A.W., & Shetelig, H., *The Viking Ships*, Oslo (1971)

Campbell, A., 'The Carpenter MacPheigh', *KIST* 51

Campbell, Lord A., *Argyllshire Galleys*, London (1906)

Campbell, M., 'The Western Voyage of Alexander II', *KIST* 22

Campbell, N.D., 'An Old Tiree Rental of the Year 1662', *SHR*, Vol. 9 (1911-12)

'Church of All Saints Staplehurst', *Archaeologia Cantiana* Vol. IX

Clark, W., *Lord of the Isles Voyage*, Ireland (1993)

Clouston, J. Storer, 'The Battle of Tankerness', *POAS*, Vol. 6 (1927-8)

Fenton, A., 'The Currach in Scotland', *Scottish Studies* Vol. 16

Fionn, 'Gaelic Technical Terms' in *Highland News* 2/10/1897

Franck, Capt. R., *Northern Memoirs*, Edinburgh (1821)

Friel, I., *The Good Ship*, British Museum (1995)

Gunn, A., *The West Highland Galley* (MA Dissertation), Glasgow University (1986)

Hornell, J., 'The Curraghs of Ireland', *MM* 23 & 24

James, M., 'The drawings of Matthew Paris', in *Walpole Society* XIV (1925-6)

Joass, Rev J.M., 'Note on the Curach and Ammir in Ross-shire', *PSAS* XV

Laird Clowes, W., *The Royal Navy*, Vol. I (1897)

Lethbridge, T.C., 'Battle-site in Gorten Bay, Ardnamurchan', *PSAS* LIX

MacAulay, J., *Birlinn*, Harris (1996)

McGrail, S., *Ancient Boats in NW Europe*, Longman (1987)

Macinnes, Rev D., 'Notes on Gaelic Technical Terms', *TGSI* XIX

Mackenna, F.S., 'Kilchattan Graffiti', *KIST* 26

Macpherson, N., 'Notes on Antiquities from the Isle of Eigg', *PSAS* XII

Mather, J.Y., 'Boats and Boatmen of Orkney and Shetland', *Scottish Studies* (1964)

Megaw, B., 'An 18th century representation of a Highland Boat', *Scottish Studies* Vol. 5

Megaw, B., 'The Ship Seals of the Isle of Man', *Manx Museum Journal* Vol. VI (1959-60)

Morrison, A., 'The Contullich Papers', *TGSI* XLIV

Munro, R.W., 'Bloody Bay' in *Notes & Queries 16*, Society for West Highland & Island Historical Research

Olsen, O., & Crumlin-Pedersen, O., *Five Viking Ships*, Copenhagen (1985)

Rawlinson, H.G., 'The Flanders Galleys', *MM* 12

Rodgers, W.L., *Naval Warfare under Oars*, Maryland USA (1986)

Sandison, C., *The Sixareen*, Lerwick (1994)

Skene, G., 'Narrative of Prince Charlie's Escape', *Blackwood's Magazine*, Vol. 114, 1873

Stell, G., 'By Land & Sea in Mediaeval and Early Modern Scotland', *Review of Scottish Culture* No. 4 (1988)

The Earliest Ships, Conway Maritime Press, London (1996)

Tinniswood, J.T., 'English Galleys 1272-1377', *MM* 35
Young, G.V.C., *The Hebridean Birlinn, Nyvaig and Lymphad*, Isle of Man (1997)

Literature – Norse

Anderson, J., (ed.), Hjaltalin, J., & Goudie, G., (trs.), *Orkneyinga Saga*, Edinburgh (1981)
Auden, W.H., & Taylor, P.B., *Norse Poems*, Faber (1983)
Fell, C., (trs.) *Egil's Saga*, Dent (1993)
Hight, G., (trs.) *Grettir the Strong*, Dent (1987)
Larson, L.M., (trs.) 'The King's Mirror' in Ross & McLaughlin (eds.), *The Portable Mediaeval Reader*, Penguin (1978)
Magnusson, M., & Palsson, H., (trs.), *King Harald's Saga*, Penguin (1966)
Magnusson, M., & Palsson, H., (trs.), *Laxdaela Saga*, Penguin (1969)
Magnusson, M., & Palsson, H., (trs.), *Njal's Saga*, Penguin (1960)
Magnusson, M., & Palsson, H., (trs.), *Vinland Sagas*, Penguin (1965)
Palsson, H., (trs.), *Hrafnkel's Saga*, Penguin (1971)
Palsson, H., & Edwards, P., (trs.), *Eyrbyggja Saga*, Edinburgh (1973)
Palsson, H., & Edwards, P., (trs.), *Hrolf-Gautreksson*, Edinburgh (1972)
Palsson, H., & Edwards, P., (trs.), *Orkneyinga Saga*, Penguin (1981)
Palsson, H., & Edwards, P., (trs.), *Seven Viking Romances*, Penguin (1985)
Poole, R.G., *Viking Poems on War and Peace*, Toronto (1991)

Literature – Gaelic

Bateman, M., (trs.), *Gàir nan Clàrsach / The Harps' Cry*, Edinburgh (1994)
Campbell, J.L., 'The Royal Irish Academy Text of Birlinn Clann Raghnaill', *Scottish Gaelic Studies* IX
Carmichael, A., *Carmina Gadelica*, (Vols. 1 & 5), Scottish Academic Press, Edinburgh (1984 & 1987)
Dwelly, E., *Gaelic-English Dictionary*, Birlinn (1993)
Macalpine, N., *Pronouncing Gaelic-English Dictionary*, Glasgow (1975)
MacDiarmid, H., (ed.), *Golden Treasury of Scottish Poetry*, Edinburgh (1993)
Macdonald, A. & A., *The Poems of Alexander Macdonald*, Inverness (1924)
Mackenzie, A.M., (ed.), *Orain Iain Luim*, The Scottish Gaelic Texts Society, Scottish Academic Press (1973)
Maclennan, M., *Gaelic Dictionary*, Acair & Mercat (1992)
Macleod, A., *Sar Orain*, Glasgow (1933)
Nicolson, A., 'The Bark of Clanranald', *An Gaidheal* (1877)
Thomson, D., *Introduction to Gaelic Poetry*, London (1977)
Thomson, D., *Alasdair Mac Mhaighstir Alasdair Selected Poems*, The Scottish Gaelic Texts Society, Scottish Academic Press, Edinburgh (1996)
Watson, W.J., (ed.), *Scottish Verse from the Book of the Dean of Lismore*, The Scottish Gaelic Texts Society, Scottish Academic Press, Edinburgh (1978)

Literature - Latin & Mediaeval

Campbell, A., (ed.), *Encomium Emmae Reginae*, London (1949)
Colgrave, B., *The Life of Bishop Wilfrid*, Cambridge (1927)
Mackenzie, W., (ed.), *The Bruce*, London (1909)
McDiarmid & Stevenson, *Barbour's Bruce*, Scottish Texts Society, Edinburgh (1980)
Vaughan, R., (ed.), *The Illustrated Chronicles of Matthew Paris*, Stroud (1993)
Webb, J., (trs.), *The Age of Bede*, Penguin (1988)
Winterbottom, M., (trs.), *Gildas: The Ruin of Britain and other works*, Phillimore (1978)

Carved Stones

Bailey, R.N., *Viking Age Sculpture*, London (1980)
Campbell, J.L., & Thomson, D., (eds), *Edward Lhuyd in the Scottish Highlands 1699-1700*, Oxford (1963)
Drummond, J., *Sculptured Monuments in Iona & W Highlands*, Edinburgh (1881)
Graham, R.C., *The Carved Stones of Islay*, (1895)
RCAHMS, *Argyll*, Vols. 1-7, HMSO (1971-1992)
RCAHMS, *Outer Hebrides, Skye & Small Isles*, HMSO (1928)
Steer & Bannerman, *Late Mediaeval Monumental Sculpture in the W Highlands*, HMSO (1977)
Stuart, J., *Sculptured Stones of Scotland*, (1856-67)
White, T.P., *Archaeological Sketches in Scotland: Kintyre*, Edinburgh (1873)
White, T.P., *Archaeological Sketches in Scotland: Knapdale*, Edinburgh (1875)

Land-assessment

Bangor-Jones, M., 'Land Assessments & Settlement History in Sutherland and Easter Ross' in Baldwin, J.R., (ed.), *Firthlands of Ross and Sutherland*, Edinburgh (1986)
W Lamont, W., 'House' and 'Pennyland' in the Highland and Isles, *Scottish Studies* Vol. 25 (1981)
MacGregor, L., & Crawford, B., (eds), *Ouncelands and Pennylands*, University of St Andrews (1987)
McKerral, A., 'Ancient denominations of Agricultural land in Scotland', *PSAS* (1943-4)
McKerral, A., 'The lesser land and administrative divisions in Celtic Scotland', *PSAS* (1950-1)
Macqueen, J., 'Pennyland and Davoch in South-Western Scotland', *Scottish Studies* Vol. 23 (1979)
Marwick, H., 'Leidang in the West', *POAS* Vol. 13 (1935)
Marwick, H., 'Naval defence in Norse Scotland', *SHR* XXVIII (1949)
Megaw, B., Note on 'Pennyland and Davoch in South-Western Scotland', *Scottish Studies* Vol. 23 (1979)
Thomas, F.W.L., 'What is a Pennyland?', *PSAS* 18
Thomas, F.W.L., 'Ancient Valuation of Land in the West of Scotland', *PSAS* 20

Highland and Scottish

Barrow, G., *Robert Bruce & the Community of the Realm of Scotland*, Edinburgh (1988)

The Book of Dunvegan, Vols. 1&2, Aberdeen (1938-9)

Campbell, M., *Mid Argyll: An Archaeological Guide*, (1984)

Campbell, M., *Mid Argyll: A Handbook of History*, (1970)

Campbell, M., 'Robert I & Tarbert Castle', *KIST* 34

Cheape, H., 'Woodlands on the Clanranald Estates' in *Scotland since Prehistory*, Aberdeen (1993)

Cowan, E.J., 'Norwegian Sunset – Scottish Dawn' in *Scotland in the Reign of Alexander III*, Edinburgh (1990)

Craven, J.B., *Records of Argyll & the Isles*, Kirkwall (1907)

Duncan, A., & Brown, A., 'Argyll & the Isles in the Earlier Middle Ages', *PSAS* 1956-7

Fergusson, C., & Mackenna, F.S., 'Is the site of Tarbert's "Peel" now identified?', *KIST* 34

Fraser, I., 'Gaelic & Norse elements in coastal place-names in the Western Isles', *TGSI* Vol. L (1976-8)

Graham-Campbell, J.A., 'The Viking-age Silver & Gold hoards of Scandinavian character from Scotland', *PSAS* 107

Grant, I.F., *Highland Folk Ways*, (ch. 12), Edinburgh (1995)

Grant, I.F., *The Macleods*, London (1959)

Johnson & Boswell, *A Journey to the Western Islands of Scotland & The Journal of a Tour to the Hebrides*, OUP (1974)

Knox, J., *Tour through the Highlands*, (1776)

Macdonald, J., *Tales of the Highlands*, Inverness (1907)

MacInnes, Rev. J., 'West Highland Sea Power in the Middle Ages', *TGSI* 1974

Mackay, W., (ed.), *Chronicles of the Frasers*, SHS, Edinburgh (1905)

Mackenzie, W.C., *History of the Outer Hebrides*, (1903)

McKerral, A., 'West Highland Mercenaries in Ireland', *SHR* XXX

Maclean, J.P., *A History of the Clan Maclean*, Cincinnati (1889)

Martin Martin, *A Description of the Western Islands of Scotland*, Birlinn (1994) (also includes Sir Donald Munro's description)

Miket, R., & Roberts, D.L., *The Mediaeval Castles of Skye and Lochalsh*, Skye (1990)

Millar, A.H., *Scottish Forfeited Estate Papers 1715-45*, SHS, Edinburgh (1909)

Miller, H., *My schools and schoolmasters*, Edinburgh (1889)

Munro, J. & R., (eds), *Acts of the Lords of the Isles*, SHS, Edinburgh (1986)

Murray, S., *The Beauties of Scotland*, Byway Books (1982)

Pennant, T., *A Voyage to the Hebrides*, (1790)

Ross, D., *The Glengarry Evictions*, Glasgow (1853)

Ross, W., 'Clan Neil of Barra' in Kay, W., (ed.), *Odyssey, The Second Collection* Polygon (1982)

Skene, W.F., *Celtic Scotland*, Edinburgh (1886-90)

Walker, J., *An Economical History of the Hebrides & Highlands*, Vol. II (1808)

Ireland

Hayes McCoy, G.A., *Scots Mercenary Forces in Ireland*, Dublin & London (1937)
Nicholson, R., 'An Irish expedition to Scotland in 1335', *Irish Historical Studies* XIII (1962-3)
O'Meara, J., (trs.), *Gerald of Wales The History & Topography of Ireland*, Penguin (1982)
O'Neill, T., *Merchants & Mariners in Mediaeval Ireland*, Irish Academic Press (1987)
Shaw-Smith, D., *Ireland's Traditional Crafts*, Thames & Hudson (1986)

Navigation

Binns, A., 'The navigation of Viking ships round the British Isles in Old English & Old Norse sources' in *Fifth Viking Congress* (1968)
Lindsay, A., ('methodized' by Nicholas d'Arville) 'The Navigation of King James V round Scotland', *Miscellanea Scotica* III, Glasgow (1819)
Lindsay, A., *A Rutter of the Scottish Seas*, NMM (1980)
Marcus, G.J., 'The Navigation of the Norsemen', *MM* 39
Waters, D., *The Art of Navigation in England in Elizabethan & Early Stuart Times* Parts I-III, HMSO (1978)

Index